The Bible Speaks Today
Series Editors: J. A. Motyer (OT)
John R. W. Stott (NT)
Derek Tidball (Bible Themes)

The Message of
Psalms 1—72

Kevin Ray

Titles in this series

The Message of Psalms 1—72

Songs for the People of God

Michael Wilcock

InterVarsity Press

InterVarsity Press
P.O. Box 1400, Downers Grove, IL 60515-1426
World Wide Web: www.ivpress.com
E-mail: mail@ivpress.com

Inter-Varsity Press
38 De Montfort Street, Leicester LE1 7GP, England
World Wide Web: www.ivpbooks.com
E-mail: ivp@uccf.org.uk
© *Michael Wilcock 2001*

InterVarsity Press® is the book-publishing division of InterVarsity Christian Fellowship/USA®, a student movement active on campus at hundreds of universities, colleges and schools of nursing in the United States of America, and a member movement of the International Fellowship of Evangelical Students. For information about local and regional activities, write Public Relations Dept., InterVarsity Christian Fellowship/USA, 6400 Schroeder Rd., P.O. Box 7895, Madison, WI 53707-7895.

Inter-Varsity Press is the book-publishing division of the Universities and Colleges Christian Fellowship (formerly the Inter-Varsity Fellowship), a student movement linking Christian Unions in universities and colleges throughout the United Kingdom and the Republic of Ireland, and a member movement of the International Fellowship of Evangelical Students. For information about local and national activities write to UCCF, 38 De Montfort Street, Leicester LE1 7GP, England.

All Scripture quotations, unless otherwise indicated, are taken from the Holy Bible, New International Version®. NIV®. Copyright ©1973, 1978, 1984 by International Bible Society. Used by permission of Hodder and Stoughton Ltd. All rights reserved. "NIV" is a registered trademark of International Bible Society. UK trademark number 1448790. Distributed in North America by permission of Zondervan Publishing House.

The extract from A. E. Housman's A Shropshire Lad on page 101 is used by permission of The Society of Authors.

USA ISBN 0-8308-1244-X

UK ISBN 0-85111-506-3

Typeset in Great Britain by The Midlands Book Typesetting Company.

Printed in the United States of America ∞

British Library Cataloguing in Publication Data

A catalogue record for this book is available from the British Library

Library of Congress Cataloging-in-Publication Data

Wilcock, Michael.
  The message of Psalms/Michael Wilcock.
    p. cm. —(The Bible speaks today)
  Includes bibliographical references.
  Contents: v. 1. Psalms 1-72—v. 2. Psalms 73-150.
  ISBN 0-8308-1244-X; v. 2—0-8308-1245-8
  1. Bible. O.T. Psalms—Commentaries. I. Title. II. Series.
  BS1430.3 .W55 2001
  223'.207—dc 21   *2001024407*

18	17	16	15	14	13	12	11	10	9	8	7	6	5	4	3	2	1
16	15	14	13	12	11	10	09	08	07	06	05	04	03	02	01		

Contents

General
preface

The Bible Speaks Today describes three series of expositions, based on the books of the Old and New Testaments, and on Bible themes that run through the whole of Scripture. Each series is characterized by a threefold ideal:

- to expound the biblical text with accuracy
- to relate it to contemporary life, and
- to be readable.

These books are, therefore, not 'commentaries', for the commentary seeks rather to elucidate the text than to apply it, and tends to be a work rather of reference than of literature. Nor, on the other hand, do they contain the kind of 'sermons' which attempt to be contemporary and readable without taking Scripture seriously enough.

The contributors to The Bible Speaks Today series are all united in their convictions that God still speaks through what he has spoken, and that nothing is more necessary for the life, health and growth of Christians than that they should hear what the Spirit is saying to them through his ancient – yet ever modern – Word.

ALEC MOTYER
JOHN STOTT
DEREK TIDBALL
Series Editors

Author's preface

'The unfolding of your words gives light,' says the psalmist. Of the many current ways of unfolding the Word of God, a very effective one is that which was devised by the editors and publishers of The Bible Speaks Today series. I witnessed the birth of the series, and have watched its growth, sustained now over three decades with no signs of flagging so far – an extraordinarily long shelf-life for what I suppose the trade calls 'religious paperbacks'.

It was a great privilege to be invited to write for it once more, twenty-five years after my first contribution, and especially to be asked to take on so big a task as an exposition of the entire Psalter. For that, and for their unfailing help, encouragement, and patience, now as on previous occasions, I am truly grateful to Alec Motyer, Frank Entwistle, Colin Duriez, and all the folk at IVP.

'You must have accumulated plenty of sermon outlines on the Psalms over the years,' said the editor, hoping to persuade me that this might not be quite such a mammoth job as it seemed. Yes, I have, and I don't think a single one of them appears here! This book started again from scratch, with scarcely a glance at all those old preaching notes.

Surplus to present requirements they may be, but they do represent attempts throughout my ministry to unfold the Word to real people confronting the questions of real life in the church and in the world. That means chiefly the four congregations to which I have been appointed since ordination: most recently St Nicholas, Durham, and before that St Faith, Maidstone, All Souls, Langham Place, London, and Christ Church, Southport. To each of them I owe a great deal, and from the pleasant pastures of retirement I send my thanks to them too.

At Southport the unforgettable Fred Pickering, who as it happened had himself been vicar of St Nick's Durham before I was born, eased my way into the life of the ministry with the kindest (and most endearingly eccentric) oversight, and put up with a very green curate's earliest essays in church-based preaching. That is why his name appears on the dedication page.

I wonder whether the other that stands with it will be known to any readers of this book? 'Mac' was a Christian gentleman of the same generation as Fred, who in a way that I think is rare today taught English to generations of schoolboys, including me, at Bromley Grammar School. If now I have the words to write about the Word, he is one of the reasons. The Word is immeasurably greater than any words of ours, but every good gift is from above, and deserves to be recognized.

MICHAEL WILCOCK
EASTBOURNE
APRIL 2000

Begin here

About this book

Austin Farrer, who wrote thought-provokingly about the Revelation of St John,[1] once said that the Bible was the only good book he knew which ought to be read backwards. We may think we know what he meant; but still, we would say, the normal way to read any book – even the Bible – is to start at the beginning and go steadily through to the end.

Yet the people who do read the Bible in sequence from Genesis to Revelation are probably not much more numerous than those who read it from Revelation to Genesis. And confronted with the easier task of reading just one segment of the book, we are, ironically, no more likely to work through that from start to finish, either, if it happens to be the Psalter. A church liturgy may cherish the hope that all 150 psalms be said or sung in the course of every month; but few outside a cathedral choir would even attempt the enterprise. Speaking generally, and not I think too cynically, a love for the Psalms tends to mean the use of just a selection of them, limited, occasional, and in no sort of order.

To the faithful souls who do practise a systematic reading of the Psalter, I want to say, 'Isn't it mind-stretching? Do you not enthuse about it to all your Bible-reading friends?' Having only recently discovered its value for myself, I am hoping that this book of mine may commend it to others.

A detective story

The publishers and editors of The Bible Speaks Today series have always said that it consists not of commentaries but of expositions. 'What *is* the difference?' asked a friend not long ago, and it occurred

[1] Austin Farrer, *A Rebirth of Images* (London: Dacre, 1949); *The Revelation of St John the Divine* (Oxford: Clarendon, 1964).

to me that the relation between the two is rather like that between a dictionary and a novel. One is for consulting, the other is for reading. Rare is the bird who like Lord Peter Wimsey's brother-in-law, the policeman Charles Parker, makes time to *read* Bible commentaries. Much as their authors might like them to be worked through in order, they are much more likely to be dipped into, as a dictionary is consulted about a particular word. But dip here and there into a novel, and you will miss the point. If it is a detective story – the name of Dorothy L. Sayers' famous sleuth brings the genre to mind – it actually *requires* to be read in order, as the clues are planted and the red herrings laid down. Read chapter 27 before chapter 8, and your frustration will be your own fault.

The writing of an exposition of the Psalms along these lines has several consequences. Where space is at a premium, it saves unnecessary repetition, because it can take for granted that readers will recall explanations given ten or twenty pages earlier. In case they have after all forgotten, it can point them back to previous psalms which it assumes they will have read, and it will do that far more often than it points ahead to later psalms which it does not assume them to have read. It deals one by one, as they arise, with matters that in a commentary would all be brought together in a substantial introduction (which is why this one is relatively brief).

A travel guide

The book of Psalms itself, of course, is not like a novel, even if that may be a good way to describe an exposition of it. The Psalter is a collection, an anthology, a hymnal, a book of songs. We might even think of it as a photograph album, full of pictures that show us a variety of places in a land of spiritual experience.

Not a novel, then. Such a book will not have a plot. But it may have a plan; and as one sets about explaining the photos, one may well recognize connections and sequences among them, and find oneself producing what is in effect a travel guide. It may even become increasingly clear that the album is not a miscellany, but the record of an actual journey or journeys. The resulting exposition will be very different from much Psalms study of the last hundred years. Let me try to explain why.

Many of the most influential twentieth-century scholars in that field were concerned to classify the Psalms into various types, to rearrange them accordingly, and to comment on them as thus rearranged. For all the value of their work, it had its drawbacks. Michael Goulder points out one of them: 'An author shows his mastery of the subject by moving at ease from 110 to 2, and thence to 132; to Exodus 15 and 1 Samuel 2 and Jonah 2. The dazzled student soon suppresses as naïve his instinct that it is proper to study 1 before 2, and that there is something curious in beginning a book on the Psalter with the 110th or 89th psalm.'[2]

Suppose, however, that we were to understand Psalm 1 to be the port of entry to this strange new country, and the step from 1 to 2 to be the first stage of a journey. We should be taking seriously the work of the unknown compilers; and, as Goulder says,'the oldest commentary on the meaning of the psalms is the manner of their arrangement in the Psalter: that is, the collections in which they are grouped, the technical and historical notes they carry, and the order in which they stand'.[3]

A study book

One way or another, then, whether what follows is thought of as a detective story or as a travel guide, its prospective readers have the right to hope that it will be readable, however daunting its size. It is, all the same, a study book, and I cannot promise them a fast read, or even an easy one. There are lots of footnotes! They really will need to have a Bible open beside them; many expositions in this series have incorporated the Bible's text, but the inclusion in these volumes of what is far and away its biggest book would have made them prohibitively fat and expensive. With so many different Bible translations available, the most helpful one for a reader to choose will be the New International Version, simply because it is on that that this book is based. That choice in turn was made not because the NIV is necessarily the best (even today the most accurate for study purposes is still the RV of 1885), but because at the time of writing it is perhaps the most widely used. Others that have been referred to are noted below, in the list of abbreviations.

The same list includes details of a number of the books mentioned in the footnotes. When I was first invited to contribute these volumes to the series, I anticipated with relish the feast of good things that awaited me in the pages of Luther and Calvin and Spurgeon, to say nothing of many more recent commentators. Alas, life is too short. In the event there has been time for far less background reading than I should have liked, and I have had to be very selective, choosing one commentary because it is thorough, another because it is perceptive, a third because it is stimulating, and so on.

[2] Goulder, *Korah*, p. 8.
[3] Ibid., p. 1. Norman Whybray's *Reading the Psalms as a Book*, JSOTSup 22 (Sheffield: Sheffield Academic Press, 1996) has a 25-page survey of recent studies on the Psalms that do, unlike many of their predecessors, concentrate on the book's biblical order and arrangement.

Two other lists are appended. Since technical aspects of Hebrew poetry will be touched on as they arise, instead of being brought together in an introduction, it may be useful to have a reminder of where those first mentions and explanations are to be found. And it may be of interest for the reader to be able to locate metrical versions and paraphrases of the Psalms that have been noted in the text. They are listed below with the respective psalm numbers alongside.

List of abbreviations

Alexander	J. A. Alexander, *The Psalms* (Edinburgh: Elliott & Thin, 1864)
Allen	L. C. Allen, *Psalms 101 – 150*, WBC (Waco: Word, 1983)
Anderson	A. A. Anderson, *The Book of Psalms*, NCB (London: Oliphants, 1972)
AV	Authorized (King James) Version (1611)
Blaiklock	E. M. Blaiklock, *The Psalms of the Great Rebellion* (London: Lakeland, 1970)
Brueggemann	Walter Brueggemann, *The Psalms and the Life of Faith*, ed. Patrick D. Miller (Minneapolis: Fortress, 1995)
BST	The Bible Speaks Today
CBSC	The Cambridge Bible for Schools and Colleges
Clements	Roy Clements, *Songs of Experience* (Fearn: Christian Focus, 1993)
Cohen	A. Cohen, *The Psalms* (Hindhead: Soncino, 1958)
Craigie	Peter C. Craigie, *Psalms 1 – 50*, WBC (Waco: Word, 1983)
Delitzsch	F. Delitzsch, *The Psalms,* 3 vols. (Edinburgh: T. & T. Clark, 1880)
GNB	Good News Bible (London: HarperCollins, 1994)
Goldingay	John Goldingay, *Songs from a Strange Land* (Leicester: IVP, 1978)
Goulder, 'Fourth Book'	M. D. Goulder, 'The Fourth Book of the Psalter', in *Journal of Theological Studies* 26.2 (1975)
Goulder, Korah	M. D. Goulder, *The Psalms of the Sons of Korah*, JSOTSup 20 (Sheffield: Sheffield Academic Press, 1982)
Goulder, Return	M. D. Goulder, *The Psalms of the Return*, JSOTSup 258 (Sheffield: Sheffield Academic Press, 1998)
ICC	International Critical Commentary

JB	Jerusalem Bible (London: Chapman, 1971)
JSOTSup	Journal for the Study of the Old Testament, Supplement Series
Kidner	F. D. Kidner, *Psalms 1 – 72* and *73 – 150*, TOTC (Leicester: IVP, 1973 and 1975)
Kirkpatrick	A. F. Kirkpatrick, *The Psalms*, CBSC (Cambridge: CUP, 1902)
Lewis	C. S. Lewis, *Reflections on the Psalms* (London: Fontana, 1961)
LXX	The Septuagint, the (pre-Christian) Greek translation of the Old Testament
Manning	B. L. Manning, *The Hymns of Wesley and Watts* (London: Epworth, 1942)
Motyer	J. A. Motyer, 'The Psalms', in *The New Bible Commentary, 21st Century Edition*, ed. D. A. Carson et al. (Leicester: IVP, 1994)
NASB	New American Standard Bible (Philadelphia: Holman, 1973)
NCB	New Century Bible
NEB	New English Bible (Oxford/Cambridge: OUP/CUP, 1970)
NICNT	New International Commentary on the New Testament
NIV	New International Version (London: Hodder & Stoughton, 1984)
NRSV	New Revised Standard Version (Oxford: OUP, 1989)
NT	New Testament
OT	Old Testament
RSV	Revised Standard Version (London: Collins, 1952)
RV	Revised Version (Cambridge: CUP, 1885)
Shepherd	John Shepherd, 'The Place of the Imprecatory Psalms in the Canon of Scripture', in *Churchman* 111.1, 111.2 (1997)
Spurgeon	C. H. Spurgeon, *The Treasury of David* (London: Passmore, 1869)
Tate	M. E. Tate, *Psalms 51 – 100*, WBC (Waco: Word, 1990)
TNTC	Tyndale New Testament Commentaries
TOTC	Tyndale Old Testament Commentaries
VanGemeren	W. A. VanGemeren, 'Psalms', in *The Expositor's Bible Commentary*, ed. F. E. Gaebelein (Grand Rapids: Zondervan, 1991)
Watson	J. R. Watson, *The English Hymn* (Oxford: Clarendon, 1997)

WBC	Word Biblical Commentary
Weiser	Artur Weiser, *The Psalms*, Old Testament Library (London: SCM, 1962)
Wenham	J. W. Wenham, *The Enigma of Evil* (Guildford: Eagle, 1994)

List of technical terms

Please note that page references are preceded by the volume number.

List of related hymns

Hail to the Lord's Anointed (Montgomery) – Ps. 72   1.249
How pleased and blest was I (Watts) – Ps. 122   2.224
How weak the thoughts and vain (Wesley) – Ps. 49   1.179
I lift my eyes to the quiet hills (Dudley-Smith) – Ps. 121   2.222
I'll praise my Maker while I've breath (Watts) – Ps. 146   2.275
I love you, O Lord, you alone (Idle) – Ps. 18   1.61
Jesu, lover of my soul (Wesley) – Ps. 32   1.111
Jesus shall reign (Watts) – Ps. 72   1.249
Joy to the world (Watts) – Ps. 98   2.104
Let us with a gladsome mind (Milton) – Ps. 136   2.249
Lift up your heads (Montgomery) – Ps. 24   2.13
Lord of the worlds above (Watts) – Ps. 84   2.47
Not to us be glory given (Dudley-Smith) – Ps. 115   2.181
O God, our help in ages past (Watts) – Ps. 90   2.74
O praise ye the Lord (Baker) – Ps. 150   2.285
O worship the King (Grant) – Ps. 104   2.121
Pleasant are thy courts above (Lyte) – Ps. 84   2.47
Praise him, praise him, praise him (Perry) – Ps. 148   2.280
Praise my soul the King of heaven (Lyte) – Ps. 103   2.117
Praise the Lord of heaven (Browne) – Ps. 148   2.280
Praise the Lord of heaven (Dudley-Smith) – Ps. 148   2.280
Praise the Lord, ye heavens, adore him (anon) – Ps. 148   2.280
Safe in the shadow of the Lord (Dudley-Smith) – Ps. 91   2.79
Shine, mighty God (Watts) – Ps. 67   1.233
Sweet is the work (Watts) – Ps. 92   2.82
The God of love my shepherd is (Herbert) – Ps. 23   1.85
The heavens declare thy glory, Lord (Watts) – Ps. 19   1.73
The King of love my shepherd is (Baker) – Ps. 23   1.85
The Lord is King (Conder) – Ps. 96   2.96
The Lord my pasture shall prepare (Addison) – Ps. 23   1.85
The Lord's my shepherd (Scottish Psalter) – Ps. 23   1.85
The spacious firmament on high (Addison) – Ps. 19   1.71
There is a safe and secret place (Lyte) – Ps. 91   2.79
This earth belongs to God (Idle) – Ps. 24   1.87
Through all the changing scenes (Tate/Brady) – Ps. 34   1.116
Unto the hills around (Campbell) – Ps. 121   2.222
We love the place, O Lord (Bullock/Baker) – Ps. 26   1.94
When all thy mercies (Addison) – Ps. 71   1.246
When Israel out of Egypt came (Wesley) – Ps. 114   2.180

In affectionate memory of
Joseph Cort McPhail
who loved words
and
Frederick Henry Pickering
who loved the Word

BOOK I
(Psalms 1 – 41)

The Preamble: Psalms 1 – 2

We are to see Psalm 1, and probably Psalm 2 also, as the inspired introduction to the whole book. Not that that is a good word for it. 'Introductions', like 'prefaces' and 'forewords', are what dull dogs like me stitch on at the front end of their work (though in this instance I have tried to avoid doing so); whereas for the original compilers, the right way into such a book of songs must itself be a work of art. For his 'multitude of Angels', who thought the same, Milton found a more beguiling word:

> With *Praeamble* sweet
> Of charming symphonie they introduce
> Thir sacred Song.[4]

Hence our heading.

Psalm 1 sings of the choice between two ways that each of us has to make; Psalm 2 unveils the cosmic confrontation which that choice reflects.

Psalm 1

There are simple words in this first psalm (three at the beginning, two more near the end) which should catch our attention. Each raises two questions, one to check our understanding and the other to challenge our assumptions.

1. Blessed (v. 1)

The first question is, What does this word mean? The versions differ; some translate it 'happy' or 'fortunate'. What matters is what the psalm says it means. It describes a life of delight and fruitfulness,

---

[4] John Milton, *Paradise Lost*, III.367–369.

with a sense of worth, which contrasts with the worthlessness of the wicked; and the delight is primarily a delight in God's directing of our ways.

It is striking that the very first word of the entire book of Psalms should be this one. Surely it is far more important (this is the second question) that we should be righteous, or obedient, or loving, than that we should be merely *happy*? Yes, in the short term; but from his original creating of his people right through to his final redeeming of them, Scripture is clear that God's long-term purpose for them is that they should be blessed. The psalmists celebrate every foretaste of that heavenly promise.

The Psalter, which thus from its very beginning is making us think, at once follows a surprising adjective with a surprising noun: <u>Blessed</u> is the <u>man</u>.

2. Man (v. 1)

The first question here is the modern one of inclusive language. For many centuries the English word 'man' has been both gender-specific (meaning male) and generic (meaning human), as it still is in the New International Version of the Bible, on which this book is based. But increasingly in the last few years of the twentieth century the generic use has been under attack in many parts of the English-speaking world. Quite suddenly (as such changes go) there arises a generation which simply does not know that 'man' can mean, or ever did mean, something else besides 'adult human male'. Why, it will ask, should Psalm 1:1 bless the man and not the woman?

In the resulting disagreement, one party, taking the narrower use to be the language of the future, abandons the generic use, while the other is unwilling to forfeit what it considers a perfectly good usage for no very good reason.[5] I have other aims in this book than to join this particular battle, but I do personally side with the latter, and should say that since 'man' here includes both genders, 'Why man rather than woman?' is not a real question. But 'Why man rather than God?' is. Practical theology, which must begin with holiness rather than happiness, must also surely begin with God rather than man? The world always, and the church too often, is man-centred when it should be God-centred.

[5] Man and God, man and beast, men and angels, are just a few of the useful, simple, time-honoured phrases which historically have nothing to do with gender but which are obviously under threat. See Gordon Wenham's remarks in *Genesis 1 – 15* (Waco: Word, 1987), p. lii; though also D. A. Carson, *The Inclusive Language Debate* (Leicester: IVP, 1998). The Psalter has a great deal to say about 'man' in the generic sense, and my preference for this historic usage will often show through. It does after all have a very long and respectable pedigree. I hope that those who may be offended by it will be patient with one who is equally offended by the current alternatives.

However, in this respect also Psalm 1:1 lays foundations for the whole Psalter. It does begin with God, a God who has already taken the initiative. The holy relationship between him and the psalmists has already been made, so that they are God-centred from the outset. Their songs are a response – the many-faceted response of the 'man' God has 'blessed'.

3. Not (v. 1)

In this case we ask first *what* the blessed man does not do. That question is readily answered from the text. More far reaching is the question of *why* the psalm seems more interested in what he doesn't do than in what he does do. Does it give grounds for the classic sneer that Bible people are negative people?

In fact this 'not', like the contrast between righteous and wicked later in the psalm, highlights the importance of *definition*. A biblical faith and life are *not* that, *but* this. On the broad scene, this attitude in the psalmists challenges the whole range of modern -isms, from liberalism to post-modernism, which shy away from the notion of objective truth and error, right and wrong. On the personal front, it challenges the individual to repeated choices between clearly defined ways of believing and acting.

The Psalms express joy, awe, doubt, confidence, anger, praise. They do so with heartfelt emotion. But behind all of them is a definite theology, which is clear as to what is and what is not acceptable.

4. Judgment (v. 5)

When we ask what is pictured in verse 5, it may well be in the first instance an Israelite community met for the day-to-day administration of justice, where bad people have no right to officiate. But it certainly means more than that. The Psalter will sing often of the great supernatural tribunal which is reflected in every such local court. Before God's judgment seat, it is a question not of whether the wicked man should himself stand up as counsel or witness, but of whether his case will stand up, when he is the prisoner in the dock.

That courtroom is a permanent, present reality, in which God's judgment may be passed and executed at any time. Near the beginning of Bible history, Abraham actually watched 'the Judge of all the earth do right' in destroying Sodom and Gomorrah.[6] It is also the scene of the coming 'last judgment' which, according to John's vision in the last book of the Bible, will bring our world to an end.[7]

[6] Gen. 18:25.
[7] Rev. 20:11–15.

These judgments, whether they take place in our time or beyond it, are eagerly awaited by the psalmists, who thus encourage us in the confidence that bad men do not in the end get away with their wickedness. On the other hand, we should learn equally the healthy respect due to a Judge who has every right to include us ourselves among the bad men.

5. Assembly (v. 5)

The question of how to define the fifth of these basic words can be answered simply. The *assembly* is what the New Testament will call the 'church'.

The question of what that implies needs a fuller answer. Two Hebrew terms are used here and in Deuteronomy 4:10 ('Assemble the people before me to hear my words').[8] Between them they shape the true notion of what the church is: the Lord's people belonging, relating, and actually meeting together in the Lord's presence, listening and responding to him – not a building, not an ordained priesthood, not a denomination or organization,

> But where Christ's two or three
> In His name gathered are;[9]

or, indeed, his two or three hundred, or even the countless myriads which come together in the heavenly Jerusalem.[10]

Even the most individualistic of the psalmists would recognize that God's concern for him personally is bound up with God's promises to that great assembly, 'the blessed company of all faithful people'.[11] All their poetry is to be read in the light of this. Throughout Psalm 1 *righteous* and *wicked* are plurals; both our present experience and our future destiny (v. 6) depend on which of the two companies each of us belongs to, not in name only but (as *the way* implies) in practice.

Psalm 2

In Acts 13:33 the apostle Paul quotes a sentence which, he says, 'is written in the second Psalm'. So it is; but, oddly, one ancient version of Acts specifies 'the first Psalm' instead. Was its editor mistaken? Probably not, for he no doubt had in mind one of the old Psalters whose 'first Psalm' was a combination of our Psalms 1 and 2.

---

[8] ʿēdâ (Ps. 1:5); qāhāl (Deut. 4:10).
[9] F. T. Palgrave, 'O Thou not made with hands'.
[10] Heb. 12:22–24.
[11] The 1662 Book of Common Prayer: the second post-communion prayer.

It is not hard to see why the two should have been bracketed as a joint preamble to the whole book. The pairing begins and ends with definitions of those who are *blessed* (1:1; 2:12). Within it, the private world of the first psalm opens out into the public world of the second; the personal is followed by the cosmic; in airport terminology, one is 'domestic' and the other 'international'. Psalm 1 talks the everyday language of wisdom books like Proverbs and Ecclesiastes, while Psalm 2, raising its eyes to world affairs beyond the control of ordinary people, speaks as the books of the prophets do of a great God in control behind the scenes.

One way in which Psalm 2 amplifies Psalm 1 is by showing us another majestic figure alongside 'the LORD' (1:2, 6), namely his appointed King, his Son, his *Anointed One* (2:2). So this is the first of the 'royal' psalms, relating originally, it seems, to what we should call the coronation of Israelite kings in Jerusalem, the *holy hill* of Zion (v. 6). Since the passing away, long ago, of that political system, it has been in another 'Mount Zion', namely 'the heavenly Jerusalem',[12] that the 'assembly' of 1:5 has gathered. The identity of the King installed there is no mystery to Christian readers.

1. What the rebels say (vv. 1–3)
We can only guess which, if any, of the kings of Judah had to cope with the rebellion of subject nations described here. Perhaps this was a regular form of 'coronation service' which was not confronting an actual situation, but rather envisaging a possible one.

From apostolic times onwards the anointed King whom the nations reject has been *the* Anointed – in Hebrew, the Messiah; in Greek, the Christ, as is made clear when the New Testament quotes these verses.[13] It is not just the political powers of this world which have no desire to be ruled by him. There is scarcely a commercial or intellectual or cultural interest anywhere on earth which would not resent his claims on it.

2. What the Lord says (vv. 4–6)
Few of those who reject God think much about him; none, I dare say, ever thinks of his actually ridiculing them! And while a God who derides, scoffs, rebukes, and terrifies is disconcerting enough, even worse is one who speaks as this one does in verse 6. The *I* is emphatic, and the tone must be one of cold anger: 'You may conspire and rebel, but *I*, you see, have already decided who shall finally rule in your world. I have spoken, and there's an end of it.'

That is a word to astonish the pundits whose judgments are deferred to in every television chat-show and every serious newspaper,

---

[12] Heb. 12:22.   [13] Acts 4:25–26; 13:33; Heb. 1:5; 5:5.

and to dismay every grandee and tycoon whose unwilling ears are made to hear it. 'A race of pigmies is face to face with a giant,' says Weiser, speaking of the 'manikins' whom God 'mocks'.[14]

3. What the King says (vv. 7–9)

These too are the words of God, though in this case it is the King who speaks them.

If in the days of the psalmists they were uttered by a newly crowned ruler in Jerusalem, they used the high-flown language of divine sonship and of a universal inheritance to mean that God formally recognized the new king (as he had previously recognized David, and before him Israel itself),[15] and gave him great authority. But when now in the end of the ages the line of anointed kings, long since extinct, has burst into life again with *the* Anointed King, this one is in the deepest and fullest sense 'declared with power to be the Son of God'.[16]

And as is shown by the three references to these verses in Revelation,[17] his own people, the church, share in the worldwide spread of his kingdom's authority – a just contrast to the pretensions and final downfall of the powers of this world.

4. What the psalmist says (vv. 10–12)

The fierceness of Psalm 2 may have come as a surprise. It should certainly be a tonic. In these closing verses there is no doubt about the wrath of God, the fear it inspires, or the destruction it threatens. Yet it is the same Lord in both this psalm and the previous one; so here on the grand scale, as in Psalm 1 on the personal level, the call is still that people should be wise, and the promise is still that they should be blessed.

Kiss the Son is only one suggested translation of the much-debated text of verse 12a. If it is correct, it repeats in this last section the partnership between God and his Anointed, his King, his Son, which has appeared in each of the first three sections. Old Testament people might honour each successive king of Israel with the kiss of homage; their book of praises is now in our hands, and with it we may honour King Jesus with a like reverence and love.

The first David Collection: Psalms 3 – 41

In the rest of the first book of the Psalter, practically every psalm has a heading which includes the name of David. Further 'David' psalms will appear later, particularly in Books II and V.

[14] Weiser, p. 112. [15] 2 Sam. 7:14; Exod. 4:22. [16] Rom. 1:4.
[17] Rev. 2:27; 12:5; 19:15.

We should note at once four things about this outstanding man, the greatest of the kings of Israel, as the Bible presents him. First, he was a man with *special experience*. It was not simply that a great variety of things happened to him, but also that he responded to them in a great variety of ways. His was an emotional, even mercurial, character, with ups and downs in his inner life corresponding to those in his outward circumstances. He was 'subject to like passions as we are', as James says of Elijah.[18]

Then he was a man with *special gifts*. As well as those which fitted him for kingship, he had those of a poet and musician, as Old Testament history records.[19] The phrase 'of David' at the head of many psalms does not necessarily mean 'by David'; they could 'belong to' him in various other ways (about him; for his use; dedicated to him; in a collection under his name; and so on). But there is generally no strong reason why it should not mean authorship, and in some cases – for example Psalm 18 – it clearly does. So here is one who feels what we often feel, but who can express it in words more telling and more memorable than most of us could put together; and such poetry is a gift not only from God to him, but from him to us.

Thirdly, he was a man with a *special calling*. He was 'the man anointed by the God of Jacob' as well as 'Israel's singer of songs' – anointed, that is, as king; and that recalls us to Psalm 2, and highlights the remarkable dual role of David the psalmist. As God looks at him, he is one with his people (and with the rest of us) in his frail and fallible humanity. But as Israel (and we) look at him, he stands alongside God in his delegated majesty as the Lord's anointed. Both in his likeness to the rest of us, and in his unlikeness, he inspires confidence in those who make his psalms their own. In psalms of authority, he gives us words God wants to say to us; in psalms of frailty, words for us to say to God.[20] On the one hand, in him God sees and understands all human weakness. On the other hand, to him God gives all the resources of divine grace to help his people in time of need.

And that brings us of course to the fourth point, that David was a man with a *special significance* in the overall scheme of Bible truth. For the pattern I have just described points forward to what the New Testament says about 'great David's greater Son'.[21]

[18] Jas. 5:17 AV.   [19] 2 Sam. 1:17–27; 22:1–51; 23:1–7.
[20] 'Al other scriptures do teach us what God saith unto us,' wrote Anthony Gilby, one of the translators of the 1560 Geneva Bible, but the Psalms 'teach us what we shall saie unto God'. A similar saying is attributed to the fourth-century theologian Athanasius.
[21] James Montgomery, 'Hail to the Lord's Anointed'. See p. 1.249

The previous paragraph alluded to the passage in Hebrews (4:14–16) which links kingship and priesthood, the representation of God to man and the representation of man to God, in the person of our Lord Jesus Christ. Whoever may have composed any particular psalm, again and again we shall find that its words might well have been heard – and in some cases certainly were heard – both from the lips of that first great king, and from those of his far greater Descendant. They ask to be heard from our lips also, perhaps far more often than they are.

Psalm 3

The story of the rebellion against King David by his favourite son Absalom is told in detail in 2 Samuel 15 – 19. It is to the earliest days of that period that Psalm 3, according to its heading, belongs. Was it written by David at the time? Or afterwards, as he relived those traumatic events? Or was it by, or about, or for, some later 'David', one of this king's descendants going through a similar hard time? Was the heading added later still by the book's editors?

Whatever the history of the compiling of the Psalter, headings of this kind do belong to it in its final form, and are part of canonical Scripture.[22] There is little reason why the heading of this psalm, for one, should not be taken at its face value.

1. Common experience (vv. 1–2)

Trouble, and a lot of it, has come the way of the psalmist. Perhaps even his friends are shaking their heads sadly and (like Job's comforters) adding to his discouragement. Such trouble was certainly David's experience at the time of the revolt. More than one of his successors would find themselves in similar trouble. The greatest of them was no exception, as we know from the accounts of the sufferings of Jesus in the Gospels. And any number of God's people, humble as well as exalted, have found at some time or other that these verses aptly express how things are with them.

2. Thought-provoking words (vv. 3–4)

We have just read in Psalm 2 of 'Zion', Jerusalem, God's 'holy hill', the place where his 'Son' – David, in the first instance – has been installed as king. Absalom's revolt has dislodged David from that place. He is no longer in control. Yet though the usurper's overwhelming forces have apparently taken over in Jerusalem (2 Sam. 16:15), they have not dislodged the Lord. Zion is still his holy hill, and from it he still controls the situation.

[22] They should not therefore be relegated to footnotes, still less omitted altogether, as the manner of some English translations is.

It is as if the compilers of the Psalter set out first, in Psalms 1 and 2, the underlying reality, the royal privileges of God's sons (at that time the Davidic king and his people, in our days Jesus and his people);[23] then from Psalm 3 onwards the earthly realities which even such privileged people have to face. David, installed on the holy hill by a God who defies the rage of nations, now chased off it by an impudent upstart like Absalom? In theory, unthinkable! In practice, a common experience. But however far from the holy hill we seem to be, the lines of communication, 'I cry ... and he answers', are unbreakable. Psalm 2 has already told us what God's answer is.

3. Waking thoughts (vv. 5–6)

The words *lie down and sleep* will recur in Psalm 4, and because of them, that is thought of as an evening psalm. Here in Psalm 3 they are followed by *I wake again*, and we can see how this psalm could have developed from a personal prayer of David's, to a 'royal' psalm for a time of political crisis, then to a general prayer for protection, then to a particular psalm for morning use.

E. M. Blaiklock calls it and four others 'The Psalms of the Great Rebellion',[24] and imagines the germ of it in David's mind as he wakes in camp a day or two after his escape from Jerusalem. Blaiklock's picture is imaginative, but psychologically true. First the brain is a clean slate, 'briefly washed' in sleep. Then, within moments, the facts of one's dismaying situation crowd back in. Next, however, just as David might be wishing he had not woken up, there comes the realization that the very fact of his waking shows the Lord's power – the power which sustains the whole framework of human life, and is in control of all its circumstances, including David's present trouble.[25]

4. Well-grounded confidence (vv. 7–8)

The psalmist knows where to find grounds for his confidence. The word of God, once spoken, is always 'living and active',[26] and already we have seen his word to Abraham in Genesis 15:1 ('I am your shield') claimed now, centuries later, by our writer (*You are a shield around me*, v. 3). Now he goes back to the formative days of the exodus, and knows he can use afresh the grand old Israelite liturgy of Numbers 10:35 ('Rise up, O Lord! May your enemies be scattered') and Numbers 6:22–27 ('This is how you are to bless the Israelites ... "The Lord bless you and keep you"').

---

[23] Eph. 2:6; Col. 3:1; 1 Pet. 2:9; Rev. 1:6.
[24] E. M. Blaiklock, *The Psalms of the Great Rebellion* (London: Lakeland, 1970).
[25] Ibid., pp. 19–28. [26] Heb. 4:12.

Thus it is words already ancient in his day that the psalmist finds to be a living basis for his assurance. And what an assurance it is! For God's blessing is guaranteed, and guaranteed to God's people, the 'assembly' of Psalm 1. So on the one hand both the psalmist, and every other individual who identifies with that people, are in the end secure. And on the other hand, though practically 'all the men of Israel' have rebelled,[27] any such revolt is bound in the end to fail.

Psalm 4

Like many of the psalms, this one divides into roughly equal sections, or stanzas.[28] In its first stanza (v. 1), the psalmist cries to his Lord in distress. In the second (vv. 2–3), he speaks to the men who are his enemies. In the third (vv. 4–5), he turns to his friends, less able to cope with his stressful situation than he is himself. And in the fourth (vv. 6–8), where he speaks to God again, he is able now to do so with confidence.

To make personal use of the psalm, we need to think ourselves into the psalmist's frame of mind. For that purpose it will be helpful to note four facts about him, rather than to follow his four stanzas in strict order.

1. A conviction about prayer

Psalm 4 is a companion piece to Psalm 3. Both seem to belong to the same author and the same circumstances, and certainly talk the same language. Here again the psalmist is in trouble (v. 1), here again there is a lot of it (v. 2). In this psalm, as in that, he speaks of his *glory* – a special gift from God, something to glory in – and appeals for God's blessing in the ancient words of Numbers 6:24–26 (vv. 2, 6). There he sleeps and reawakens, here he lies down again to sleep, and the two psalms may be contrasted as a morning prayer and an evening one; but each is a cry to God which expects an answer.

For the psalmist is convinced that prayer is a necessity. In his greatest distress (and there will be worse times than Absalom's revolt), prayer is his greatest resource. Even when he is blaming God, he still cries to God. Against all the odds, he is sure that there must still be an ultimate framework of right, upheld by the *righteous God* (v. 1), behind all the wrongs which God allows to happen.

---

[27] 2 Sam. 16:15.

[28] A plainer word would be 'verses', like those into which hymns are divided. But to use this term would obviously cause confusion with the numbered 'verses' of the text of the Bible.

2. No delusions about his enemies

What lies behind the 'glory' phrases of 3:3 and 4:2? Perhaps something like this: 'What glory!' says David, 'God has given me a kingdom.' 'What a shame!' laughs Absalom, 'it belongs to me now.'

Absalom has captured the kingdom by lies ('he stole the hearts of the men of Israel').[29] Deception is the stock-in-trade of the enemies of God's people, most of all of the great enemy Satan, who is 'a liar and the father of lies'.[30] He and those he uses *love delusions* (v. 2). But they are themselves deluded. Deep down, the psalmist knows that in spite of everything – and his circumstances really are black – *the LORD has set apart the godly for himself* (v. 3), and the enemy cannot in the end succeed.

3. No delusions about his friends

The psalmist's friends, not his enemies, are in view in verses 4–8. Friendship does not blind him to their failings; and in encouraging them, he encourages himself. Some of them are angry, some despondent; well, anger can be a positive good, if the heart is right with God (vv. 4–5), and despondency can be cured by looking to the light of God (v. 6). Physical blessings can be a pointer to corresponding spiritual blessings, as he can testify (v. 7). And much as he no doubt appreciates his supporters, he reminds them that it is the Lord *alone* who can enable any of them to *dwell in safety* (v. 8).

The psalmist might have said of his friends, as Job said of his, 'Miserable comforters are you all!'[31] But it was 'after Job had prayed for his friends' that things began to go right for him again.[32]

4. No delusions about himself

In verse 1 the cries for help, the distresses, and (if this is what *merciful* implies) the sins are all real. The psalmist's belief in a *God of righteousness* does not mean that he imagines such things ought not to happen, or pretends they don't, or is too ashamed to admit they do. Rather, he calls to this righteous God as one who will put things right; not necessarily by spiriting the troubles away, but by giving his servant an inner peace in spite of them (v. 8).

Many an inexperienced believer will have been perplexed by the contrast between Psalm 1 and those that follow so hard on its heels. How to square what seems its complacent optimism ('Whatever he does prospers') with the traumas of real life? The question will come

[29] 2 Sam. 15:6.
[30] John 8:44. C. S. Lewis's chapter on 'Satan' in *A Preface to Paradise Lost* (London: OUP, 1942) sheds much light on this Bible truth.
[31] Job 16:2.   [32] Job 42:10.

to the fore again halfway through the Psalms, with 73, and again at the end, with 150. In the meantime we learn from them to hold on in faith, not only through distress but also through perplexity.

Psalm 5

Several words and turns of phrase from the last two psalms reappear in this one, and it is, like them, a cry to God from a believer assailed by many enemies. All three could well be 'psalms of David' in the same sense, expressing David's feelings at the time of Absalom's revolt.

If so, it could also be the next morning psalm, meaning not just the next one suitable for morning use (v. 3), but one for the 'next morning', when Tuesday's prospects are, at first, as gloomy as Monday's were. With Psalm 3 the king woke to his first day of exile, with Psalm 4 that day ended, and with Psalm 5 he wakes again to the same situation, but now with maturer thoughts about it. He sees the broader scene. His opponents represent all God's opponents, *the wicked* (v. 4), and his supporters represent *the righteous* (v. 12). The Psalter opened with the making of that basic distinction in Psalm 1.

All five stanzas of Psalm 5 are addressed to God, but in them the two kinds of relationship between God and man alternate. The psalmist speaks about 'you and me', then 'you and them', and so on: 'you and me', 'you and them', and finally 'you and me' once more.

1. People whom God condemns

Bad people, with seven ways of describing them and six ways of describing what God thinks of them, are the subject of stanza 2 (vv. 4–6). *Arrogant* is a word we might be inclined to apply to the psalmists themselves when they say, as they often do, *But I ...* (v. 7), claiming to belong with the righteous, not the wicked. There was much in the life of David, for example, that was not at all righteous. But his heart was God's, and he bowed to God's authority. That is the opposite of arrogance.

Stanza 4 (vv. 9–10) tells us that the bad heart has bad effects, and comes to a bad end. It expresses itself in words that harm; the great rebellion was a case in point, with the *intrigues* of Absalom[33] and the *destruction* proposed by Ahithophel.[34] It stands condemned by God; the verb *declare ... guilty* is the opposite of the great New Testament verb 'justify', and the crime for which this is the verdict is, as it is throughout Scripture, that *they have rebelled against* God. Absalom's determination to put himself on the throne in David's place illustrates perfectly this most basic of sins.

---

[33] 2 Sam. 15:1–12.   [34] 2 Sam. 16:23 – 17:4.

2. People whom God justifies

The ground on which God declares people guilt*less*, on the other hand, is not their goodness, any more than it is in the great New Testament passage on justification, Romans 3. In fact the description of the wicked in this psalm is applied by Paul in that chapter to 'the whole world'.[35] No; in Old Testament as in New the ground of one's justification is simply faith in a God of grace.

The odd-numbered stanzas spell this out. In the first (vv. 1–3), the psalmist recognizes the Lord as *my King and my God,* a higher authority whom he, king though he may be, is bound to obey and to trust. The third (vv. 7–8) tells how much he values God's *house* or *temple,* the place where God is to be met with, whether the tent of earliest times or the building of more recent times;[36] and how much he desires God's *righteousness* and God's *way,* so that his whole lifestyle shall be governed by the divine word. The fifth (vv. 11–12) rejoices in God's *protection* and *favour,* and supremely in his *name,* Yahweh, the Lord. The meaning of that name had been established in the days of the exodus: an almighty, saving God, whose undeserved love – his grace – rescues and blesses his people, destroying his enemies as he does so, and makes them his own by an unbreakable covenant. In contrast to the wicked (*not a word from their mouth can be trusted,* v. 9), he really is who and what he says he is: "I AM WHO I AM ... This is my name for ever."[37] It is the entrusting of oneself to this God which is 'counted ... for righteousness'.[38]

Psalm 6

The sixth psalm is the most emotional so far, and for that reason raises some important questions.

1. A question of expression

The idea that spontaneous praise and prayer are somehow better, more real, than those which are thought out and 'composed', is a foolish one. The psalmists, indeed all the great hymn writers, would have no patience with it. Even when they themselves went through the kind of turmoil described in Psalm 6, they could afterwards, or even at the time, look objectively at it, and shape it into a poem which God's people have valued ever since. Like every other psalm this is a '*work* of *art*', in the sense that effort (work) and skill (art) were put into the making of it. It is worth noting some of our

[35] Rom. 3:19; Rom. 3:13a = Ps. 5:9b.
[36] The ark was kept in both kinds of structure before the temple was built in Solomon's time: 1 Sam. 3:3 (?); 7:1; 2 Sam. 7:2.
[37] Exod. 3:14–15.   [38] Gen. 15:6 RV.

writer's methods; they will recur throughout the Psalter.

He used parallelism (Hebrew poetry 'rhymes' not in the sound of its word-endings but in its meanings):

Rebuke me not in your anger / Discipline me not in your wrath.

He used the device known as chiasmus ('crossover'), phrases balanced on either side of a pivot:

Lord, heal me / My bones suffer // My soul suffers / How long, Lord?

He used repetition: *bones* and *soul* may contrast the physical and the mental/spiritual, or (more likely) be parallel ways of saying 'the real Me'[39] or a comprehensive way of saying 'the whole Me', but both of them suffer[40] in verses 2–3, and so will the enemy in verse 10 – the same word three times.[41] His poem was set to music: the *director* would rehearse it to *sheminith* (*eighth* – conceivably the *stringed instruments* accompanying the voice line at an octave interval). By such craftsmanship his deep feelings were expressed more, not less, effectively.

2. A question of background
Was he ill? Neither *bones ... in agony* nor the ambivalent word *heal* necessarily implies illness. But regardless of his state of health, two other things certainly are implied as background to the psalmist's *anguish*. One is his sin: he needs God's mercy (vv. 2 and 9) and fears God's anger (v. 1). The other is the malice of his enemies (vv. 7, 8, 10).

These and the other pieces of the jigsaw – the threat of death (v. 5), the emotional turmoil (vv. 6–7), the suddenly renewed confidence in the closing verses – fall into place if, with Blaiklock, we take the heading of Psalm 3 ('A psalm of David. When he fled from his son Absalom') to cover at least four consecutive psalms, and thus to include this one. The rebellion of Absalom is now seen by David to be the result of his own sinful mismanagement of his family and his kingdom. The rebels are many (*all*, three times), death and destruction seem a real possibility, and the fact that he still dotes on his ungrateful son sharpens his grief. But then he is reminded of

---

[39] 'Bone' (*eṣem*) is often translated as '(it)self', 'same' or 'very' (e.g. Exod. 24:10; Lev. 23:21; Exod. 12:17).

[40] A strong word; 'shaken to the depths', suggests Kidner. The Greek word used here in the LXX (see p. 1.38, n. 64) appears also in Matt. 14:26; John 12:27.

[41] NIV scrambles the effect, alas, by translating the repeated *bāhēl* in three different ways.

God's unbreakable promises to the House of David, and persuaded that, in spite of all, those promises are for him, not for Absalom. *Away from me* is not peevish, but imperious: it is the king who speaks.

3. A question of theology

This is the first psalm to provide a piece of another jigsaw, the Old Testament picture of life after death. Psalm 16 will give us more, but for the moment we have simply the bleak statement which the psalmist addresses to God in verse 5, *No-one remembers you when he is dead.*

Jesus teaches us that the basic fact of an after-life is implied far back in the Bible story. He is not referring to Sheol (the *grave* in v. 5), which throughout the Old Testament denotes simply 'the place of the dead', good and bad alike, and does not in itself tell us anything about that place. Rather, he is speaking specifically about the dead *rising*, that is, about *life* after death: 'Have you not read in the book of Moses, in the account of the bush, how God said to him, "I am the God of Abraham, the God of Isaac, and the God of Jacob"? He is not the God of the dead, but of the living.'[42] In other words, when God says long after Abraham's death that he is still Abraham's God, he is talking about a relationship between two persons who in some sense are still both living, even though one of them has undoubtedly died.

But of what that life after death would *mean*, of what you would *do* in it, the Old Testament people had little idea. In verse 5, the word *remembers* has to do not with memories but with memorials, that is, commemorations. David certainly believes that after this life he will still belong to God, and be aware of God; the divine *anger* (v. 1), presumably provoked by sin on his part, must be a temporary thing, since he is casting himself in penitence on the covenant love (v. 4) of Yahweh, the covenant-keeping Lord; verse 5 is not therefore the cry of a despairing sinner.[43] But what he cannot imagine is how he will be able after death to *express* his awareness of God. How is anyone in that land of shadows able to commemorate, to celebrate, God's great doings? *Who praises you from his grave,* when voices and harps and temples have all (to the best of David's knowledge) been left behind?

We New Testament people are much more fully informed, now that 'Christ Jesus ... has brought life and immortality to light

---

[42] Mark 12:26–27, quoting Exod. 3:6.
[43] Weiser's view (p. 131), that the psalmist 'believes that death completely severs every bond between God and man', is a very superficial reading of this text.

through the gospel'.[44] We know that though this present life is full of good things, and is God's perfect plan for us for the time being, the next life will be even better, indeed infinitely better. But for all his limited view, the psalmist has a lesson for us. What he least wanted to leave behind in this world (he has by now discovered that he has not lost it after all!) was the opportunity to serve and praise God. He had his priorities right.

4. A question of use

Whether or not David was its author, Psalm 6 puts into words the traumatic experience of one servant of God, and it has been preserved for others to make it their own. First the desperation, and then the renewed confidence, have often come the way of God's people, whether as a people or as individuals.

This is not a matter of our experience merely happening to coincide with that of the psalmist. Jesus himself takes up a phrase from each end of this psalm: 'My heart is troubled' (John 12:27) echoes verse 3,[45] as he looks towards his death; 'Away from me, you evildoers!' (Matt. 7:23) echoes verse 8, as he looks towards his return. All who identify with him, who 'want to know ... the power of his resurrection and the fellowship of ... his sufferings',[46] are bound to find themselves at some time, in some measure, following the path of the rejected King and of his distant ancestor David. But they too can rediscover their confidence in God's promises, and express the whole experience in the words of this most heartfelt of psalms.

Psalm 7

Psalms 1 and 2, the preamble to the book, offered us two complementary ways of looking at God and his world. Psalm 7 now combines them. The down-to-earth practicality of Psalm 1 and the wisdom books is here both at the beginning, where the *ifs* of verses 3 and 4 recall the protestations of Job 31, and at the end, where the trouble-maker's fate in verses 14–16 recalls Proverbs 26:27 and 28:10. The sublime vision of Psalm 2 and the prophetic books is here at the centre, where in verses 6–9 the Most High – El Elyon, the God of all nations[47] – presides as Judge over the universal court.

But notice in particular in the heading of this psalm a link with Psalm 3. Leaving aside *shiggaion*, presumably a musical term whose

---

[44] 2 Tim. 1:10.   [45] The equivalent Gk. verb; see p. 1.32, n. 40.   [46] Phil. 3:10.
[47] First proclaimed by that name as the God of both Abraham the Hebrew and Melchizedek the non-Hebrew, in Gen. 14:18ff.

meaning we can only guess at,[48] we find that this sequence of five psalms, all in some sense *of David*, is pinned at either end to the biblical narrative by a reference to events in David's life. Psalm 3 is 'of David. When he fled from ... Absalom', Psalm 7 is *of David, which he sang ... concerning Cush* (whoever he may be).

As we pursue these clues, we shall notice two things about the way the psalmist writes. There is vivid picture language throughout: David's opponent is like a lion, a pregnant man (!), and a digger of holes; God is a judge in a courtroom and then an armed warrior. And there is chiasmus, the poetic device we first noticed in Psalm 6: the poem's four stanzas are about Cush/God//God/Cush.

1. Concerning Cush: a lion (vv. 1–5)

This man *Cush, a Benjamite,* represents a crowd of enemies who are attacking the psalmist with false accusations. We know nothing else about him, though his very obscurity suggests that he really existed (what would be the point of mentioning him otherwise?). But we do know that there was no love lost between David and the tribe of Benjamin, both before he first came to the throne and after he regained it at the death of Absalom.[49]

How might we fit together such information as we have?

First, we have seen how not only Psalm 3 but also the three following psalms would not be out of place in the story of Absalom's revolt. Next, we find that there was a Benjamite (though he is not called Cush) who at that same time did exactly what this one is described as doing, fierce as a lion in his loyalty to Saul, David's predecessor.[50] It is not hard to hear his accusing words behind those of verse 4: 'Once you were with Saul, and you betrayed his trust; then you turned against him, and you stole his kingdom.'[51] Next, three of these psalms are linked by 'glory', for verse 5c should read, '[Let him] *lay my glory* in the dust.' It means the honour of being God's chosen king (3:3), which Absalom wants to take from David (4:2), and which Shimei the Benjamite will be delighted to see him lose (7:5).[52]

The word *selah*, which occurs in the same three psalms,[53] is often thought to mean an interlude for music or meditation when a psalm

---

[48] Perhaps from a verb 'to wander' (therefore wild, rhapsodic music?) – though it is hard to see why.

[49] See 1 Sam. 18 – 27 (Saul was a Benjamite); 2 Sam. 20.

[50] See 2 Sam. 16:5ff.

[51] There is much debate over v. 4, as the variety of translations indicates. The NIV's is as good as any.

[52] Most translations miss the link; the ever-faithful RV, finding *kābôd* in all three places, translates it as *glory* in all three places.

[53] Pss. 3:2, 4, 8; 4:2, 4; 7:5.

was used in public worship.[54] With the network of connections just noted, it seems a distinct possibility that *selah* might indeed mean an interlude, but one with a different purpose. Perhaps it shows where singing was to give place to the reading of related scriptures – in this case accounts of the events which (depending on one's view of the headings) either gave rise to Psalms 3 to 7, or illustrate them so remarkably.[55]

2. Concerning God: a courtroom (vv. 6–9)

The psalmist would like his name cleared by the judgment of a human court (it is this, I think, that is primarily in view in 1:5), but he appeals beyond that to the divine *rule* of the One who will *judge the peoples* (vv. 7–8, as in 2:8–9).

A risky step! True, you can be far more sure of getting justice in the latter courtroom, but there the Judge *searches minds and hearts* (v. 9) with infinite thoroughness. You may get more than you bargained for – 'Everything is uncovered and laid bare before the eyes of him to whom we must give account'[56] – and you may be vindicated in much slower and stranger ways than you expected.

How could the psalmist dare to maintain his *righteousness* and *integrity* (v. 8) before such a court? Is not this the very arrogance that 5:5 deplores? No. The case of Shimei's slanders shows what is meant by the innocence claimed in verses 3–5. David was protesting not that he was sinless, but simply that he was innocent of this particular charge. As he fled from Jerusalem, he knew he deserved God's 'discipline' and 'wrath' (6:1) for all sorts of things, but not for those of which this Benjamite was accusing him.

3. Concerning God: an armoury (vv. 10–13)

People who object to the violence of the Old Testament are really objecting to the fierceness of the Old Testament God. They think he ought to be grandfatherly and mild, and they ask what he is doing with shield and sword, bow and arrows.

The psalmist gets this divine armoury into focus. God is still in verse 11 the *judge*, and the *righteous* judge, that he was in verses 6–9. The odd picture of an armed judge means that he is active, and effective, in the pursuit of justice. This court has teeth; it does not deal in idle threats.

---

[54] Note the phrase *For the director of music* in the headings of Pss. 4, 5, and 6. We shall find it also in many later psalms.
[55] The suggestion is Goulder's, in respect of other parts of the Psalter. We shall return to it at the beginning of Book II with Ps. 44 (see p. 1.157, n. 399) and Ps. 46 (see p. 1.167).
[56] Heb. 4:13.

The fact that God is a righteous judge means that he uses his armour impartially. His *wrath* cuts both ways. The AV translators felt they had to insert three extra words to make sense of verse 11: *God is angry with the wicked every day*. But in fact God's daily anger affects everyone. We may be innocent in one respect, yet must fear it because of our guilt in another.

Even so, the stanza's main intention is to comfort. Just as the *man* who *does not repent*[57] feels the edge of God's sword, so the *upright* man benefits from his shield. The armoury of his wrath is constantly mobilized to save as well as to punish, and it is precisely by dealing with the wicked that he rescues the innocent.[58] So far from being embarrassed by the fierceness of the biblical God, we ought to be grateful for it. It guarantees that sooner or later everything will be as it ought to be.

4. Concerning Cush: a pregnancy and a pit (vv. 14–17)

The doom of the wicked, from one point of view God's anger against them, is from another their own malice recoiling on themselves. We might add to the armoury of verses 12–13 a weapon of which the Bible world had never heard, namely a boomerang, and put it into the hand of the psalmist's enemy!

With its startling picture of a pregnant man, verse 14 recognizes that the growth of an evil deed is real and inexorable, from its conception to its completion.[59] But verses 15–16 add the picture of a pit into which the man who has dug it falls himself. The evildoer is finally destroyed by his own wickedness.

In the process God rescues those who have cried to him for help. As Craigie puts it, what he does is 'to direct the consequences of evil away from the innocent and turn them back upon their perpetrators'.[60] The supreme instance is when he raises his Son from death, and his Son's people with him, and death itself is destroyed.

Verse 17 is not therefore a doxology merely tacked on at the psalm's end, a formal 'nod to God'. The whole poem celebrates *his righteousness*. In a world full of evil he will be seen in the end to have 'done everything well',[61] and put everything right.

---

[57] The NIV marginal reading of v. 12 must be correct.
[58] See on Ps. 5:11–12, p. 1.31.
[59] The usual translations of *šeqer* (NIV *disillusionment*) are 'falsehood' or 'lies', and false accusation is of course the particular evil in the case of David and the Benjamite.
[60] Craigie, p. 103.   [61] Mark 7:37.

Psalm 8

In three or four places here, "'the Hebrew," as the margin of the RV candidly notes, "is obscure"'.[62] The NIV, however, with its own 'margins' or footnotes (which hint at some of the problems), gives a sufficiently clear idea of this splendid psalm.

Notice first a few features of the translation before us. (a) Though it does not explain the musical term *gittith*,[63] it does highlight a poetic device to add to those we have met earlier. 'Inclusio' means beginning and ending a literary unit with the same words, which in this case 'include' the bulk of the psalm between two identical shouts of praise. (b) It gives two versions of verse 2. *Strength*, in the margin, represents the original Hebrew; *praise*, in the text, represents the Greek translation of the Old Testament, the LXX,[64] which Jesus quotes in Matthew 21:16, as we shall see. (c) It does the same with verse 5; *God* (mg.) is the obvious meaning of the Hebrew, *heavenly beings* (text) is a possible meaning preferred by the LXX and quoted in Hebrews 2:9.

But what is the psalm saying, and what is it doing in this position in the Psalter?

1. The story so far

We cannot miss its echoes of Psalms 3 – 7. The remembering, or 'being mindful', of 6:5, the glory of 3:3, 4:2, and 7:5, the avenger of 7:3–5, and the enemies in all five psalms, are here in this one as well.

On the other hand there are differences. Psalm 8 moves away from the individualism of 3 – 7 with the word *our*, while its cosmic, prophetic scope, not to mention its use in the New Testament and its familiarity even today, hark back to Psalm 2, which displays the same features.

If the compilers reckoned that the intervening psalms were all related in some way to the David-and-Absalom story, the group would have been well framed by Psalms 2 and 8. Perhaps the germ of the latter came to David the shepherd boy, marvelling at the night sky above the hills of Bethlehem (8:3). But it is David the king before and after the great rebellion – that is, realizing at his accession (Ps. 2) and more fully after his restoration (Ps. 8) the privilege of being God's deputy – who provides a richer background to the sequence.

---

[62] Kirkpatrick, p. 37, referring particularly to the words *You have set* (v. 1).

[63] *Gittith* means someone or something – a tune? an instrument? a ceremony? – from Gath; perhaps the marching song of David's bodyguard, some of whom, as the history of the rebellion tells us (2 Sam. 15:18), were Gittites. (So was Goliath!)

[64] The Septuagint (*septuaginta* is Latin for 'seventy', hence LXX), from the group of scholars supposed to have made this translation in Egypt in the third century BC.

2. *The joyous slaughter of sacred cows*

So familiar is verse 1 that we can easily miss its shameless political incorrectness. The Bible world, like ours, was pluralistic, awash with all sorts of different beliefs: in the view of any correctly thinking person, all of them valid, but none of them actually 'right' in such a way as to make the rest wrong.

Not so the psalmist. The LORD, the God of Israel and the Bible, is not just *our Lord*, he says, but *the* name, the only name, to be honoured *in all the earth* and even *above the heavens*. Little Israel is right, and the rest are wrong.

What is more, those with opposing ideas are not to be listened to for their helpful insights, as is urged by some, but rather put to *silence*; and that, not by equally powerful champions, but by the simple-hearted and dependent. Such *infants* hold the position of *strength*, which when Jesus quotes these words[65] means that the children's *praise* of him on Palm Sunday is right, and that those who would tone it down are wrong.

Verses 3–8 are equally 'incorrect', even apart from the NIV's traditional use of the word *man* to signify the human race.[66] What is the fashionable view of man's littleness? That it is ludicrous to imagine God, if there is a God, centring his interest on the inhabitants of this tiny planet. And of man's greatness? That the inhabitants of this tiny planet nevertheless have the ability to control their own destiny. Psalm 8 contradicts both views. Little, yes; great, yes; but only because it was God's plan first to create this immense setting for man, and then to appoint him ruler over it.

3. *The first man and the last man*

This is not only the theme, but also the plan, of our psalm. In verses 1–5, the first half of Genesis 1's creation story (summed up in v. 3) provides the vast stage for a drama in which man, though diminutive, is the central character. In verses 6–9, the second half of that story (summed up in vv. 7–8) describes the world over which he wields the delegated rule of its majestic Maker.

That authority[67] is given to man first in the person of Adam.[68] It is renewed to Noah after the flood,[69] and later embodied in the kingship of David and his successors. While in a broad sense it has never ceased to be the responsibility of the human race in general, it really 'comes true' – is 'fulfilled', to use the biblical term – in Christ, the true Man, Saviour, and King. Of course 'we do not yet see

[65] Matt. 21:16.   [66] See p. 1.20.
[67] *Māšal*, the verb behind *ruler* in v. 6, is used of God himself in Pss. 22:28; 66:7; 103:19; and elsewhere.
[68] Gen. 1:26, 28.   [69] Gen. 9:2.

everything in subjection' to him, says Hebrews 2:5–9 NRSV. But because of his crucifixion (says Hebrews) and resurrection (says Eph. 1:19–22), that glory is already his, and one day we shall see it revealed – shall see everything, even death, 'under his feet' (says 1 Cor. 15:24–27).

All three of these New Testament letters are quoting Psalm 8. They tell us that it is only when Christ crucified and risen stands at the centre that the pieces of the jigsaw – the picture of creation and of man's position in it – fall into place. Of all that God created, only man is able even to ask the question of verse 4, as Kidner points out;[70] and only the man who is also redeemed by God can grasp the answer to it.[71]

Psalms 9 and 10

It is the Hebrew and English versions, and the Protestant tradition, that reckon these as separate psalms; the Greek and Latin versions, and the Roman Catholic tradition, combine them, and so, surprisingly perhaps, shall we – for reasons which will emerge.

1. Something familiar

Much here is familiar from what we have recently been reading. On the one hand, 'praise to the name of the LORD Most High' (7:17; cf. 9:2), the Redeemer of Israel and the God of all nations, from the innocent plaintiff who seeks him; on the other hand, the discomfiture of the wicked, despite all their pretensions and his seeming remoteness, when the Lord in his turn seeks *them*, to call them to account – such themes, with many recurring turns of phrase, figure repeatedly in these two as in the previous eight psalms.

There is no good reason why it should not, as before, be the experience of David, indeed his experience at the time of the great rebellion, which is described here. Both his past victories and his present tribulations are of a kind which justifies the dramatic language of Psalms 9 and 10.

2. Something new

The obvious novelty is the word *higgaion* (9:16), but alas its meaning can only be guessed.[72] Of much more significance, because it clarifies the structure, which in turn clarifies the meaning, is a

---

[70] Kidner, p. 67.

[71] These scriptures rather undermine the first verse of the popular hymn 'Jesus is Lord, Creation's voice proclaims it' (David Mansell). It is not creation, but the cross, which proclaims the Lordship of Christ, and moves people to confess it (Phil. 2:5–11). See also the praise of the Creator in Rev. 4 and of the Redeemer in Rev. 5: it is the latter, the slain Lamb, who shows the seer how things really are.

[72] It may be related to the word rendered *meditate* in 1:2 (and *plot* in 2:1!).

technique of verse-writing which appears here for the first time in the Psalter, though it is not apparent in our English Bibles. Rather as in the Western tradition of poetry the ends of lines may rhyme, in this form of verse the beginnings of lines follow a sequence: the first word in 9:1 begins with the first letter of the Hebrew alphabet, the first word in 9:3 begins with the second letter, and so on. Here the scheme is not complete, but if it were, the psalms combined would make a poem of twenty-two short stanzas with two verses each.

This 'acrostic' pattern is only one of the things that bind our two psalms together. We might note also a good many words and phrases which occur in both, while the presence of a *selah* after 9:20 and the absence of 'David' before 10:1 suggest the midpoint of a single psalm rather than a break between two. But the alphabetical scheme, though far from complete, is the major unifying factor, and a great help in seeing the point of this fascinating two-part poem.

There may have been a more regular original version, now lost. Yet for all its irregularities, whenever and however they came about, the version we do have is a remarkably consistent and shapely piece of work.

3. Technique and inspiration

> A boat, beneath a sunny sky
> Lingering onward dreamily
> In an evening of July –
> Children three that nestle near,
> Eager eye and willing ear ...

Lewis Carroll wrote the poem which begins thus as the final page of his two great books, *Alice's Adventures in Wonderland* and *Through the Looking-Glass*. It is, first, a classic English example of an acrostic, and secondly, a fine illustration of how technique and inspiration can be friends, not enemies. Within the technical constraints of making twenty-one lines of verse not only scan and rhyme, but also spell out with their initial letters the full name of the child for whom the stories were told, Carroll produced one of his finest poems. It is a real *jeu d'esprit*: a 'game' not simply 'of wit' but 'of spirit', the spirit of the people and relationships and circumstances that gave rise to it, and an expression of deep feeling.

So it is with Psalms 9 and 10. In this most artificial of forms the psalmist expresses the most profound of emotions. Let us try to see the shape and to feel the force of these psalms as they have come down to us.

First, the two psalms answer to each other like the two hinged panels known in the world of art as a 'diptych'. They are almost exactly the same length, and the whole of Psalm 9, the left-hand panel, as it were, divides neatly into ten two-verse stanzas. With one or two exceptions, these begin in the Hebrew original with the first ten letters of the alphabet. (The details are in the footnote.)[73] There is a marked change of tone at 9:13, dividing the first six stanzas from the remaining four.

Psalm 10 is more complicated. Again there seem to be ten stanzas, though the English Bible's verse numbers are no guide to them.[74] Again the tone changes after the first six (at 10:12). So does the acrostic structure, when after the many textual problems of 10:1–11 the last four stanzas complete the alphabet straightforwardly.

As now we see 9:1–12 answering to 10:1–11, and the changed tone of 9:13–20 answering to the changed tone of 10:12–18, the maker of this double poem will emerge powerfully from it.

4. Grammar and facts (9:1–12)

Immensely positive is this section – you would not guess the plight the psalmist is actually in. *Tell* of the Lord's *wonders* (9:1) and *proclaim ... what he has done* (9:11); with him injustice is righted (9:4) and the *oppressed* find a *refuge* (9:9); we notice the chiastic pattern,[75] and at the centre of it the Lord judging (9:5–8).

But the grammar too should be noticed. What gives rise to the immediacy of the verbs in the first and sixth stanzas (*I will praise*; *Sing praises*)? Verbs in the perfect tense in the second and third (9:3–6), and verbs in the future (imperfect) tense in the fourth and fifth (9:7–10); and the tenses are rich and subtle. *You have ... destroyed the wicked* means what it says; David has seen this happen in the past. But it

---

[73] Readers with no Hebrew may find the following list helpful, and will excuse its echoes of a dentist checking one's teeth. It gives the 22 letters of the Heb. alphabet in numbered order, as they relate to Pss. 9 – 10 in Craigie's reconstruction. They are transliterated not in the way preferred in the footnotes in this book, but (for simplicity's sake) as in the NIV of Ps. 119.

Ps. 9:1–12: *aleph* (1), *beth* (2), *gimel* (3); *daleth* (4) missing; *he* (5) begins the final word of 9:6; *waw* (6), *zayin* (7).

Ps. 9:13–20: *heth* (8), *teth* (9), *yodh* (10); *kaph* (11) missing, replaced by an extra *qoph* (19).

Ps. 10:1–11: *lamedh* (12); *mem* (13) missing; *nun* (14) comes halfway through 10:3b; *samekh* (15) begins an emended word in 10:5b; *ayin* (16) and *pe* (17) have been transposed, and *pe* begins the second word, not the first, of 10:7, while *ayin* begins 10:8c; *tsadhe* (18) begins a hypothetical word filling out the beginning of 10:10.

Ps. 10:12–18: *qoph* (19), *resh* (20), *sin* or *shin* (21), *taw* (22).

[74] Stanzas 1–6 begin successively with vv. 1, 3b, 5b, 7, 8c, 10, according to Craigie; stanzas 7–10 with vv. 12, 14, 15, 17.

[75] See p. 1.32.

means more. God's prophets have seen – *foreseen* – these things happening in the future, and so sure is their vision that the deed is as good as done already. Such judgments, according to 'the perfect tense of certainty, "are sure to"' fall sooner or later,[76] and on this massive encouragement the psalmist has been feeding his soul.

If the perfect tense is a kind of future, the future is a kind of present![77] To say that *the LORD reigns for ever* (9:7) means not that when time comes to an end his eternal reign will begin, but that he is as truly on the throne now as he will be then, and has in fact never been off it. So because he is eternal these future tenses – *he will judge* and *he will govern* – tell us what he is already doing, indeed what he is always doing, though often in ways we cannot see. The grammatical forms of perfect and future, what he has done and what he will do, are both in their different ways facts on which to base a faith for the present. With this too David will have fortified himself.

5. The other side of the picture (10:1–11)

Turning to the right-hand panel of the diptych and the corresponding section of Psalm 10 (vv. 1–11), we see something very different. For all that the Lord has *never forsaken those who seek him* (9:10), that is precisely what he does now seem to have done (10:1). Psalm 9:1–12 focused on God, and the wicked were mentioned only to be dismissed; 10:1–11 focus on the wicked, and God is mentioned only to be dismissed.

The wicked man *boasts* and *sneers*, utters *lies* and *threats*, *hunts down the weak* and *murders the innocent*. Secular modern people would no doubt be surprised to be told that the root of his wickedness is his atheism. This is not a consciously reached religious conviction, but an atheism-in-practice, which can quite cheerfully coexist with church attendance and the reciting of the creed. It is not so much that the wicked man of 10:1–11 believes *there is no God* (10:4 NRSV), as that he acts as if there weren't. *In all his thoughts* – the word is *schemes*, as in 10:2 – *there is no room for God* (10:4 NIV). In the same way, God's *laws are far from him*. He both distances himself from the rules, and presumes himself immune from their penalties.

You don't have to believe in God to deplore all the wickedness in the world. But if you do believe, that panorama of evil may well provoke the response of 10:1–2. This also could verge on atheism-in-practice: *There is no God* showing himself as, or where, you think he ought to. But absent though he seems to be, at least you are still talking to him.

---

[76] Motyer, on 9:15–16.   [77] On the perfect and imperfect/future tenses, see p. 1.68.

6. A prayer in the light (9:13–20)

When we describe Psalm 9 as positive and Psalm 10 as negative, we might almost be speaking in photographic terms. The two panels picture the same circumstances, but one is bright with dark shadows, the other dark with bright gleams.

This is true of both halves of each psalm, even though in the case of Psalm 9 the mood changes so violently at verse 13. We should never have guessed from 9:1–12 that the psalmist was feeling so threatened by his *enemies* and so close to the *gates of death*. Yet when in these four final stanzas he again speaks to the Lord (as he did in stanza 1, 9:1–2), his prayer for the punishing of evil and the vindicating of innocence is illuminated by a great certainty. It is true that from the eye of experience the Lord sometimes hides himself (10:1); but to the eye of faith he *has made himself known* (9:16 NRSV). The counterpart of the *wonders* by which he has revealed himself in the past (9:1) is a *terror* by which he will equally surely do so in the future (9:20), when all will be seen for what they really are.

7. A prayer in the dark (10:12–18)

That (Ps. 9) is how things are. But it is not how things seem. Like Psalm 9, Psalm 10 both began with prayer, and now reverts to it in its second part. The darkness, however, persists; the innocent are still *afflicted* and *oppressed*, and the wicked still get away with it. However much you 'trust and obey', 'belief and morality are not guarantees of happiness and stability'.[78]

Yet there are real gleams in the darkness. The wicked man, who said in 10:11, *God has forgotten*, is still saying in 10:13, *He won't call me to account*; thus (as Kidner puts it) 'his inner dialogue contradicts' the 'bold words, "There is no God"'.[79] It is the God he doesn't believe in who will, he hopes, leave him alone! God *is* there; he *does* see (10:14), he *does* hear (10:17), and his eternal reign *will* one day be revealed in power (10:16).

How realistic, finally, is the order of these two psalms! A mere religious versifier, interested chiefly in working out his acrostic, would without doubt have assumed that so far as his subject matter was concerned, naturally that should move from the darkness of experience (Ps. 10) to the light of faith (Ps. 9). David knew otherwise. He had enough ups and downs in his life to recognize how often they come in that order. When he was down in the dark, and wickedness swelled to fill the whole picture of 10:1–11, how he must have valued the providence that had first lifted him up into the

---

[78] Craigie, p. 128.   [79] Kidner, p. 71.

light, to be reassured in advance about the way things really were. And, of course, still are.

Psalm 11

There is in Psalm 11 enough that is familiar from the preceding 'David' psalms to show that it belongs with them, and enough that is new to give it a distinctive message.

1. Something familiar, something new

It talks the language of Psalms 3 – 10. Here again are the wicked and the righteous. Here again is the Lord, who will punish those and favour these. We must remind ourselves also that although he *is* *righteous* and *loves justice* (v. 7), meaning that he loves to see righteousness in human lives because it corresponds to his own character, what wins his favour is not our sinlessness but our submission. Again, therefore, he is on his throne, a judge of the rebellious and a refuge for the trusting.

Moreover, as Psalm 11's phraseology is so like that of its predecessors, and they fit so readily into the biblical history of David, that may equally well be the setting for this psalm.

Here again, then, would be David the refugee. Not, however, David in flight from his son and would-be successor Absalom, for at the time of the great rebellion he and his advisers agreed that flight was the only possible course. Psalm 11 fits much better with the events not of 2 Samuel 15 – 19, but of 1 Samuel 18 – 27, where also David was often in flight (though not, in the event, on this occasion). Then it was his predecessor Saul who threatened him.

Taking refuge in the mountains was sound advice in a number of biblical situations,[80] and faced with those earlier threats David had regularly disappeared into the unfrequented hill-country of the south. This would be the natural understanding of verse 1 – 'Flee, like a bird, to the mountain' (not 'Flee, like-a-bird-to-the-mountain'; the mountain belongs to the reality, not to the simile) – indeed, 'Flee to *your* mountain.'[81]

All this is one of the new and distinctive features of the psalm. Another is the absence from it of any form of prayer. It is, rather, a statement: a testimony, even a creed. Where every David psalm hitherto has at some point been addressed to God, this one is a proclamation about him. It declares a great strong theology, with facets not previously shown in the David Collection; a theology

[80] E.g. Gen. 19:17; 1 Sam. 14:22; 1 Kgs. 19:3–9; Matt. 24:16.
[81] See 1 Sam. 23:14, 25–29; 26:1. Some commentators take the view that *your mountain* means Mount Zion, and that David, now king, is away from Jerusalem, is advised to go back there, and repudiates the idea. This seems to me very unlikely.

which so far from being merely academic has proved itself in a time of great crisis.

2. In the dark (vv. 1–3)

In the Lord I have taken refuge.[82] Before the psalm begins the psalmist has already made a decision. We note that a decision has been necessary; there has been no one obvious course of action, and David (we assume it is he) has had to choose among various options.

But he, his advisers, and his opponents are all in some sense in the dark. His opponents lurk in the dark, *to shoot from the shadows at the upright in heart.* The biblical narrative tells how David when on the run from Saul never knew when and where he might be betrayed.[83] In the modern world, on the global scale, terrorism strikes *from the shadows* at targets which (like its motives, though in a different sense) are indefensible. And towards any of God's people, at any time, from some hidden source, *arrows* may be winging their way – not so much the 'arrows of outrageous fortune',[84] as those of a malicious spiritual foe who knows very well what he is doing.

David's advisers are not malicious. Flight to the hill-country means safety, as he and they know from experience. They are not schemers, like Shemaiah plotting Nehemiah's downfall,[85] but well-meaning friends, like Peter trying to protect Jesus.[86] But they are in the dark, in that they cannot see what David *ought* to do. Confronted by this crisis, whatever it may be, is he to run away from it, to shut his eyes to it, or to outface it? They opt for the sensible choice, because they cannot see which is the right one.

David is in the dark in that he does not know, any more than the rest do, where or what the next attack will be. But he has already made his choice: *In the LORD I take refuge.* 'We know that,' say his friends pettishly, 'but what are you actually going to *do*?' His reply must be that it matters little whether he is in the hill-country or in the city, so long as he is *in the LORD.* The important thing is attitude, not location. The main reason for their suggesting flight is that this time, in their view, *the righteous* will achieve nothing by trying to stand firm, since *the foundations are being destroyed:*[87] 'the "ground rules" on which society operates'[88] have broken down. David's retort is that this is the very time *not* to do as he has done often before, and flee to the mountain. This is the time to stay put, and to demonstrate by his faith that the 'ground rules' are still in place,

[82] So v. 1 is better translated.   [83] 1 Sam. 22:9; 23:7, 19; 24:1; 26:1.
[84] William Shakespeare, *Hamlet*, III.i.58.   [85] Neh. 6:10–13.   [86] Matt. 16:22.
[87] On this showing the NIV rightly includes v. 3 within the quotation marks.
[88] Motyer, p. 494.

despite Saul's wholesale flouting of them, simply because the Lord is still there.

3. The central fact (v. 4a)
He *is* there; the way the psalmist writes the first couplet of verse 4 states it emphatically. The stress is on the first half of each line; wherever the *temple* and the *throne* are – commentators differ over the meaning of *temple* in this verse – the great fact is not so much that he is *there* (rather than somewhere else), but that he *is* there (really existing, really present).

The second halves are not however mere padding. According to some, the temple is the physical building in Jerusalem,[89] that is, an earthly temple, contrasting with the heavenly throne; it stands for God's immanence (he is with the psalmist in this crisis), while the throne stands for his transcendence (he is over all things, including this crisis).

The Old Testament, however, represents temple and throne not as being on different planes, but as picturing different aspects of God. It is, again, not a matter of location; it is a matter of function. There were, at any rate from Solomon's time onwards, both a literal temple and a literal throne in Jerusalem; one showed how man could come to God, the other how God could govern man. Each has an eternal counterpart in heaven, which is where God welcomes all to his eternal presence and governs all by his eternal power.

When Habakkuk quoted verse 4a, long after the time of David, he followed it with the words 'let all the earth be silent before him'.[90] The ringing affirmation that *The Lord is* certainly silences the psalmist's well-meaning friends.

4. In the light (vv. 4b–7)
God is not in the dark. None of those who figure in verses 1–3 can see him, but he can see them. In fact though he seems to them both invisible and idle, he is actively doing just that – observing and examining them (v. 4b), all of them, righteous and wicked alike.

He does not, however, treat them alike. What he is doing right now, while things go from bad to worse and they see no sign of his activity, is, on the one hand, examining the righteous in a more particular way. This is the word used for testing, or assaying, precious metals. Its use in verse 5 reminds us that the righteous are not being set the kind of test they might fail, for not having scored enough goodness points. Being believers, they are already, so to speak, gold.

---

[89] Making the psalm later than David if Solomon's temple is meant, or meaning the tabernacle if the psalm is David's.
[90] Hab. 2:20.

On the other hand, being rebels, the wicked are already shown to be base metal, and there is no point in God's putting *them* through the refiner's fire. What he will do in the end (v. 6) is to punish them with another kind of fire, that which destroyed Sodom and Gomorrah in Genesis 19:24.[91]

What, in contrast, will he do for the righteous, those who are in tune with 'his nature and will: what he *is* and what he *loves*'?[92] He will bring them into the light as he is in the light: they 'shall know fully, even as' they are 'fully known'.[93] Was the psalmist speaking of the after-life? He certainly knew that it is God's gracious custom to give his people glimpses in advance of that blessed vision.

Psalm 12

Often in Old Testament times people might have spoken as the psalmist speaks here. Micah did: 'The godly have been swept from the land; not one upright man remains' (7:2). So did Isaiah: 'The righteous perish ... devout men are taken away' (57:1). So, most famously, did Elijah: 'I am the only one left' (1 Kgs. 19:10, 14).

David equally could have said these words in his refugee days, in Saul's time even more than in Absalom's, when there were so many whose word he could not trust. Psalm 11 has already pointed us in that direction. We could imagine this psalm growing out of the same circumstances. Suppose the friends who had advised him to 'flee' (11:1), and to whom he had said that he wouldn't, had then responded, 'Well, if you won't, we shall!' *Help, LORD*, cries David, *the faithful have vanished* (12:1).

The faithful, which nowadays need mean no more than 'regular churchgoers' (an example of the debasing of words which is the very theme of Ps. 12), are here those whose faithfulness to God and to others mirrors God's faithfulness to them. It is they who seem in such short supply. Verses 1–4 are about the many who cannot be trusted, and verses 5–8 about the One who can be totally trusted, specifically in their *words*.

Mention of words of guile and deceit is not however confined to the first four verses, so we shall consider the psalm not as two halves, but under two headings.

1. Words of guile

The psalmist describes such speech in several ways. In verse 2, *lies*[94] means empty talk, *vanity* (AV/RV), words with no corresponding

---

[91] The New Testament reiterates the fire theme frequently: e.g. Luke 17:28–30; 2 Pet. 2:6–9. The fire of v. 5a is that of 1 Pet. 1:7.

[92] Kidner, p. 74.   [93] 1 Cor. 13:12.

[94] The first four of these definitions are Kidner's neat coinage (p. 75).

truth behind them. *Flattering lips* means smooth talk, not only insincere praise but plausibility in general. *Deception* is double talk: *a double heart* (NRSV), literally 'a heart and a heart', readily understood today as 'doublethink' and the speech in which it is expressed. The *boastful tongue* (v. 3) *makes great boasts* (NRSV) – big talk; and the phrase *lips* which *we own* (v. 4) – *who is our master?* – means irresponsible talk, for which no-one will call us to account.

None of this talk, unfortunately, is mere hot air. It can have considerable effects. Verse 5 is in no doubt that it leads to *the oppression of the weak and the groaning of the needy*, and superhuman power is necessary to *protect* us from it. Destructive gossip, undemocratic legislation, language devalued by political correctness, the media's drowning of quality in quantity, are all examples.

All such words abuse the precious gift of communication. It is one of the 'foundations' which are being 'destroyed' (11:3). So serious a matter is the abuse of words that a society which lets it happen must be one from which *the faithful have vanished*. If they were there, they would fight it.

2. Words of truth

In linguistics as in economics, good currency drives out bad. The best is of course the Word of God. The true shows up the false, and Scripture, which is God speaking, is guaranteed true. Unlike one prominent churchman of our time, who was (we are told) 'a good preacher, though he seldom referred to the Bible',[95] those who preach from Scripture have the inestimable privilege of showing the way things really are – a great definition of preaching! – and thus of countering with words of truth the words of guile which would otherwise engulf today's world.

We must not imagine that obscurities in the Word of God affect its clarities. This psalm gives more than one example. There are half a dozen guesses as to what the last line of verse 5 means (*those who malign them*),[96] and at least three for the *furnace of clay* in verse 6.[97] None of this affects the clear message of the psalm. We must never let what we do know be obscured by what we don't know.

There is one thing which verse 5 says so clearly that we may miss it. For the first time in the David Collection, the Lord speaks. Are

[95] This contradiction in terms appeared in the obituary of Edward Carpenter, Dean of Westminster 1974–85.

[96] Something to do with 'blowing' – 'panting', and therefore 'longing' (*I will place them in the safety for which they long* NRSV)? Or perhaps 'breathing out' a curse?

[97] *Clay* is *earth* (AV/RV). On the earth? To the earth? Of the earth? A change of one letter would make the word 'gold' ('a furnace, gold purified').

these his words, or the psalmist's? Were David a poet of our own day, we should say that in such a verse he was putting words into God's mouth. But in this case it would be truer to say that God was putting words into David's mouth! In fact both are true, according to the classical doctrine of inspiration. This psalm, which is about the *flawless ... words of the LORD* and their opposite, is itself made up of those flawless words (even if we don't understand all of them), and itself has power to combat the words of guile.

Unexpectedly perhaps, Psalm 12, like Psalms 9 and 10, does not move out of darkness into light. It ends as it began, with an inclusio which might seem discouraging but is in fact merely realistic: *the faithful have vanished from among men* (v. 1) and *what is vile is honoured among men* (v. 8). The victory of true words is not instant. The weeds will continue to grow among the wheat until harvest-time.[98] We might want to insert the words 'even though' between verse 7 and verse 8; but the text as it stands makes this point forcefully – both words of truth and words of guile are ever-present realities. The true words of Psalm 12 have nonetheless made another point. The wicked say, *We will triumph* (v. 4); but that is their kind of word, and they won't. The Lord says, *I will ... arise* (v. 5); that is his kind of word, and he will. He will, in fact, have the last word.

Psalm 13

Very much at home among the David psalms, this little poem nevertheless makes its own special contribution to them.

1. Distinctive pattern, distinctive prayer

Psalm 13 has more to it than meets the eye. It divides fairly obviously into three stanzas. With the acrostic of Psalms 9 and 10 fresh in mind, I am tempted to the next best thing – the alliteration of Pain, Prayer, and Praise! In verses 1–2, the psalmist's *enemy* could be Saul, or it could be Absalom; then again it could be death (v. 3), or an illness which might lead to death, and in fact the phrase *must I wrestle with my thoughts* might mean, as in the NRSV, *must I bear pain*. At any rate, this enemy is causing real distress. Next, although the whole psalm is addressed to God, verses 3–4 are prayer in the simple and straightforward sense of petition. Finally, from past experience, or somewhere, comes a renewed confidence which leads in verses 5–6 to praise.

A different threefold division cuts across this one, for in each stanza the psalmist is concerned with God, with himself, and with his circumstances, in that order. The resulting three-by-three grid

[98] Cf. Matt. 13:24–30.

shows him (a) complaining to God in stanza 1, seeking an answer from God in stanza 2, regaining his trust in God in stanza 3; then (b) successively feeling wretched, asking for renewal, finding joy; and (c) at the end of verses 2, 4, and 6, bowing under pressure, then defying it, then rising above it.

This artful construction carries an artless message. In verse 6, in thirteen words of one syllable (still waters run deep; *good*, in particular, here means something very like Eph. 3:20), the NIV sums it up with beautiful simplicity: *I will sing to the LORD, for he has been good to me.*

So much for the form of Psalm 13. The distinctive thing about its content is the heartfelt cry of verse 1, also in monosyllables: *How long, O LORD?* As in several of the preceding psalms, something bad is happening; in this case we are not told what it is – simply that whatever it is, it seems interminable.

So we find acknowledged here in Scripture what we all know in experience, that the steady march of real time never corresponds to the rate at which perceived time moves, dawdling or cantering, disappearing in a flash or seeming to stand still. It is not only 'with the Lord' that 'a day' can be 'like a thousand years'![99]

2. Looking backward, looking forward

If we look for background for Psalm 13 in the life of David, the likeliest is the antagonism between him and Saul. From the time the older man became jealous of David's success, he 'remained his enemy for the rest of his days'.[100] As with so many of the psalms, there will have been any number of hard-pressed believers later in the Old Testament story who as time seemed to bring no end to their troubles found their own feelings expressed in these words. Indeed the cry *How long?* is echoed in John's vision of the suffering church at the end of the New Testament.[101] There we learn, as we learned also in Psalm 12, that just as there is no place, so too there is no time, which will ever be free from evil during this age.

As we now find ourselves looking forward as well as backward in time, our psalm opens up two further themes. David either would be or was already a great and successful king. He had, all the same, his share of suffering. So did all those, in Old Testament times and New, whose experience was aptly put into words by these painful songs which may well have been his. Then we realize that such words could express the cry not just of individuals, but of Israel as a nation; even the cry of the true Israel, God's faithful minority within the nation; and even that of the One who was in his own

---

[99] 2 Pet. 3:8.   [100] 1 Sam. 18:29.   [101] Rev. 6:10.

person the true Israel. We are told that on the cross he cried out a few words from Psalm 22, and to them we shall come in due course. Many more of the psalms would have been vividly real to him during those interminable six hours, not least this one. Read it again with that in mind!

Hence the remaining question: How could any of these sufferers say, *I will sing to the LORD, for he has been good to me*?

There are three answers. This is a 'prophetic perfect' such as we have seen before, and behind the psalmist's very real anguish is an equally real certainty that he *will* be lifted out of it, and will *then* say, 'God was good to rescue me.' It is also a recognition that God has undoubtedly been good to him in the past, and 'he who began a good work ... will carry it on to completion'.[102] It is, finally, a grasp of the fact that even at the time, without ever saying (as some seem to do) that evil *is* good, he could rejoice in the great truth of Romans 8:28, that God was working all things *for* good to those who love him.

Psalm 14

There is no denying the gloomy view of humanity which we find in these early psalms. We might almost wonder whether their writers were themselves infected by one of the faults of which they accuse the wicked, namely a certain manipulation of the facts! Did they really believe that *no-one* speaks truth (12:2), that *no-one* does good (14:1)? Surely God takes a more charitable view of the human race than our jaundiced poets do?

Well, here we have a God's-eye view of the matter, as *The LORD looks down from heaven on the sons of men* (v. 2), and as he sees it the situation is even worse than the first few psalms would have had us believe. That at least is how verses 1–3 of this psalm depict it, in a merciless dissection of human nature.

1. Total depravity? (vv. 1–3)

In the spirit of the wisdom books and, in this book, of Psalm 1, these verses focus on folly, the opposite of wisdom. The *fool* is far from stupid; we have to understand his 'folly' in the biblical sense, which is explained here. Verse 1 is a sequence of pictures showing how it develops, and the key words are *heart, corrupt, deeds*, and *no-one*.

The *heart* means the will, and *in his heart* means not 'privately' but 'as an act of will'. Whether or not he would call himself an atheist, the *fool* is one who has decided (like the 'practical atheist' of Pss. 9/10) that God shall have no place in his life. The will then

---

[102] Phil. 1:6.

shapes the character, which becomes *corrupt*. Character emerges in action (*deeds*), and action finds allies, and it turns out that there is *no-one* who is uninfected by this folly.

This is how God sees humanity (v. 2), and to make sure we get the message he repeats it in verses 2d–3: everyone's will has decided not to *seek God*, but to turn from him; everyone's character has *become corrupt*; action follows, and the infection is universal – *no-one ... does good, not even one*.

2. Not quite total depravity? (vv. 4–7)
A contradiction now emerges. No-one is good, said the first half of the psalm, but some people are, says the second half. What is this *company of the righteous* (v. 5) which belies the sweeping statement of verse 3?

We need a definition of our terms, and are given it by Paul in his letter to the Romans, where he quotes from this and other psalms in order to make his point.[103] All are declared unrighteous (as Ps. 5:10 has put it) because all rebel against God's law; some of the unrighteous are then declared righteous (which is the whole argument of Rom. 3) because they accept God's offer of salvation – they are 'justified' because, in New Testament terms, they have 'faith in Jesus'.[104] These are *my people* in verse 4, *the company of the righteous* in verse 5, *the poor*, whose *refuge* is the Lord, in verse 6, *Jacob ... and Israel* in verse 7; thus they make their presence felt throughout the latter part of our psalm.

For an illustration the psalmist seems to go back to the beginnings of Bible history. Universal wickedness did not have to wait for Psalm 14, let alone Romans 3, to be recognized; back in Genesis we are told that the Lord had looked down and seen it already rampant in the days of Sodom, in the days of Babel, indeed in the days of the flood – all these events have been echoed in verses 1–3.[105] He saw it again in the days of the exodus.[106] Each line of verse 4 might be expressly describing the Pharaoh of the book of Exodus: his obstinacy, his cruelty, and the repudiation of the Lord from which they sprang.[107] Verse 5 is illustrated in the showdown at the Red Sea, where God, *present in the company of the righteous*, looks down yet again, this time from the pillar of cloud, and the Egyptian army is *overwhelmed with dread*.[108] Verse 6 sums up the whole Exodus narrative, a wonderful rescue after repeated frustrations.[109] *There* – the word in

---

[103] Rom. 3:10–18 is a sequence of six OT passages, all but one from the Psalter: Pss. 14:1–3; 5:9; 140:3; 10:7; Is. 59:7–8; Ps. 36:1.
[104] Rom. 3:24, 26.   [105] Gen. 18:21; 11:5; 6:5.   [106] Exod. 3:9.
[107] Exod. 10:7, etc.; 1:8ff.; 5:2.   [108] Exod. 14:24–25.
[109] E.g. Exod. 10:8–11, 24–28.

verse 5 is emphatic – *there* was a classic example of the kind of thing we want to see today, says the psalmist, we who now worship the Lord in these modern times on Mount Zion. So verse 7 updates the Bible story which above all others shows God as the Saviour from the worst of situations.

For an application to ourselves we tend to gravitate to verses 4–7, and identify with *the righteous*. We are, after all, *his people*, those who *rejoice* that *the* LORD *is their refuge* from *evildoers*. If it is indeed the exodus story which the psalmist has in mind, that could reinforce this Egypt-and-Israel, us-and-them idea, which is true as far as it goes.

But Paul's use of verses 1–3 insists that this psalm has a deeper lesson. We may not be the *evildoers* of verse 4, but we and they alike have to identify with the *fool* of verse 1. We must go back beyond 'us-and-them' to our common sinful humanity. William Temple, when archbishop of Canterbury, was asked by a 'lay person' (to use the jargon) why Anglican clergy were of such poor quality, and replied that it was because the church had only the laity to draw them from! Just so, the *corrupt … sons of men* were all that God had to draw *his people* from, and it is for that mercy above all that we should give God what he most desires, 'our humble, thankful hearts'.[110]

Psalm 15

In Bible terms, then, the 'foolish' are not necessarily stupid; rather, they are those who care nothing for God. Similarly, the 'wise' are not necessarily brainy; rather, they are those who care a lot about God. In this sense Psalm 15 is about wisdom, and is well placed in the first David Collection alongside its predecessor, which had so much to say about folly.

1. The tabernacle reconsidered
No doubt a congregation had gathered, perhaps with alternate voices asking and answering the question of verse 1, in what some would now call an 'opening act of worship' and others an *Einzugsliturgie*.[111] An impressive word suitable for an awesome occasion: amid splendour and ritual the worshippers arrived at the *sanctuary*, fully aware that this was no place for the casual and the shoddy.

In Moses' time the *holy hill* was of course Sinai, and the *sanctuary* was the tent set up at the foot of it. Long afterwards, in

---

[110] Matthias Claudius, tr. Jane Campbell, 'We plough the fields'.

[111] I.e. entrance-liturgy. At only fifteen letters, a relatively short example of the sort of technical German word that has been unkindly likened to a trunk falling downstairs.

the time of David and Solomon, the tent was moved to its final location, and in due course replaced by a building, on the holy hill of Zion. This suited the metaphor of verse 5 better: the temple on the mountain was the kind of structure which would *never be shaken*, unlike the tent, which was made to be taken to pieces and moved around.

But the NIV's translation of verse 1 misses a miracle. The word there rendered *sanctuary* simply means 'tent'. God had first decreed the making of his tent at a time when everyone was living in tents. He proposed to do the same – to make his *home* among his people. The miraculous double resonance of that simple word is that it is *both* awesome – it was, after all, God's tent – *and* (in the British sense!) homely: in fact, and quite designedly, a foreshadowing of the incarnation, when 'the Word became flesh, and *pitched his tent* among us'.[112]

2. The ten commandments reconsidered

The relevance of this to verses 2–5a will appear in a moment. First we note that the bulk of the psalm is very like Psalm 24:3–6 and Isaiah 33:14–16, and first cousin to the lists of Christian duties in Paul's letters.[113] It looks forward to the beatitudes of Matthew 5 and back to the commandments of Exodus 20. Like the latter, it may be seen as ten easy-to-remember watchwords for the righteous life: integrity, well-doing, truthfulness; no scandal, no unneighbourliness, no defamation; discernment, faithfulness; no greed, no graft.

It is a giant step forward from pagan religion to believe that the conditions for coming into the Lord's tent are moral and not ritual – what you are, not the words you recite or the offerings you bring. It is an even bigger step to realize that they are not in the usual sense conditions at all. For this is the wonder and the uniqueness of the tent of our God. Those for whom it is only the Tent-as-Sanctuary may well be overawed by its holiness, and see qualities like these ten as qualifications they have somehow to produce from within themselves before God will admit them. But in fact the tent is also the Tent-as-Home, into which God invites those he has already made his friends. The 'ten commandments' of Psalm 15 are not conditions for people who want to belong, but descriptions of people who do belong. As with the original commandments, first he makes Israel his own (Exod. 20:2), then explains how his own are to live (Exod. 20:3–17).

So they approach with respect yet with confidence, neither overawed nor overfamiliar. Psalm 15 outlines the kind of behaviour that is appropriate for guests who are staying with God, their friend;

[112] John 1:14, literally. [113] E.g. Rom. 12:9ff.; much of Eph. 4 – 6; Col. 3:1 – 4:6.

especially since it will turn out – such is the lovely ambiguity of the word – that they will actually be *staying* with him.

Psalm 16

When we use the previous psalm devotionally, we understand a visit to God's *holy hill* in a metaphorical way. As that *sanctuary* ceased to exist nearly two thousand years ago, we have to; and there is no reason why we should not. But for a thousand years before that, the natural meaning was the literal one. The people of God would, as we should say, go regularly to church, where services would be held, with ceremony and liturgy, prayers and hymns: all the activity which is commonly but misleadingly called 'worship', and for which the technical term 'cultus' is therefore better. This was centred on the tent or temple at Jerusalem, and Psalm 15 was presumably written for it.

Important studies over the past century[114] have focused on the public use of the Psalms as the hymn book of the Jerusalem cultus – how they should be classified, how they relate to the life and literature of their time, how and when they would have been sung, and so on. We notice how many of them are 'for the director of music'. But not all of them would have been composed with the cultus in mind. Psalm 15 probably was; Psalm 16 probably was not, although in other respects the two are alike in both form and content. Both contain descriptions of people who are right with God (15:2–5a; 16:2–7), set between expressions of their sense of security in his presence (15:1 and 5b; 16:1 and 8–11). Both psalms tell us that such people will *not be shaken* (15:5; 16:8).

But there are differences between the two, which will emerge as we consider Psalm 16 in greater detail.

1. The place of refuge (v. 1)
No-one knows for sure what a *miktam* is, though the term resembles a word for 'cover', which might suit what follows. Five of the six *miktams* in the Psalter are in Book II (Pss. 56 – 60), four of them have headings relating to events in the life of David,[115] and three of *them* are about his outlaw years. In view of both its heading and its contents, this one may well have belonged originally to the same collection and have the same theme.

If so, might 'cover' have to do with concealment or secrecy? And might *refuge* mean exactly what it says? If the psalmist is David the

---

[114] Particularly those of Hermann Gunkel and Sigmund Mowinckel from the 1920s onwards, and Aubrey Johnson and Artur Weiser in the 1950s and 1960s.
[115] Such as we have already seen in Pss. 3 and 7.

refugee, in hiding from his enemy Saul, both Psalm 16 itself and the placing of it next to Psalm 15 make especially good sense.

In the face of unjust persecution, to whom does one appeal? To God, of course; and God is represented in Israel by his kings and his priests. But in this case the king is the very person of whom David is complaining, and 'Gibeah of Saul'[116] (for neither throne nor sanctuary is yet in Jerusalem) is the last place he will want to go. Similarly, not safety but treachery awaits him among the priests at Nob,[117] and in any case he will, quite literally, find no sanctuary there, for the ark is at Kiriath Jearim[118] and the tent that used to house it seems to have disappeared altogether.

So although in later, happier, times David will regularly find God 'at home' on the holy hill of 15:1, he first learns in these darker days a greater truth. While as an outlaw he keeps 'moving from place to place'[119] all over the southern wilderness, God himself is his refuge everywhere, regardless of place. This is the mirror image of the faith of Psalm 11.[120]

2. The voice of confidence (vv. 2–7)

In these next verses the Hebrew is difficult and translations vary, but we may take the NIV text as it stands. Apart from verse 5, where it blunts the point, its general meaning is clear enough.

As with Psalm 15, we have here a longer central section describing the person whom God welcomes. Verses 2–4 are in effect repeated and amplified in verses 5–7. We find in verse 2 the psalmist's declaration to the Lord, in verse 3 his delight in the Lord's people, and in verse 4 his dedication to the Lord's service. What follows stands out in vivid colours against the background of David's experience as a fugitive. Every Israelite clan is *secure* in the possession of a *portion, boundary lines*, and an *inheritance* in the Promised Land, and the Lord's presence among his people *counsels* and *instructs* them. All this David has lost. Significantly, the history of the time records these words of his: 'They have now driven me from my share in the LORD's inheritance and have said, "Go, serve other gods."'[121] Yet he is enabled by that very loss to declare, as the tribe of Levi can declare,[122] that the Lord himself is his portion (v. 5 NRSV). This is a fact in which he really can delight (v. 6), and this is a God to whose obedience he will all the more gladly dedicate himself (v. 7).

---

[116] 1 Sam. 11:4. [117] 1 Sam. 21 – 22. [118] 1 Sam. 7:1–2. [119] 1 Sam. 23:13.
[120] See p. 1.46. [121] 1 Sam. 26:19. [122] Cf. Deut. 18:1–2.

3. The path of life (vv. 8–11)

Verse 8 goes further than 15:5 in explaining who will *not be shaken*. Here in Psalm 16 is David's testimony that the Lord is real to him, and it is that personal relationship which gives rise both to the stability spoken of in this verse and to the confidence of the three that follow.

How far into the future does this confidence look? Indications of belief in an after-life have already begun to appear in the Psalter,[123] but in themselves the words of this passage do not necessarily refer to that. They could simply be about a man who, though a fugitive, can nevertheless sleep soundly (v. 9), who trusts God to preserve him from an untimely death (v. 10), and who looks forward to better times to come, enjoying blessings of a kind only God can give (v. 11). Even so, it is classical, apostolic, New Testament teaching that in these words David 'spoke of the resurrection of the Christ' and of 'the fact that God raised him from the dead, never to decay'.[124]

As far back as Psalm 2 we caught a glimpse of this question of prophecy and fulfilment. The chapters on 'second meanings' in C. S. Lewis's *Reflections on the Psalms* illuminate it wonderfully. Here we should note just two facts. It could be that when David composed Psalm 16 he was not thinking of the after-life at all (though he may have been). But in God's providence, the words he wrote were going to apply with uncanny accuracy, centuries later, to his great Descendant. With hindsight, the witnesses to Christ's resurrection realized that they had seen a man who when actually *in* the grave had not been abandoned to it, who was most truly God's Holy One, and who was now in the fullest sense seated eternally at God's right hand.

The other fact is that this was not mere coincidence. It was because of his intimate relationship with the Lord (v. 8) that David had been sure there would be life after exile. Surely such a relationship would even imply life after death? Jesus said exactly that in Mark 12:26–27, as we have seen in connection with Psalm 6. It would be surprising if David had not reached the same conclusion. The idea of an unbreakable covenant bond between the eternal God and mortal humanity already had these mind-blowing implications, even if, quite understandably, they did not burst into full bloom until (in words already quoted in connection with Ps. 6) 'Christ Jesus ... destroyed death and brought life and immortality to light through the gospel'.[125]

[123] See Ps. 6, p. 1.33.   [124] Peter, in Acts 2:24–31; Paul, in Acts 13:32–37.
[125] 2 Tim. 1:10.

Psalm 17

The psalmist is one whose heart God touches in the quiet of the night (v. 3); he knows God's path, and has a firm footing on it (v. 5); and God is his refuge (v. 7). These are only some of the numerous places where Psalm 17 echoes Psalm 16.[126] Already we have noted the links between Psalms 16 and 15, and a common theme can in fact be traced through all three.

1. Three linked psalms
'He ... will never be shaken', sings the congregation (15:5). 'I shall not be shaken', agrees the psalmist (16:8), for whom this has become a personal experience. We may well identify him with the David of 1 Samuel 24 – 26, the outlaw who has found out the hard way, when he has to leave his family home, that the Lord is his inheritance (16:5–6), and in a close brush with death that the Lord is his rescuer (16:10).

Very suitably then does Psalm 17 come next in this David Collection. It is *a prayer of David* written not after but during a time of trouble, and thus even more heartfelt than Psalm 16.

The three psalms all speak of confidence in God (future) for those who live God's way (present) because he has made them his own (past). The confidence of Psalm 15 has been tested and proved in Psalm 16, while Psalm 17 goes back to the actual testing.

2. Three urgent prayers
Hear, O LORD (v. 1) is the first of a dozen such prayers in our present psalm. Out of this barrage of appeals – even demands! – three summarize the rest. Of those in the opening verses, the crucial one is *Listen* (v. 1); in verses 6–9, it is *Show* (v. 7); in the closing verses, *Bring ... down* (v. 13).

'Listen,' says David first, 'this is the kind of person I am trying to be, Lord'; and verses 1–5 are the equivalent of the descriptions of the godly life which we have already found in the previous two psalms (15:2–5a; 16:1–4).

'Show,' he continues, 'show again the signs of your power in my life!' For the godly life is an effect of God's grace, not of David's exertions. If he pleases God it is only because God has first taken hold of him. It was thus that the Lord took hold of his people at the time of the exodus, showing his wonders, his covenant love, his salvation, and his right hand, 'four highly-charged Hebrew words' in verse 7.[127] The last psalm also had pleaded that special relationship (16:5–8).

---

[126] Cf. Ps. 16:7, 11, 8, 1.
[127] Kidner, p. 87. All four figure also in Exod. 15:2, 11–13.

What is new in Psalm 17, and is not in either of the previous two, is something due to the immediate threat from David's enemies. The words *bring them down* sum up the third group of prayers. We have in 1 Samuel the historian's account of the time; these verses might well be the victim's version of it. 'They have tracked *us* down, they now surround *us* … *He* is like a lion hungry for prey' (as vv. 11–12 should read) – in other words, 'Saul and his forces were closing in on David and his men', says 1 Samuel 23:26. In a moment we shall begin to consider the vindictive tone of this and other psalms; but we ought to recognize at once that in the circumstances David might simply be crying out with a good deal of urgency, 'Lord, it's either them or me!'

3. Three puzzling questions

What David says about the Lord cannot be faulted. He proclaims the four great exodus-words of verse 7. To them he adds the divine promise of answered prayer, the human metaphor of a protection as instant as the automatic blinking of an eye to guard its pupil (its *apple*), and the picture from the animal world of wings that surround even more closely than his enemies do (vv. 6–9). Such is God to him.

What he says about himself, however, raises a question we have touched on already – that of his self-righteousness (vv. 1–5). What a prig he seems! But we need to realize what his *righteous plea* (v. 1) is, and what it is not. He is not claiming either to be perfect, or to be sufficiently good for God to owe him a favour. His plea *is* a claim, but simply that of a misrepresented man: he insists that what Saul believes about him is not true – he is not the king's enemy, as the events of 1 Samuel 24 and 26 show. More than that, his innocence in this particular respect is a cause for wondering thankfulness. 'By the word of your lips I have kept myself from the ways of the violent: had you not taught me, Lord, that Saul is your chosen one and therefore sacrosanct, I could easily' – the story of Abigail in 1 Samuel 25 shows how easily – 'have done something I should have bitterly regretted afterwards.'

What David says about his enemies raises the question of his seeming vindictiveness, certainly in verse 13, and in verse 14 too if its second part is not about satisfying *the hunger of those you cherish*, but about filling *them*, the wicked of verse 13, *with what you have stored up for them* (NRSV), meaning their punishment. It must however put a different complexion on the matter when we recall that Saul, whom as the Lord's anointed David repeatedly refused to harm, was increasingly often a violent and evil man. David's prayer is that such wickedness be dealt with, not by him, but by the only one who has the right to do it – the Lord himself.

What he says, finally, about the outcome of all this, raises the question of his insight. Is he a prophet, expressing in verse 15 a very New Testament doctrine of life after death? The answer is surely the same as that of Psalm 16.[128] Held in the bond of the Lord's *steadfast love*, the NRSV's regular term for the very special love expressed in his unbreakable covenant (17:7), David knew that the nightmare of persecution would end, and that God's presence with him in the future would be as real and as sure as it had been in the past. And if he should ask himself whether this would hold good even when life itself came to an end, the 'spirit of prophecy' that was in him (for 'he was a prophet')[129] must at the very least have retorted, 'And why not?'

Psalm 18

Of the first eighteen psalms, this one would be outstanding if only for its length, with more than twice as many verses as the next longest, and ten times as many as the shortest. As we shall see, it is outstanding in other respects too, a vivid and powerful song of thanksgiving. The first three stanzas of Christopher Idle's modern metrical version, 'I love you, O Lord, you alone', well render the first quarter of it, and the last one summarizes the rest.

Nine significant phrases will lead us through it. Each represents one of the sections into which it may be divided, and each looks beyond its own section and thus colours our reading of the whole.

1. 'I love you, O LORD' (vv. 1–3)

And how he loves him! With a Hebrew word whose English equivalents you or I might have hesitated to use, which indeed is used nowhere else in the Old Testament quite as it is here, the psalmist bursts out at once with his affection, even his passion, for his beloved Lord. A flood of metaphors follows, showing something of what this God means to him. We shall consider shortly what lies behind the graphic picture language of verse 2; but already there is no denying the fervour of these three introductory verses.

Even scholars who hold that *Of David* does not normally mean 'By David' are likely to make an exception in the case of Psalm 18. With a string of supporting references to the psalm itself, Kirkpatrick thus describes its author: he is 'a distinguished and successful warrior, general, and king' who

has had to contend with domestic as well as foreign enemies ... and has received the submission of surrounding nations ... He looks back upon a life of extraordinary trials and dangers ... from

[128] See p. 1.58.   [129] Rev. 19:10; Acts 2:30.

enemies among whom one was conspicuous for his ferocity ... He
appeals to his own integrity ... yet ... shews a singular humility
... he owes to Jehovah's grace whatever he has or is. These
characteristics ... point to David, and to no one else of whom we
have any knowledge.

And words as personal and direct as those we have just been noting
are surely David's own, Kirkpatrick continues, and not 'a
composition put into his mouth by some later poet'.[130]

Furthermore, the psalm is reproduced almost in its entirety in the
history of David's times as chapter 22 of 2 Samuel. There, it is clearly
meant to be taken as a song of his own composing, celebrating the
end of strife both internal and external (ch. 21), and belonging to the
period described in 2 Samuel 8:13–18, the zenith of David's career.
Though there are wonderful psalms still to come in Book I of the
Psalter, Psalm 18 is in this sense the high point of the collection.

2. 'In my distress' (vv. 4–6)

It was in distressing circumstances that David had called to the
Lord, and had found that his prayer was heard, as he says in these
verses. The metaphors of verse 2 have already suggested what those
circumstances were. The first *rock* was the cliff in the Desert of
Maon, the second (a different word) was the Crags of the Wild
Goats in the Desert of En Gedi, the *fortress* and the *stronghold*
were the cave of Adullam. All are located in Israel's southern
wilderness, and all are described in the accounts of David's years
as an outlaw persecuted by Saul, in the closing chapters of 1
Samuel. At such places David had often cried to God to be his
deliverer and his *refuge*, his *shield* (for defence) and his *horn* (for
attack).[131] Certainly Saul is the individual *enemy*, at the head of an
army of *foes*, to whom Kirkpatrick's comment refers and whom we
shall meet in verse 17.

Such is the *distress*, the 'straits', out of which David called to the
Lord. In Hebrew as in English the word means 'narrow', and
anyone with the slightest tendency to claustrophobia will understand
David's thankfulness to the God who eventually rescued him from
every such tight corner, from the *cords* and the *snares* (v. 5), and
brought him out, as we shall see, *into a spacious place* (v. 19).

---

[130] Kirkpatrick, p. 85.
[131] 1 Sam. 22:4; 23:24–29; 24:2, 22. Ps. 17 is David's call for help at the time of the
1 Sam. 23 incident.

3. 'Consuming fire, dark clouds' (vv. 7–15)

If verse 6b is rephrased within quotation marks, as Kidner suggests, the response to it is dramatic indeed. 'Let him hear my voice, let my cry come to him,' David prays, and behold an earthquake! The nine verses that follow are a remarkable description of the Lord's coming to the rescue of his servant.

We need to read them through biblical glasses. First, we shall ask ourselves, as David's original readers would have done, not what the startling imagery looks like, but what it means. If we try to picture God with nostrils puffing smoke and a mouth spewing coal (v. 8), 'these images ... offend our sense of dignity and beauty'.[132] The ancient Greeks, who had a strong aesthetic sense and liked their gods to be beautiful, would have laughed them out of court, as mere grotesqueries. But to the Hebrews they were vivid images, not for the *mind's eye*, but for the *mind itself*, and the prime consideration was not aesthetics but truth – in this case, how effectively they conveyed the fact of God's anger and judgment.

Secondly, we shall not be troubled by suggestions that the representing of God in terms of the convulsions of nature was originally a heathen idea, and that Israel got it from the Canaanites. The facts are otherwise. In the beginning was the truth of God; in due course God used nature, the world which by then he had made, to illustrate it; the Hebrews had the revealed version, the pagan nations a garbled one.

Thirdly, much of what these verses portray had once happened quite literally in the experience of his people Israel. We have only to recall the events of the exodus to realize that the plagues of Egypt possibly, the crossing of the Red Sea probably, and the descent of God on Mount Sinai certainly, are all in mind here. Exodus 9, 10, and 15, and especially 19, are the chapters to link with the verses of this section.

Of course God's rescuing of David did not 'look like' his rescuing of Israel in the time of Moses, any more than he himself 'looked like' a fire-breathing ogre on either occasion. But in fact if not in appearance, what happened to David was an exodus-type deliverance. It was the God of Moses who had come to his aid, even though what his eyes saw was not *consuming fire* and *dark clouds*, but a weary band of outlaws still alive when their enemy abandoned the chase, went off to fight somebody else, and perished. So today, what our eyes see is unlikely to 'look like' either event, yet we may still be able to say of some current experience of our own, 'The LORD

[132] R. C. Trench, *The Epistles to the Seven Churches in Asia* (London, 1861), pp. 42–43. An excellent passage which relates to the equally 'grotesque' vision of the risen Christ in Rev. 1:4–20, and which is worth studying in full.

has done this', the Lord of Moses and of David, 'and it is marvellous in our eyes'.[133]

4. 'Into a spacious place' (vv. 16–19)

In this section the exodus-God who had rescued the people of Israel now reaches down to rescue the individual David. 'All this cosmic drama, just for *me*?' he might have said (note how often that little word appears in these four verses). But such is God's care for the one as well as for the many. And as Israel was brought out not only into freedom in the wilderness but eventually into the *spacious place* of the Promised Land, so David's rescue broadened out from mere survival, first to freedom, then to honour, then to kingship.

There is more still to this repeat of patterns. The Israel whom God had saved from Egypt is known to the Old Testament as God's servant, as God's firstborn son in whom he delights, and as a nation of kings and priests and therefore God's anointed.[134] It cannot escape us that this same calling, in almost every respect, is according to Psalm 18 also that of one particular Israelite, who is likewise God's servant (in the heading) and God's anointed (v. 50), in whom God delights (v. 19); and with the anointing comes also the sonship, as we shall see.

And here we begin to descry something even more astounding as we look into the future than what we have seen in linking David with his past. For there will be another of the same nation, even the same family, who will be his heir in all these respects. Luke, who speaks within a few verses of both God's servant Israel and his servant David,[135] speaks in another place, also within a few verses, of both his servant David and his servant Jesus.[136] And Jesus is of course God's anointed, his Christ, and his firstborn son in whom he delights;[137] and we know into how spacious a place he has been raised from his *distress* and *the cords of the grave* (vv. 5–6).

5. 'He has rewarded me' (vv. 20–24)

The words with which the last section ended, *he delighted in me*, are far reaching. Moses and Israel in the time of the exodus, David in his time, our Lord Jesus Christ at the turning point of history, and we his people in our time, can all say that God delights in us. The claim opens up a theology as spacious as the place into which David has been brought, as spacious as the Bible itself. The following section (vv. 25–29) will show something of what it implies.

What in these present verses it *seems* to imply is a different matter. This section is a warning against taking things at face value. *He*

---

[133] Ps. 118:23.   [134] Is. 49:3; Exod. 4:22; Is. 62:4; Exod. 19:6.   [135] Luke 1:54, 69.
[136] Acts 4:25, 27.   [137] Matt. 16:16; Col. 1:15, 18; Matt. 3:17; 17:5.

rescued me because he delighted in me (v. 19), and apparently he delighted in me because I am righteous; *according to the cleanness of my hands he has rewarded me* (v. 20). Next, protestations about the good things I have done and the bad things I have not done alternate three times over (vv. 21–23), and the inclusio which frames the whole section is completed by the renewed insistence that this is why the Lord has rewarded me (v. 24).

If this is not Little Jack Horner sitting in his corner and saying 'What a good boy am I,' then what is it?

Well, it is the last theory but one in a mystery novel, which accounts for practically all the clues, and turns out in the final chapter to be totally wrong. Apart from anything else, such a theory is in this case *psychologically* wrong. It depicts a man who reckons that the basis of his relationship with God, and therefore the most important thing in his world, is his own good character. I do not recognize in that portrait the man of verses 1–19, who is in love with God, who sees God bringing blessing out of every crisis of his life, who marvels that God should have done all these things for *him*. The most important thing in that man's world is his God.

So we are not to imagine that it was David's virtues which originally endeared him to the Lord. The springs of that first delight were not in David's deserving but in God's undeserved and unaccountable love, exactly as Moses had said in Deuteronomy 7:7–8: 'The LORD ... set his affection on you' for no other reason than that 'the LORD loved you'.

No, the claim and the reward in verses 20–24 are not the making of a relationship; they arise within a relationship which has already been made. David's righteousness here is something more than a plea of genuine innocence in the face of a particular accusation, as it was in Psalm 17,[138] but something considerably less than a presumption that he can deserve God's grace. It is in fact a confidence that those who out of love for the Lord want to walk in *the ways of the LORD* (v. 21) will find that the blessings of the Lord will come to meet them there. He delights to reward obedience.

6. 'You save the humble' (vv. 25–29)

One of the best tools for grasping the import of a Bible passage is the study of its structure, and one of the best ways of discovering its structure is to work out how it most naturally breaks down into manageable sections. In the second half of Psalm 18, for example, we notice that five verses (20–24) speak *about* God (*he has rewarded me*), then five verses are addressed *to* him (*You save the humble*); there are five more about him (*He is ... the Rock*), and finally eleven

[138] See p. 1.60.

almost entirely to him (*You have made me the head of nations*), before the doxology of verses 46–50. We can divide the psalm accordingly.

Here in verses 25–29, then, David speaks to God. But what he says to him is in fact what he believes about him. That is, he makes his creed his prayer. This should be our regular practice much more than it is: taking up what God has told us he is, and returning it to him as praise and challenge. David's own famous prayer responds to God's word to him in precisely this way: '*Do* as you have *said*' (2 Sam. 7:25 JB).

God's truth is the first article of this creed, and particularly that aspect of it of which David has just spoken. Those who want to be true to God's word will find that he too is true to it, to their great encouragement. On the other hand, he is *crafty with the devious*, as the Jerusalem Bible puts it. This version of verse 26b sounds odd, but is simply the other side of the coin, for those who 'get across' God will find that by his very straightforwardness he is bound to 'get across' them; he 'must needs be at cross-purposes with the wicked'.[139] This is what lies behind the 'repentance of God' paradox: he both can and cannot 'repent',[140] because when he changes his purpose towards us (which does happen), it is we who have moved across from his unchanging goodwill to the penitent to his equally unchanging antagonism to the self-assured, or vice versa.

God's grace is the other article of this creed. Verse 27 tells us who it is for, verses 28–29 what it does. 'The humble' is a misleading term if it makes us think of the unctuous, fawning Uriah Heep, in Dickens's *David Copperfield*, who is 'well aware', as he himself tells us, that he is 'the 'umblest person going'. Better to read 'the *humbled*', those who have really been brought low and who know they have neither resources nor deserts.

The effects of grace, God's undeserved goodness to such people, are to bring light into their life and (what is more) to keep it burning, and to provide the very resources which they lack in coping both with people (*a troop*) and with things (*a wall*). David is no doubt thinking of some of the achievements which climaxed with his accession to the throne, for instance his defeat of the Amalekite raiders in 1 Samuel 30 and his capture of the Jebusite city of Jerusalem in 2 Samuel 5; and Scripture is going to speak of the dynasty which he will found as a lamp which will be handed on from generation to generation down the centuries.[141] Again the

---

[139] Kirkpatrick, p. 94.

[140] The apparent contradiction is startling in 1 Sam. 15:11, 29, 35, where the same word is used twice to say that God does not repent and twice to say that he does. This is brought out by the older translations, including the RSV.

[141] 1 Kgs. 15:4.

psalmist King is quoting his own experience as he sings the praises of God.

7. 'He is ... the Rock' (vv. 30–34)

In this section David reverts to speaking *of* the Lord instead of *to* him, and he emphasizes more and more how real this God is.

The God of David's creed is celebrated in verses 30–31 as the God of David's history also, for again the psalm is using the language of the exodus. It is in the two great 'Songs of Moses', Exodus 15 and Deuteronomy 32, that the uniqueness of the Lord, the perfection of his ways, and his name The Rock are first spoken of like this.[142] It is at Sinai that the God of the perfect way first utters publicly and comprehensively the flawless word. It is Moses his mouthpiece who commands his people to fix these words in their hearts and minds, to 'tie them on their hands and bind them on their foreheads', to teach them to their children and to talk of them incessantly, above all to observe and obey them.[143] To immerse oneself in his words is the way of blessing, and it is what is meant by 'taking refuge in him'. From the time of Moses right down to the time of David those who have done so have found him to be, in every circumstance, their shield.

Thus history has shown the God of Israelite theology to be a real God. Theology may seem to many practically minded people an 'airy nothing'; but a series of historical events belonging to their own not-so-distant past, rehearsed repeatedly and enthusiastically by every succeeding generation of Hebrew children, gives it 'a local habitation and a name'.[144]

And verses 32–34 make it even more real, for here the God of David's creed becomes not only the God of his history but also the God of his experience. Now, in his own age, amid the practicalities of warfare and politics and leadership, David becomes strong and sure-footed, and delightedly gives God the glory for every one of his abilities and achievements.

There is an obvious and very clear distinction between the giver and the receiver of these gifts. Yet there is also an identification between them which makes us wonder. *As for God, his way is perfect*, says David; yet this God *makes my way perfect* too. And for four hundred years the ways of the Davidic kings enthroned at Jerusalem were intended to represent the ways of the Lord, who was himself the real King of Israel. There was never any question, of course, but that the one was the original and the other merely a

---

[142] Exod. 15:11; Deut. 32:4, 15, 18, 30–31.
[143] Cf. Deut. 11:18–25.
[144] William Shakespeare, *A Midsummer Night's Dream*, V.i.16–17.

reflection. The earthly reigns of David's descendants and the heavenly reign of David's Lord would in the nature of things always run parallel, and surely, therefore, could never converge.

Or could they?

It is with that question in the back of our minds that we begin to consider the next section.

8. 'You have made me the head of nations' (vv. 35–45)

On the face of it, as we read the NIV, this section is full of praise for what David has already experienced of God's help in his military successes. But the translations, and the commentaries, do not speak with one voice. Some say that this is David's past experience, others that it is his future expectation. If we are unfamiliar with the Hebrew language, these conflicting opinions confront us with what may seem one of its oddest features. For us, the verbs in a sentence mostly describe either what happened in the past, or what is happening in the present, or what will happen in the future. That is what we mean, broadly speaking, by the tenses of a verb. Hebrew tenses are not like that, although confusingly they use the terms 'perfect' and 'imperfect', which in Western languages denote two types of past tense. Hebrew is more interested in whether the action of a verb is continuous (imperfect) or has been completed (perfect). It often leaves us to infer from the context whether that action is past, present, or future.

These technicalities explain why in verses 37–38 the NIV has *I pursued* and *They fell*, the JB *I pursue* and *They fall*, and the RV *I will pursue* and *They shall fall*. Surely one translation must be right and the others wrong? But no, the verb forms cannot in themselves answer that question, and any of the three versions could be correct.

This may seem to us a weakness in Hebrew, which must have made it difficult for God to express himself as clearly as he might have done if a different language (English, dare we suggest?) had been available to him at the time! But a parallel between this part of Psalm 18 and the account of another historic military campaign, leading to the capture of another throne, sheds light on the matter.

The Bayeux Tapestry, like a high-class medieval strip cartoon, depicts the last successful invasion of England, by William of Normandy in 1066. We could describe its pictures in terms of Hebrew tenses: 'Here William has given the order to embark' (perfect), 'and these are his ships crossing the Channel' (imperfect). 'Now here is the English king Harold falling down' (imperfect); 'an arrow has struck him in the eye' (perfect). (So William doubtless thought!) We happen to know that all this is taking place in the past, and was already past history when the tapestry was made 900 years ago.

But suppose the ladies of Bayeux had embroidered their pictures not as a record after the event, but as propaganda beforehand, to boost Norman morale. In that case our description, and the Hebrew tenses, would be exactly the same; but the whole thing would concern not what *had* happened but what they hoped *would* happen.

These are the ambiguities of Psalm 18. In these verses it too is setting before us a series of pictures. Here in verse 40, for example, we see David destroying his foes, God having made them turn their backs in flight.[145] Here in verse 43 God is making him the head of nations, and subjecting to him people he has not hitherto known. We can detect the mix of perfects and imperfects. But is the scene as a whole set in the past, the present, or the future?

Finding an answer to this question matters less than we might think. If we worry about the time-reference of these pictures, we are missing the point. They certainly did happen historically; it is important to recognize that the God of Scripture does act in history. But it is equally important to recognize that he is the ever-living, ever-active God, and he repeatedly works in the same ways. As it was a Moses-deliverance which rescued David, so it is a David-triumph which exalts Jesus – has done, and will do. When we hear this voice from the past, the king of Israel saying, *you have made me the head of nations; people I did not know are subject to me*, we realize how both the grammar and the theology are going to be carried forward from the Old Testament into the New; for in Revelation 11:15 we hear 'loud voices' from the future telling us the same thing – 'The kingdom of the world *has become* the kingdom of our Lord and of his Christ'. A 'prophetic perfect', they call it:[146] even the technical term has a touch of glory!

9. 'Unfailing kindness to his anointed' (vv. 46–50)

Grand themes converge in these verses, the doxology which completes this splendid psalm.

The divine titles of *living Lord* and *blessed Rock*[147] come together in its opening line. During the redrafting of a Christian organization's basis of faith, one keen member of the group was eager to replace all its nouns by verbs, to make it 'more dynamic'. The spirit was willing, but the thought was weak, for 'basis' means

---

[145] Or having *given me their necks* as in the AV, if v. 40 is the same 'picture' as v. 39; cf. Josh. 10:24 ('*ōreṗ* means both 'back' and 'neck').

[146] In English, that is. The Greek word *egeneto* is in fact an aorist, but requires to be translated by an English perfect (*has become*) or its equivalent.

[147] So most English versions except the NIV.

'foundation', and who wants a foundation that won't keep still? Static nouns are as necessary as dynamic verbs. Verse 46 does not confuse the two ideas; it treats them as complementary. For Moses and David and Isaiah, and equally for Paul and (in my view) for Jesus himself, the Lord is the immovable Rock.[148] Yet at the same time he is vibrantly alive; he *is* dynamic – he is verb as well as noun. David's career is testimony to that 'tireless energy', and his throne is secure in that 'endless stability'.[149]

The past (vv. 47–48) meets the future (vv. 49–50). David can look back over all that God has done for him, the *consuming fire* and *dark clouds* which although picture language for perhaps one special rescue, represent also many other experiences of God's timely help. He can look forward to many more such experiences, both for himself and for *his descendants*. And it may be that he sees further still into the future; because the word for *descendants* is *seed* (v. 50 AV), and Paul could have written about David what he wrote about Abraham in Galatians 3:16: 'The promises were spoken to Abraham and to his seed. The Scripture does not say "and to seeds", meaning many people, but "and to your seed", meaning one person, who is Christ.' So far from narrowing the line of promised blessing, this remarkable perception broadens it unimaginably, for the millions of us who receive the promises because we are in Christ are far more numerous even than the countless physical descendants of David or Abraham.

There is a third convergence in verse 49, which is quoted in one New Testament passage (Rom. 15:9) and illustrated by another (Luke 2:32). In the words of Simeon which Luke quotes, in the baby Jesus 'a light for revelation to the Gentiles' meets the 'glory' of God's 'people Israel'. This too is an immense New Testament truth anticipated by David. It is as the king of Israel that he is praising God. But he finds non-Israelites who have been his antagonists (vv. 43, 47) now joining him in those praises; and we catch a far-off glimpse of the true Israel of God in Revelation 7:3–10, the 'great multitude … from every nation' which stands 'before the throne' in heaven.

Finally, at this climactic moment in Book I of the Psalter the 'wisdom' of Psalm 1 and the 'prophecy' of Psalm 2 come together. The cosmic vision of the latter, picturing the confrontation between 'the kings of the earth' and 'the LORD and … his Anointed One' (2:2), is embodied in an actual flesh-and-blood man. This man's 'delight is in

---

[148] Deut. 32 (five references); the Psalms (eighteen); Is. 44:8 (and three others in Isaiah); 1 Cor. 10:4; and surely men who knew their Hebrew scriptures would have understood Jesus' words in Matt. 16:18 in this way.

[149] The phrases are Kidner's, p. 96.

the law of the LORD', and though he now 'prospers' (1:2–3), he has had a hard time of it, in down-to-earth practical terms, on his way to be 'installed' as 'King on Zion' (2:6). It is the voice of wisdom, of Psalm 1, which David and David's Son and David's Son's people must heed as they cope with the practicalities of daily life. Verses 20–23 of our present psalm are their ambition. But their shining hope is what the prophetic voice of Psalm 2 has promised; what verse 50 here calls *great victories … unfailing kindness … for ever.*

Psalm 19

We come now to one of the most memorable psalms in this or any other part of the Psalter. Hardly any of the first eighteen have classic English hymns based on them; this has not one but two, both of which we shall have reason to quote.

1. Three voices

Of all the myriad voices of creation, the psalmist tunes in to those of the heavens, and among them the sun in particular tells him something about God. In modern times, superstitious people (like the pagans of old) 'hear', by way of astrology, more than the heavens are actually saying, while secular people hear less than they have to tell. For those who are seriously listening for a divine word, the voices of what is called 'natural religion' can be confusing, for the beauty of nature says one thing, its harshness another; but one idea at any rate comes over clearly – how wonderful must the Maker of all this be!

Joseph Addison's fine version of these lines, 'The spacious firmament on high', makes the point well. Sun and moon, stars and planets, 'utter forth a glorious voice, For ever singing as they shine, "The hand that made us is divine."' Incessantly (v. 2) and universally (v. 4) *they pour forth speech,* even though *there is no speech,*[150] and any willing hearer can get the message.

After the voice of the skies (vv. 1–6) the voice of the law speaks (vv. 7–9). The commentaries detail the meanings of *law* and its five parallel nouns, and the adjectives and verbs that go with them. The six little sentences are worth meditating on; some are quite startling.

With echoes from the New Testament in our ears – 'law brings wrath', 'the letter kills'[151] – we may not have imagined *the law of the LORD … reviving the soul.* But we need to grasp that here in the Old Testament 'law' is a wonderfully comprehensive word, meaning all that God wants us to know about himself. There is no life for the

---

[150] The NIV's insertion of *where* into v. 3 is unjustifiable, and quite alters the sense. The translation in its margin is right.
[151] Rom. 4:15; 2 Cor. 3:6.

soul without that. *Statutes* are the firm principles to whose validity the Lord testifies. On them simple people like us can build their lives. *Precepts* are precise rules for living: a new thought for some, perhaps, that detailed obedience is the *right* way to *joy*. Similarly *commands*, which have authority and are to be obeyed, sound like unwelcome restraints, yet will lead us out into *radiant ... light*. *Fear* means that what this voice tells us is, in both senses of the word, venerable: time-honoured truth, permanently valid, and therefore to be revered. *Ordinances* are in Moffatt's translation *rulings*, God's decisions on practical questions of human behaviour. They are *righteous*, not *altogether* (meaning 'absolutely'), but 'all together' (meaning 'the whole lot')!

Law might seem an unlikely source of delight; yet, as the transitional verse 10 says, for God's servant that is what it is. His is the third voice, which now speaks in verses 11–14.

He hears the first two voices rightly, because he has a right relationship with the Lord. He is the Lord's *servant*, as he says twice, and the Lord is his *Rock* and *Redeemer*. He is well aware of his sin (vv. 12–13), but, to anticipate what Jesus says in Matthew 5:48, he would like to be perfect as his God is perfect (for that word in v. 7 is the word for *blameless* in v. 13) – particularly in his speech, since that motif has run through the rest of the psalm.

2. One theme

The obvious differences between verses 1–6 and the rest persuade some commentators that Psalm 19 could not have been composed as a single poem, that the two parts separately represent two different types of psalm, and that when combined they are something of a hybrid.

C. S. Lewis, as a specialist and a professional not in biblical but in literary studies, and as a poet himself, took a different view. To his mind, the psalmist felt

> so close a connection ... between his first theme and his second that he passed from one to the other without realising ... First he thinks of the sky ... Then he thinks of the sun ... Finally, of its heat; not of course the mild heats of our climate but the cloudless, blinding, tyrannous rays hammering the hills, searching every cranny ... Then at once, in verse 7 he is talking of something else, which hardly seems to him something else because it is so like the all-piercing, all-detecting sunshine.[152]

[152] Lewis, p. 56.

Lewis had written similarly, in an earlier book, of 'that glorious, *sustained* image from the XIXth Psalm where the Sun and the Law became fused in the poet's mind, both rejoicing, both like a giant, like a bridegroom, both "undefiled," "clean," "right," and "there is nothing hid from the heat thereof"'.[153]

A second feature binds the psalm into one. The fact that the Deity is called *God* in its first part, and *the Lord* in its second part, is a pointer towards rather than away from its unity. It is precisely the limitation of the voice of his world that it can tell us only about God the Creator; we have to heed the voice of his law to learn that he is also the Lord, the Redeemer.

And behind that observation lies a deeper unity yet, shown to us in a second scripture which runs parallel to this one.

3. Two scriptures

Whatever is meant by the words *of David* at the head of these psalms, we have seen how readily we can find appropriate settings in the history of David's time for most of the first eighteen. Psalm 19 is not so easy to place, unless the germ of it was there in the shepherd boy's sunlit days (and starlit nights for Ps. 8?) on the hills of Bethlehem.

But if now one were planning a service in which psalms, hymns, and readings were all to be integrated, so as to highlight God's message and focus his people's attention on it (an important responsibility for church leaders, in my view), how should one go about it? With this psalm as starting point, two or three hymns would choose themselves: Addison's, as quoted above, or even closer to the psalm as a whole, Isaac Watts's:

> The heavens declare thy glory, Lord;
> In every star thy wisdom shines;
> But when our eyes behold thy word,
> We read thy name in fairer lines.

A scripture reading, though? The books of Samuel, with their many parallels to earlier psalms, here seem to fail us. Well, Romans 10:18 quotes verse 4 of this psalm, and Paul has already spoken in Romans 1 of the voice that all can hear: 'What may be known about God is plain to them, because God has made it plain to them. For since the creation of the world God's invisible qualities – his eternal power and divine nature – have been clearly seen, being understood from what has been made, so that men are without excuse' (vv. 19–20).

[153] From Lewis's foreword to his wife Joy Davidman's *Smoke on the Mountain* (London: Hodder & Stoughton, 1955), pp. 8–9. My italics.

This in turn leads us to an obvious Old Testament reading, namely the creation narratives of Genesis. The God who has brought David through much political turmoil and enthroned him in Jerusalem (1 and 2 Sam. provide the relevant readings), is still his Rock and Redeemer in Psalm 19 as in Psalm 18, but his poetic inspiration is now free to range further afield, and to take up the themes of other scriptures. Where better to start than with Genesis 1? The heavens and the *firmament* of our verse 1 (NRSV), and the sun of verses 4–6, are all there (Gen. 1:1, 6, 16).

Follow the reading through, however. The God who 'created the heavens and the earth' in chapter 1 is in chapter 2 'the LORD God' who 'commanded the man', giving him a law which if he obeyed it would ensure his happiness. There we find verses 7–10 of the psalm. And verses 11–14? Chapter 3 of Genesis shows how easily the human heart can be seduced by yet another voice, that of the Tempter. If Adam and Eve, who in one sense knew better than we do both *the glory of God* and *the law of the LORD*, could trade in these things for the illusory gratifications of sin, how much more should we pray to be kept in the law and away from the illusion?

Psalms 20 and 21

Although they are not bound together as closely as Psalms 9 and 10, these also, like that earlier pair, form a 'diptych', facing each other like two hinged panels. Particular words and turns of phrase, and a similar structure, are found in both, and their themes complement each other.

The Church of England's 1662 Book of Common Prayer contains, as its title indicates, forms of words – liturgies – for communal worship when God's people meet. It includes for use 'upon several [i.e. various] occasions' a prayer 'In the Time of War and Tumults' and a thanksgiving 'For Peace and Deliverance from our Enemies'. Repeatedly down the ages such gatherings have used such prayers, not least in the period of Bible history in which the Psalms were written. Psalms 20 and 21 relate to a time of warfare, the first as the 'Tumults' are beginning, the second to celebrate the 'Deliverance' as hostilities are brought to an end.

1. A prayer 'In the Time of War'

Psalm 20 is not just a prayer, but a mini-service. Its welter of pronouns, *you* and *we* and *he* and *I*, is confusing at first, but in fact they clarify the structure.

Verses 1–5 are addressed by *us*, to *you*, about *him*. *We* are the gathered people of God, the congregation. *You*, as it turns out, means the king, the Lord's anointed (vv. 6 and 9). The *he* to whom *we* refer is the Lord. This section is not a direct prayer, but an oblique one, like 'God bless you.' It is to their king that the people speak, as he is about to lead an army to battle: *May he* [i.e. the Lord] *send you help.*

Then in verse 6 *I* am speaking, an individual voice: a prophet or a priest or a Levite, or perhaps the king himself (if the latter, he would here of course be speaking about himself in the third person).

In verses 7–8 *we* speak again, about God and about our enemies, and finally in verse 9 we speak *to* God, about the king.[154]

All this may seem complicated, but it represents a simple six-part rite (bearing in mind the *selah*-pause after v. 3). It may well have run like this:

> (vv. 1–3) address to the king (all);
> (*selah*) Scripture reading (?);[155]
> (vv. 4–5) address to the king (all);
> (v. 6) individual response (the king?);
> (vv. 7–8) declaration of faith (all);
> (v. 9) final prayer (all).

The liturgy is bound together as poetry by the repeating of a number of its words, as a kind of rhyme or echo: for example, 'May the Lord answer (... answer ... answer), because we pray in the name (... the name ... the name) of the God who saves (... who saves ... who saves).'[156] An inclusio, hidden by the NIV's *in distress* (v. 1) and *when we call* (v. 9), frames the whole: 'Answer *in the day of distress*'; 'Answer *in the day of calling*'.

2. A thanksgiving 'For Peace'

Psalm 21 mirrors its predecessor, not only in theme (before the battle, *May he give you the desire of your heart*, 20:4; after it, *You have granted him the desire of his heart*, 21:2),[157] but in structure and language too.

It forms a similar six-part liturgy:

> (vv. 1–2) address to the Lord (all);
> (*selah*) Scripture reading (?);
> (vv. 3–6) address to the Lord (all);

[154] Following, like most translations and commentaries, the NIV text rather than its margin.

[155] See pp. 1.35–36.

[156] The 'victory' and 'save' words in 20:5, 6, 9 (and in 21:1, 5) are all related (the Heb. verb is *yāša'*).

[157] The correspondence is not as exact in Hebrew as in English, but is sufficiently close.

> (v. 7) individual response (the king, or another?);
> (vv. 8–12) declaration of faith (all?);
> (v. 13) final prayer (all).

In the first six verses the congregation speaks not to the king, as in Psalm 20, but to the Lord. On the other hand, the 'declaration of faith' of verses 8–12 is addressed to the king. Again an awareness of the Hebrew tenses[158] gives depth to the psalm. Those of verses 1–6 are generally perfects, looking back to what God *has done* in the (very recent) past. Thus encouraged, the king *is trusting* in the Lord (v. 7), a present confidence; and the imperfects of verses 8–12 are what we should call futures – as it were pictures of what is to come, the king laying hold on the rest of his enemies and the Lord's fire consuming them.

As with Psalm 20, we find words at the beginning which are echoed later – *joy*, *salvation/victory*, and (as another inclusio) *strength*. At the same time, *salvation* also forms a link between the psalms, as do *trust*, *right hand*, and the *requests* and *desires* of the king.

3. 'Upon several occasions' in those days?

By yet other links (20:8; 21:12) we can see how both of them connect with the great Psalm 18, particularly its verses 37–45. In the glory years of David's reign, which are the background to that psalm, Bible history describes a variety of occasions for which these two would have been appropriate: 2 Samuel 8, 10, and 12 mention campaigns against Philistia, Moab, Ammon, and Aram. In later times, liturgies composed by David for the beginning and the end of such a campaign would surely have been valued by his successors Asa, Jehoshaphat, and Uzziah.[159]

Jehoshaphat followed this pattern when he was mobilizing against an invading army. He and 'the assembly of Judah' cried to the Lord, recalling as they did so what the Scripture said had been done for Israel in the past in the Lord's name. Thereupon one of the Levites was inspired to declare, 'The battle is not yours, but God's,' and the choir 'stood up and praised the LORD'. Victory followed; the enemy was destroyed, and 'the fear of God came upon all the kingdoms ... when they heard'. Asa's experience was similar, except that in his case the fear of the Lord in some mysterious way actually brought about the enemy's defeat.

If *selah* does mean the point in a liturgy where Scripture is to be read, what reading would suit here?

---

[158] See on 18:35–45, p. 1.68.   [159] 2 Chr. 14:8–15; 20:1–30; 26:3–8.

Nowadays we might parallel Psalms 20 and 21 with one of these Chronicles readings, and in their day the Chronicles people might have related them to one of the aforementioned David stories. It is not hard to go one stage further back, and to imagine David beginning to compose these psalms ('May the LORD answer you in the day of distress; may the name of the God of Jacob protect you') with a key passage from Genesis in mind: the journey to Bethel of Jacob, his nation's great ancestor, to '"build an altar to God, who answered me in the day of my distress" ... They set out, and the terror of God fell upon the towns all around them so that no-one pursued them'.[160]

4. 'Upon several occasions' in these days?

There are no such occasions in these days. All that world has come to dust. None of today's nations, rulers, or conflicts corresponds to Old Testament Israel, her kings and her wars. But since God's people do still exist, though in a different form, the pattern remains the same, and the people of God today must face their conflicts with the same strategy.

First they identify with their King. He has offered the great sacrifice without which his enterprise and their hopes and prayers are vain (20:3). He goes out to battle on their behalf. Knowing from Scripture how his predecessors have been blessed (20:1), they look forward to his victory (20:4, 9), because it is already assured (20:6). They are confident that they will share that victory (20:7–8), since they belong, heart and soul, to him. The God who bound himself by covenant to Jacob and his family and to David and his nation has by the same covenant bound himself to their descendant Jesus and his church. They have therefore total confidence in him through whatever conflict may lie ahead.

If Psalm 20 stresses the identity of the King with his people, Psalm 21 celebrates the unity between the King and his Father God. He emerges from the bitter conflict of Calvary, and from every other conflict, crowned with glory and victory (21:3, 5). The *length of days, for ever and ever* (21:4), which for his Old Testament ancestors was either an exaggerated compliment or at best the promise of a long line of descendants, is for him literal truth. His appearing and his wrath (21:9) are scarcely distinguishable from God's (21:6, 9).[161]

There is warfare and warfare in this life. What the world considers a war worth fighting may well not seem so to us. We have it on good authority that 'our struggle is not against flesh and blood, but against

---

[160] Gen. 35:1–5.
[161] *Presence* (21:6) and *appearing* (21:9) represent the same Hebrew word, *pānîm*.

... the spiritual forces of evil in the heavenly realms'.[162] The closer we get to the kind of war that really must be fought, the closer we need to get to the King who will fight it for us, and to the rest of his people who will pray to that end with us. That will be the time for Psalms 20 and 21.

Psalm 22

What would people who knew the accounts of the death and resurrection of Jesus, but little else of the Bible, make of this extraordinary psalm? It must be the risen Jesus himself (surely they would say) who is here recording his thoughts and feelings after the event. We know otherwise; and the fact that these words were written not after, but centuries before, the event, is what gives them their peculiar interest.

What was the psalmist writing? From our point of view, Psalm 22. But not of course from his. 'The compilers of our Psalter have got to No. 21, and I am busy on the next one'? No, that is not at all what he would have said. But what he *would* have said is much debated. The variety of suggestions as to what he himself understood this psalm to be recalls the old rhyme about the blind men who tried to describe an elephant from the feel of the beast. To one its trunk suggested that it was a kind of snake, to another its side felt like a wall, a third concluded from one of its legs that it must resemble a tree-trunk, a fourth found its tail and said it was a rope. None was wholly wrong, yet none was wholly right. So did the author of this psalm believe himself to be writing prophecy, or liturgy, or poetry? Was he putting an actual experience into words, and if so, whose?

1. Psalm 22 as prophecy
My God, my God, why have you forsaken me? The fearful cry of verse 1 takes us instantly across the years to Calvary. Only those with no feeling for the *mot juste* would speak of our Lord's 'quoting' or even 'using' these words at such a moment of agony. They were as genuinely his own as they had been the psalmist's.

But the fact is that we do find them on the lips of both. And when we also find, in verse 7, the mocking of which the passion narratives in the Gospels speak, and the hurling of insults and the shaking of heads; in verse 8, another sentence 'quoted', this time by the Jewish leaders (*He trusts in the LORD ... Let him deliver him*); in verses 14–15, the pains of crucifixion detailed, and in verses 16–18 the sufferer surrounded, stared at, even pierced, and his garments shared out by lot – when we find all this, we are not surprised that Psalm 22 should be thought of as prophecy.

[162] Eph. 6:12.

The question is what that means. Ezekiel in the Old Testament and John in the New tell how they were caught up by the Spirit of God, and shown 'the shape of things to come'.[163] Such revelations have happened. But if Psalm 22 is about the death and resurrection of Jesus *and about that alone*, then the psalmist found himself as it were temporarily inhabiting the body of Jesus, and describing *from the inside* an experience which bore no relation to his own place and time. No doubt it could have been so; but both as a psalm and as a prophecy these lines would then be so very unlike anything else in Scripture that one would be inclined to say, 'There must be more to the elephant than this.'

2. Psalm 22 as liturgy

Nearly all the David psalms so far have been in the first person singular. They lend themselves to use in our personal devotions, especially if our church tradition has been one which seldom if ever includes psalm-singing in its congregational worship. But when 'I cry aloud' (3:4) gives way to 'We will shout for joy' (20:5), clearly something different is happening. Psalms begin to appear which are suited, or intended, for corporate use. In this respect 22 is like 20 and 21. Although it is *I* who speak throughout, this is *my praise in the great assembly*, and *in the congregation* I *will praise you* (22:25, 22).

So we come to the subject of liturgy: forms of words for the gathered people of God to use, the frameworks into which those forms fit and the occasions for which they are designed. There have been times when academic study of the Psalms has seen them chiefly as an expression of individual piety (not that the churches have ever ceased, in practice, to use them congregationally). But many of the famous twentieth-century names in this area of study, such as those mentioned earlier,[164] moved in the opposite direction, and were concerned to explore the Psalter as liturgy. When and where would it have been used *corporately* in Bible times? How did it relate to the cultus, the whole formal religious life of Israel as a community?

Three guidelines directed these explorations: hints in the psalms themselves, evidence from the rest of the Old Testament (temple worship, recurring events such as the great festivals, one-off special occasions), and parallels in contemporary non-Israelite religions of the Near East. Certainly many of the psalms fit readily into the known outline of Israel's religious observances. The festival of Tabernacles in particular would be one of these, the king's accession (as we have seen in Ps. 2) would be another. In fact these two would

---

[163] The title of H. G. Wells's novel of 1933. A horse of a different colour.
[164] See p. 1.56, n. 114.

have been one, if, as some think, the latter were re-enacted annually at the former.

The explorers were pushing out into more uncertain waters when they linked these rituals closely with the religions of surrounding nations. Was there any justification *in Scripture* for the king annually to go through a ritual 'marriage', 'death', and 'resurrection' – still more, to personify as he did so a God who was likewise marrying, dying, and rising? And further, although the reconstructions of such supposed 'cultic dramas' can be dramatic indeed, hugely exciting and involving, one may properly have doubts about the whole principle of re-enactment. Like the sacrifice of the mass, what such rituals make relevant and vivid is (or ought to be) an historical event, not a mythical one, and an event which is meant to be made relevant and vivid *in a different way*. For old Israel, the exodus-event had happened once and for all; for us, the Christ-event has happened once and for all; in the Hebrew festivals, and in Christian worship, it is not by re-enactment but by faith that their reality was and is borne in upon the people of God. The rituals are signposts, which point beyond themselves to certain destinations. We were never meant to make pilgrimages to signposts.

What does all this say about Psalm 22? It tells us on the one hand that we have every reason to make use of such a psalm not only for private devotion, but also liturgically, for *praise in the great assembly*. But it tells us on the other hand that 'a ritual humiliation at an annual festival in Israel', though that 'would provide a plausible setting',[165] is surely not what the psalmist composed it for.

3. Psalm 22 as poetry

If the psalmist was not transcribing a prophecy or composing the script for a religious drama, was he perhaps writing a poem? Rather than recording the words of the Christ, predictively, or putting words into the mouth of the king, liturgically, was he imagining how an idealized voice might express the truth he had in mind?

It was a profound and far-reaching truth, which figures in different ways in other parts of Scripture also. It was a pattern which would in fact be fulfilled in the experience of the Messiah, when eventually he came. But Israel did not need to look that far ahead – indeed, did not need to look ahead at all – in order to see it. In David's time it was her most significant national memory: her suffering in, and rescue from, Egypt. Five hundred years later she would be able to look back on a repeat of the pattern, her exile and then her restoration in the days of the Babylonian and Medo-Persian empires.

[165] Kidner, p. 105.

One who is often called the 'suffering servant', who appears elsewhere in the Old Testament (notably in Is. 42 – 53) and in some sense stands for the whole people of God, is portrayed as the speaker of these tremendous lines. The misery and the entreaty of verses 1–21 and the ecstatic praise of verses 22–31 are thus expressed by the corporate voice of Israel speaking through this imagined representative. If we were able for a moment to loosen the bonds that, to our minds, tie Psalm 22 so closely to the gospel narratives, we might admire the psalmist's poetic achievement all the more.

Yet this is still only a partial view of the psalm. Not only is it impossible, in practice, to separate this Old Testament scripture from its New Testament connections; it is almost as difficult to suppose that the writer was writing in a detached and objective way about someone else's experience, even if that someone was the nation to which he belonged. It is hard to believe that this is his poem and not also his own experience – not just something he has written, but something he himself has known and felt.

4. Psalm 22 as experience

Turning back to the traditional view, that in the case of this psalm *of David* means 'by David', we are hard put to it to find any episode in the great king's life quite as traumatic as the one depicted here. When *a band of evil men ... encircled* him, as in his outlaw days, and later, when Absalom rebelled against him, he was never brought quite as low as this. When the exposure of his adultery and murder really did abase him,[166] he was crushed by guilt but not by insults; in Psalm 22 the reverse is the case.

If it is not about (and by) David, but about (and by) some later Davidic king, Hezekiah is the likeliest candidate; another psalm of his is recorded in Isaiah 38. In the language of this one, the *dogs* that *surrounded* him were invading Assyrian armies; the Lord *listened to his cry for help* and rescued him, and 2 Chronicles 32:23 tells us that as a result 'he was highly regarded by all the nations' (reminding us of v. 27 here). However, there is no hint that Hezekiah ever felt forsaken or unheard by God, or was ever isolated among (let alone despised by) his people.

Another suggested author is the prophet Jeremiah, whose own book reflects much that is said here – the appeal to God's saving work in the past (32:17–22), the people's contempt (37:2), the call from the womb (1:5), the isolation and the pain (37:15–16), the promise of restoration (33).

Our psalm must surely be a transcript of experience, and not a clever invention by an 'ivory tower' poet. And if its author went

166 See 2 Sam. 11 – 12.

through such public trauma and emerged into such public acclaim, it is hard to believe he was someone whose name has been completely forgotten. Which of the noted names, then, should be front runner?

So many of these psalms in Book I not only bear the title *of David*, but fit readily into the David narratives in the books of Samuel, that in spite of the problems recognized above I should want to fit this psalm in with the rest, even though it is not clear where it would belong. After all, David certainly could have written such words; his reputation as a psalmist is secure in the Old Testament, and his status as a prophet is vouched for both there and in the New Testament.[167]

The apostolic testimony to this is Peter's address on the day of Pentecost, in Acts 2. There David's confidence in God, in Psalm 16:10, is taken to mean that God would rescue not just him, but Christ, not just from dying, but from death. We are thereby given a pointer towards a parallel understanding of Psalm 22. It would be a composition of David's, about one of the distresses which we have considered above, and to which earlier psalms have alluded (4:1; 18:6). To our eyes even the worst of them might not seem as terrible, nor its outcome as glorious, as what is described here. But a combining of the man's mercurial temperament, his 'poet's eye, in a fine frenzy rolling',[168] the heightened sensibilities of a mind under great pressure, when everything seems larger than life and twice as fraught, and a sense of destiny fed by the far-reaching promises of 'the word of the LORD' that 'came to Nathan' in 2 Samuel 7, might well produce Psalm 22. As with Psalm 16, the Spirit of prophecy would be seeing to it that David's words about himself were intensified to the point of depicting, more than adequately, his great Descendant's infinitely deeper experience of the same pattern of death and resurrection.

5. 'The sufferings of Christ' (vv. 1–21)
Peter, who referred to that earlier psalm in Acts, could well be thinking of this one in his own first letter, when he is, appropriately, writing about Old Testament prophecy. His phrase 'the sufferings of Christ and the glories that would follow' (1 Pet. 1:11) sums up the two parts of it.

Verses 1–21 may be divided into six sections of varying length, with a brief and striking tailpiece. In the first section David is overwhelmed by his own misery, which contrasts with the positive things he can yet say about God in the second section, introduced

---

[167] 2 Sam. 23:1–3; Acts 2:30.
[168] William Shakespeare, *A Midsummer Night's Dream*, V.i.12.

by the words *Yet you* in verse 3. The third and fourth sections are paired similarly, and so are the fifth and sixth, as follows.

For David, for Christ after him, and for all of us who share 'the fellowship of his sufferings',[169] the relationship with God must take precedence over everything else (vv. 1–2). However awful the experiences of verses 6–8 and 12–18, first and worst is the sense that God is distant (*so far from … me*) and silent (*you do not answer*). But at any rate we begin where we know we ought to begin, and that in itself is a sign of hope.

As with his grasp of his own situation, so with his grasp of God, David starts in the right place (vv. 3–5). Before any appeal to God's love and mercy comes a recognition of his majesty and holiness. Along with that is a conviction that he is a God who makes himself known, not only in word but in action, and in saving action at that; and that he has in fact done so in the days of *our fathers*. Of all this David is convinced. Where would even the most pious of us be without a good strong theology like that?

According to the NIV margin, this second section also tells us that God is *enthroned on the praises of Israel*, a phrase which can be crudely misunderstood. He is indeed present where his people praise him; not however as one who is compelled to answer the door if the carol singers sing loudly and badly enough,[170] but as one who gladly does so when he hears the voices of friends as eager to meet him as he is to meet them.

But I (begins the third section) have cried to this God and have got no answer. Again, God matters more than I do, so that even worse than my opponents' sneers at me are their sneers at him. 'He is supposed to delight in this servant of his', they say in verses 6–8; 'he delights, but he doesn't deliver!'

Yet you (begins the fourth section) have proved yourself real and active, loving and trustworthy, not only in your people's past but in my own past, right from the very beginning: from the breast, even from the womb (vv. 9–11). Jesus, of course, could say to his Father, 'you loved me before the creation of the world'.[171] But even we may join with the hymn writer, 'His love in time past Forbids me to think He'll leave me at last In trouble to sink.'[172]

With the sustained cry of agony in verses 12–18 (the fifth section) we are once more inside the skin of the sufferer. Bulls and lions and dogs are no doubt metaphors for his enemies, but his own physical pain sounds horribly real, and not metaphorical at all. Whatever David went through that was like this, the suffering of Christ *was* this, and far more besides. His followers therefore can expect no easy

---

[169] Phil. 3:10 AV/RV.   [170] Cf. 1 Kgs. 18:26.   [171] John 17:24.
[172] John Newton, 'Begone, unbelief!'

ride; the way they are following is the way of the cross.[173]

But you, cries the suffering servant for the third time, as the sixth section begins, and now it is the direct appeal of verses 19–21: Come, deliver, rescue. Verse 20b may still be familiar in the quaint AV, RV, and Prayer Book translation, *my darling from the power of the dog*. *My darling* is 'my only one', 'all I have left', the word used of Abraham's son and of Jephthah's daughter,[174] each of whom in their respective stories was about to be sacrificed. In this case 'all I have left' is 'my precious life', me myself. That is what David, and we, most fear losing. But it is what Christ was prepared to lay down for us.

Good punctuation is sparing of dashes and italics, but if ever it were proper to use them it would be in verse 21: 'Rescue me from the mouth of the lions; from the horns of the wild oxen – *you have answered me!*' The first two thirds of the psalm end with this totally unexpected cry from the psalmist, a single Hebrew word and the last in the verse. 'The Hebrew vividly reveals the lightning change in his mood,'[175] for rescue has come, interrupting him in the middle of a sentence, and 'the glories that ... follow' now open up immediately before us in verses 22–31.

6. 'The glories that would follow' (vv. 22–31)

The change of tone at verse 22 is so marked that some have believed the remaining verses were once separate, the present psalm being a stitching together of earlier poems of two different types, 'lament' and 'praise'. But there is of course no reason why the concept of a two-act drama should have been foreign to even the earliest psalmists. The dual pattern of conflict and resolution was there before them in the real-life events of David's career as a whole, as well as in the particular circumstances to which Psalm 22 refers. It was a drama which was in due course to be replayed on the grand scale, in the humiliation and exaltation of the Christ.

The contrast between the wretchedness of the first part of the psalm and the joy of this part is obvious. There is another contrast alongside it: the isolated *I* of verses 1–21 suddenly finds himself in a *great assembly* (v. 25). We recall this as part of the basic theology laid down in Psalm 1; it is a people, not just individuals, that the Lord saves, which is a comfort to the lonely, though on the other hand a challenge to loners.

Here in verses 22–26 the assembly is that of Israel, and Israelite law provides a background to the curious connection between vowing and eating. If we piece together the relevant passages in

---

[173] Matt. 16:24.   [174] Gen. 22:2; Judg. 11:34.   [175] Cohen, p. 64. Cf. NIV mg.

Leviticus and Deuteronomy,[176] we may picture David expressing his gratitude to God by bringing to the priest the foodstuffs required for a 'fellowship offering', and having a portion of them formally returned to him for a festive meal, to which he invites not only family and friends but others less fortunate, even outsiders.

Table fellowship which brings together the risen Jesus and his people has been central to the church's life ever since the first Easter Day. When considered one by one, none of those earliest joyful gatherings would have looked much like a *great assembly*.[177] The very first, at Emmaus, was precisely the mere 'two or three' with Jesus 'among them' that was foreseen in Matthew 18:20 (NRSV). But the Lord, as he looked along the line of history and not only at sections cut across it, could see the ever-increasing company of the *descendants of Israel* who would celebrate with him *for ever* his deliverance from death.

For Israel-by-grace, even more than Israel-by-race, was going to spread to *all the ends of the earth*, and to draw its adopted children from *all the families of the nations*. Verses 27–31 transcend all the boundaries. What God has done for his suffering Servant will become a blessing to rich and poor, powerful and helpless, Jew and Gentile, this generation and *people yet unborn*. As Kidner says, 'Now David's language overflows all its natural banks.'[178] He was, in his time, held in high regard by the surrounding nations. To that extent these words are true of him and his age. But as with the account of his suffering in the first part of the psalm, what a cooler man in a cooler moment might have expressed more moderately is here heightened, by passion and inspiration, to convey a greater truth than David's time could know. The first part ended with a cry of praise to God, *You have answered me*; this, echoing it, with a cry of praise about God, *He has done it*.

Psalm 23

Only a vandal, surely, would want to take to pieces the best-loved psalm in the book! I promise to put it together again, having perhaps shown in the process that it is even more special than we thought.[179]

---

[176] E.g. Lev. 7:11–21; Deut. 12:11–19; 14:23–29.

[177] Luke 24:30, 41–43; John 21:13.

[178] Kidner, p. 109.

[179] The metrical versions that make Ps. 23 readily available for congregational use include George Herbert, 'The God of love my shepherd is'; Henry Baker, 'The King of love my shepherd is'; Joseph Addison, 'The Lord my pasture shall prepare'; the 1650 Scottish Psalter, 'The Lord's my shepherd'.

1. The making of a little masterpiece

The Lord is described as *my shepherd*, and as nothing else throughout the six verses. Not surprisingly the simple but profound metaphor has often been taken to govern the whole psalm, so that all of it is about the relationship between shepherd and sheep. (Who, by the way, was better qualified to write such a poem than David, whom the Lord 'took ... from tending the sheep ... to be the shepherd of his people'?)[180]

The awkwardness is that in verse 5 the metaphorical sheep seem to have a doubly metaphorical table laid for them. Many commentators therefore believe that the final verses change the picture from that of a shepherd and his sheep to that of a host and his guest. It is not difficult to locate in David's later experience the literal spreading of a table for him by his friends at Mahanaim, practically *in the presence of* his rebel son Absalom, 'camped' just down the road 'in the land of Gilead'.[181]

A different division of the psalm notes that the first half speaks about the Lord (*he leads me*, vv. 1–3), while the second half speaks to him (*you are with me*, vv. 4–6). But this too is awkward; the 'halves' are far from equal. A better proportioned analysis suggests not two but three pictures: the sheep and its Shepherd (vv. 1–3), the traveller and his Companion (v. 4), and the guest and his Host (vv. 5–6), each expressing one aspect of David's confidence: *I shall not be in want, I will fear no evil, I will dwell in the house of the* LORD *for ever.*[182]

Even so, the single-theme view has much to commend it. A little devotional classic from, I think, the 1930s puts it persuasively. W. A. Knight's *The Song of our Syrian Guest*[183] has no pretensions to scholarship, but simply describes the day's work of an Eastern shepherd, still (at that time, at any rate) unchanged over the centuries.

2. The message

According to Knight, *green pastures* and *quiet waters* mean of course rest and refreshment for the sheep. Restoration is the rescuing of the animal 'from forbidden and fatal places', where in one way or another its life (its *soul*) is in jeopardy. In difficult terrain the shepherd, 'proud of his good name', knows where to find the *right paths*; and since these may 'lead through places that have deadly perils', he carries a cudgel and a crook, 'for defence and ... guidance'.

The scene does not change at verse 5, which has in mind first the shepherd's skill in clearing a feeding-ground of dangerous creatures

---

[180] Ps. 78:70–71.   [181] 2 Sam. 17:24–29.   [182] Motyer, p. 500.
[183] Stirling Tract Enterprise / Marshall, Morgan & Scott, n.d.

and poisonous plants, and then, on the return to the sheepfold in the evening, his ointment for small injuries and his 'large two-handled cup ... brimming' with water for the weary flock.

It is easy to see the equivalents of all this lifelong *goodness and love* in the experience of the believer; and Psalm 16 has already opened up for us what was, and is, meant by *for ever*.

There is another kind of background, provided yet again by the events of the exodus. Even before his family's enslavement in Egypt began, Jacob could speak of 'the God who has been my shepherd all my life'. After the Israelites had been rescued from slavery, Moses could remind them that in the wilderness 'You have not lacked anything,' and promise them that in Canaan too 'You will lack nothing.' The words for *green pastures* and *quiet waters* correspond to the 'dwelling' and the 'rest' to which God was leading them. Sinai was where he made his 'name' known. The wilderness was the 'land of ... the shadow of death'. It was there nevertheless that God 'spread a table' for them.[184] From the exodus onwards, shepherd-language was used to describe all their leaders, including David himself.[185]

In other words, the confidence of Psalm 23 is that of one who is steeped in the theology of those earlier days, when God made his covenant with his people. David knows *that God*. And since he is the eternal Lord, his people are not surprised to find him as the New Testament Shepherd too: the good Shepherd, the great Shepherd, the chief Shepherd who will one day appear with 'glory that will never fade away', and who 'will lead them to springs of living water'.[186]

Psalm 24

You could say that Psalm 24, like Psalm 23 (and like Caesar's Gaul), is divided into three parts. A tiny hymn about the power of God the Creator is followed by an 'entrance liturgy' about the holiness of God the Lord and a 'procession liturgy' about the victories of God the King. But, again like the last psalm,[187] this one works properly only when reassembled, and taking it as a whole there is one particular historical occasion to which it is ideally suited.

---

[184] Gen. 48:15; Deut. 2:7; 8:9; Exod. 15:13; Num. 10:33; Exod. 34:5–7; Jer. 2:6 (NIV mg.); Ps. 78:19.

[185] 2 Sam. 7:7; 5:2.

[186] John 10:11; Heb. 13:20; 1 Pet. 5:4; Rev. 7:17.

[187] Unlike its predecessor, however, this psalm is conspicuous by its absence from most modern hymn books and song books, except in the form of Christopher Idle's splendid version 'This earth belongs to God'.

1. A very special occasion

Much the most likely setting for this psalm, as for some others,[188] is David's bringing of the much-travelled ark of the covenant to Jerusalem, its final home. The events of that time are recounted in 2 Samuel 6 and 1 Chronicles 15 and 16.[189] The ark, the gold-plated chest containing the stone tablets of the law, signified the presence of God among his people. 'That unique occasion', its installation in Israel's royal city, was in many ways 'the greatest day in David's life'.[190]

God comes emphatically first in the Hebrew text: '*The Lord* owns the earth; *the Lord* founded it.' Israel believed the inhabited world to be, not an island floating on the sea, but *terra firma* raised above it (v. 2). The sea represented chaos, and the Lord had imposed order on it and 'fixed limits for it', as the magnificent poetry of Job 38:8– 11, echoing Genesis 1:9, says ('This far you may come and no farther; here is where your proud waves halt').

Verses 1–2 have told us that we are never out of God's presence. There is, in a different sense, no coming into his presence, without the four qualifications of verse 4. For he who made all places also made one special *holy place* where he promised to meet with his people in a special way: in David's time and for a thousand years after, the hill of Zion. To meet God there required right living, right thinking, a right relationship with him, and a right relationship with one's fellows. But these things were a righteousness (*vindication*) which could only be received, not achieved: things which the God who saves from sin gives to *those who seek him*.

That 'seeking', that humble longing for God, was the basic requirement for those who would come to meet with him on Mount Zion. But what qualified *him* to be there was very different. The glory and the might of verses 7–10 are military glory and might. For *the LORD Almighty*, the older translations had 'the LORD *of hosts*', of armies. He was there by right of conquest. We read in 2 Samuel that 'David grew stronger and stronger' (3:1); he 'captured the fortress of Zion, the City of David' (5:7), and 'the LORD gave [him] victory wherever he went' (8:14). David's victories were the Lord's victories, and as the great gates of the ancient Jebusite city rose before the approaching procession, they were, in recognition of his glory, not shut in defiance but open in welcome.

---

[188] Ps. 132, and perhaps 68. We find in 1 Chr. 16:7–36 that 96, 105, and 106 are quoted as having been used on this occasion.

[189] For what lay behind them, see 1 Sam. 4:1 – 7:1 and 1 Chr. 13.

[190] Kidner, p. 127.

2. A climax

That great day was more than the culmination of David's career. It was the end of a far longer journey, which brought the ark to Jerusalem not just from Kiriath Jearim but from the place where it had originally been made in the days of Moses, Mount Sinai. For this psalm too looks back to the days of the exodus. 'The LORD is my strength ... he has become my salvation ... The LORD is *a warrior*,' was the cry of the Israelites as they left Egypt. You will bring us, they sang to God, to 'the mountain of your inheritance – the place, O LORD, you made for your dwelling, the sanctuary, O LORD, your hands established. The LORD will reign for ever and ever.'[191]

The composite psalm which according to 1 Chronicles 16 was used later on that day of celebration[192] traces its origins further back still. It was rooted, we are told, in the covenant made with Abraham, Isaac, and Jacob. Indeed, it was from these very gates, from the *ancient doors* of the city then called Salem, that the august figure of the priest-king Melchizedek had stepped forth to give Abraham the blessing of 'God Most High, Creator of heaven and earth ... who delivered your enemies into your hand'.[193]

One might even say that the day of the ark's arrival was in one sense the climax of all Bible history up to that point. We have already seen how verses 1–2 reflect something of Genesis 1, the imposition of order on chaos. But from the moment of Adam's fall, the possibility of renewed chaos has always been present, and the incessant warfare that has plagued humanity is the most obvious sign of it. While his people are a nation, then, the Lord will be a warrior, *the LORD mighty in battle*, overcoming chaos still as he gives David victory everywhere. Today, as the ark arrives, Jerusalem, the city of peace, becomes the dwelling-place of both the lesser king and the greater King.

3. A starting point

The fact that *the earth is the LORD's* means of course that its Maker and Owner expects his tenants to look after it, and to do so in his way. But for Psalm 24 it means more than that. Almost from the outset there have been those who would spoil it *and everything in it*. A remaking has been necessary. Central to God's plans is the remaking of people. If we see the need and long for the privilege, he calls us to meet him in his *holy place*. To that place he comes as *King of glory, the LORD mighty in battle*, for he has declared war on the forces of destruction. To that place we come as *those who seek him*,

---

[191] Exod. 15:2–3, 17–18. The context makes plain that they envisaged not Sinai but a mountain in the Promised Land.
[192] See n. 188 above. The reference here is 1 Chr. 16:15–18.   [193] Gen. 14:18–20.

to be ourselves remade, and to be recruited into 'the King's own army ... Round his standard ranging.'[194]

Where today is the hill of the Lord?

The installing of the ark in Jerusalem, from one point of view the end of a process, is from another a starting point. It establishes the Old Testament pattern for our New Testament days. The two kings, human and divine, are now one: Jesus Christ, the King of glory. Wherever his Spirit and his church are, there the gates of the city stand open for all who will enter. There now is the true 'Mount Zion ... the heavenly Jerusalem, the city of the living God', as we learn from Hebrews 12:22 (a key NT scripture we noted in both Ps. 1 and Ps. 2, and to which we shall have cause to return). The only requirement is that as creation was once just as he wanted it, so we too should seek to be just as he wants us, 'right loyal, Noble, true, and bold', as the Havergal hymn says, 'on the Lord's side', to 'serve the King'.

Psalm 25

A number of the psalms we have already considered shed light on this one.

1. Its shape: Psalms 9, 10, and 18

Psalm 25 is the Psalter's second acrostic, another alphabet poem like the combined Psalms 9 and 10. What was said there about the mechanics (and the inspiration) of such psalms applies here equally. With two or three small amendments the initial letters of these twenty-two verses will spell out the Hebrew alphabet, except that the final verse begins with an extra *pe*. It may be a kind of appendix, or 'Amen', as we shall see.

None of these acrostics is merely an assortment of twenty-two beads, connected only by the alphabetical string on which they are threaded. Like the rest, this one can be divided into sections which are fewer and therefore larger, and which clarify what it is driving at. Here Psalm 18, though not itself an acrostic, has provided guidance. In the latter part of that psalm we noticed that prayer-sections alternate with creed-sections; that is, the Lord figures throughout, but what the psalmist says *to* him alternates with what he believes *about* him.[195]

The same feature is obvious in Psalm 25, divides it helpfully, and gives it a well-proportioned shape. As it stands unamended, with its slightly irregular alphabetical pattern, it has three equal sections, prayer/creed/prayer, but in the middle of the middle section an extra

---

[194] Frances Ridley Havergal, 'Who is on the Lord's side?'   [195] See pp. 1.65–66.

one-verse prayer is inserted. In other words, the first seven verses are spoken to God; then seven verses about him are divided, three and four, by the interjected prayer of verse 11; and the final seven verses are again addressed to him.

2. Its theme: Psalm 1

I shall not be the only preacher to have based sermons on the subject of guidance on texts taken from Psalm 25. It has a good deal to say about guiding and showing, about paths and ways, and specifically about God showing *his* ways to *me*.

Preacher and hearers alike may have in mind a particular kind of situation: namely the facing of some personal choice which warrants a special pointer from God. The pointer is needed, they feel, when an important decision has to be made, and both possibilities seem equally *good* but neither seems obviously *right*.

I believe that in fact such situations are rare, and are in any case not what Psalm 25 is about. When we set its 'guidance' texts in the context of the whole psalm, and read that, in its turn, against the background of Psalm 1, a different picture emerges. For it is out of Psalm 1 that Psalm 25 grows. Both are wisdom poetry: both say, 'If you are wise, these are the down-to-earth practical ways in which you will walk: you will choose the "way of the righteous", not the "way of the wicked".' Both point forward to the regular New Testament use of the 'walk' metaphor for practical Christian living, and of 'the Way' as an early title for Christianity itself.[196]

And when we pray in the words of Psalm 25 *Show me your ways ... teach me your paths ... guide me in your truth* (vv. 4–5), we mean the ways, the paths, and the truth that God has already made known once and for all in the pages of Scripture. 'The secret things belong to the LORD our God, but the things revealed belong to us and to our children for ever, that we may follow all the words of this law.'[197] What has he told us? That he is in fact guiding us all the time, whether or not he shows us how. That he is far more interested even than we are in our getting to where he wants us to be. That he cares much more about our willingness to obey what he *has* shown us than about our cleverness in puzzling out what he hasn't shown us. These things are facts. The better we know him, and these facts about him, the less we shall feel the need for 'requests for special guidance ... the basically pagan search for irrational pointers and omens'; we shall instead be 'laying the foundation for right decisions' which are 'personal and mature'.[198]

---

[196] The 'Way', Acts 9:2 and several other times in that book; the 'walk', repeatedly in the letters of Paul and John.
[197] Deut. 29:29.   [198] Kidner, p. 116.

3. Its circumstances: Psalm 3

Why should Psalm 25 present the following of God's way as something much less simple than it seems to be in Psalm 1?

Like its companions here in the middle of Book I, this psalm comes in any case from a more complex world than that of the early part of the book, which is, I take it, that of the fugitive David, generally concerned with little else than keeping out of the clutches of either Saul or Absalom. But for the David of Psalm 25, finding God's way is further complicated by two factors which Psalm 1 does not mention. One of them is first foreshadowed in Psalm 3; the other does not appear at all before this point.

We begin with the former. After the two introductory psalms which I have called the 'preamble', the very first words of the main body of the Psalter are, 'O LORD, how many are my foes!' (3:1). David's enemies, having made frequent appearances in those early psalms, now raise their heads once again. In Psalm 25 they are making it difficult for him and his people to concentrate on living 'peaceful and quiet lives in all godliness and holiness'.[199]

The other factor is, surprisingly, new to the Psalter. There have been hints of the psalmist's consciousness of guilt, for example in Psalm 6, but up to now not a single mention of the noun 'sin'. 'Sinners' have come on the scene occasionally, true, but they are always other people – nobody admits to being one! At last here in verse 7 David recognizes that his troubles have to do not only with external forces, his enemies, but with internal ones as well, his own *sins* and *rebellious ways* – not unlike Paul's phrase 'fighting without and fear within'.[200] If he cannot see the way ahead, it is as likely to be due to his own bias towards sin as to the antagonism of others.

4. Its value

I may use Psalm 25, therefore, as a prayer for guidance, provided I grasp what that means and what it involves, as expressed in the central credal section.

The first section, verses 1–7, begins with my focusing on the Lord, trusting in him, and waiting expectantly for him. It ends with my praying that he for his part will remember me, but not my rebellions – that he will separate the sinner from the sin – and in particular that he will remember his *love*, the covenant love that we noted in connection with 17:7.[201] I don't want supernatural omens to point out the way I ought to go; I just want to see more clearly the way he regularly works. It is there plain to behold in Scripture; but the deceitfulness of the world and the devil, and of my own flesh, confuse my view of it.

---

[199] 1 Tim. 2:2.   [200] 2 Cor. 7:5 RSV.   [201] See p. 1.61.

I do believe that if I am humble and obedient, penitent and reverent and expectant (says the centre section, vv. 8–15), then though I am a sinner he will guide and bless me. He will guide me *without necessarily telling me how*. What he confides in me is not the details of the plan, but *his covenant*, the fact that he has bound himself to me by steadfast love. The little extra prayer for me to slot into the middle of my creed (v. 11) reminds me that what I need is not information but forgiveness.

The prayer of the final section, verses 16–22, is a recognition of the forces arrayed against one who seeks to learn God's way. There are enemies who see this precious intimacy between the believer and his Lord as their key target. The maintaining of it must therefore be my chief aim.

All this has been in the first person singular. Has it sounded selfish? Lord, says the little tailpiece, what I have been asking for myself is wrapped up in your promise to rescue not just individuals but your whole people. So bless us every one in the way I have asked you to bless me. 'Peace and mercy to all who follow this rule, even to the Israel of God.'[202]

Psalm 26

David had a good deal of experience of the *evildoers* (v. 5) and *bloodthirsty men* (v. 9) who lurk in the background of this psalm. As with so many of the psalms in Book I, we can reasonably assume that he was its author, though suggestions as to when he might have written it can only be guesses.

1. Protestations

When we are faced yet again with David's extraordinary eagerness to say how blameless he is, we may think that like the Player Queen in Hamlet he 'doth protest too much'.[203] But it is only when we look at Psalm 26 in isolation, indeed at selected verses from it, that David seems a self-righteous prig. Set all this protestation in the context of similar psalms, and they shed much light on it.

Psalm 25:21 helps by translating the word here rendered *a blameless life* (vv. 1 and 11)[204] as 'integrity' – that is, an undivided heart. At bottom, David's heart really is the Lord's, however badly he sometimes lets him down. That is why Psalm 25 can at the same time both admit his sin and protest his integrity.

Psalm 17:1–5, and before that Psalm 7:1–8, have shown David blameless in another sense: particular charges against him are unfounded.

[202] Gal. 6:16.   [203] William Shakespeare, *Hamlet*, III.ii.242.
[204] So NIV. AV/RV/NRSV are consistent with *integrity* in all three places.

Back in Psalm 1, the Psalter begins with a theology which polarizes all shades of grey into a black-and-white contrast, dividing everyone into those who despite their sins are 'the righteous' and those who for all their respectability are 'the wicked'.

2. The core of the protestations

It is there at the beginning of the book that we find our best clue to Psalm 26: the individual (1:1–3) seen as part of an assembly (1:5).

Here in verses 6–8 we can visualize even more clearly than in Psalms 15 and 24 people assembled for a ceremony at the tabernacle or the temple. We can understand how a latter-day hymn writer could transmute the scene of verse 8 into a nineteenth-century Anglican church building – 'We love the place, O Lord, Wherein thine honour dwells' – complete with its 'font' and its 'board' (i.e. communion table!).[205]

But the important thing is not the building. It is the meeting of the Lord's people with him and with one another, whatever the place.[206] That is the 'assembly' of Psalm 1, and it reappears here in verse 12, with its counterpart, the *assembly of evildoers*, in verse 5.

The core of David's protestations is his claim to *abhor* the one assembly, the 'anti-church', and to identify with the other. It is not a matter of temperament or taste, but of 'spiritual alignment'. He has declared his allegiance. For the church is people, *these* people and not *those* people, and in spite of all his sins and failures – indeed, because of them – it is with these that he belongs.[207]

3. Pleas

So it is not conceit that is expressed in the plea of verses 1–2. Rather, it is an attitude like Paul's: 'Not that I have already ... been made perfect, but I press on'; or Peter's: 'Lord, you know all things; you know that I love you.'[208] It is a plea that the divine Refiner should *test, try, examine* David, to demonstrate not that the metal is *pure* (it isn't; hence the need for refining), but that it is *precious*. It really does belong in the Refiner's workshop.

Conversely, David's plea for rescue and mercy in verses 9–11 is a plea that God will not *take away [his] soul along with sinners*; that is, that he will be distinguished from those of the other *assembly*, those who do not want to belong in God's company.

---

[205] William Bullock. The more familiar version has several alterations by Henry Baker.

[206] Cf. on the tabernacle, Ps. 15, pp. 1.54–55. Today Jesus is himself the tabernacle, and may be worshipped anywhere: 'Neither on this mountain, nor in Jerusalem', but 'in spirit and in truth' (John 4:21, 24).

[207] This paragraph owes much to Kidner's comments; and see VanGemeren, p. 240.

[208] Phil. 3:12; John 21:17.

4. The basis for the pleas

If we ask David on what grounds he prays as he does, he answers both at the beginning and at the end of the psalm, 'My blameless life'! We have seen that that does not mean quite what we might have thought it meant. Both pleas, and the verses between them too, spell out the true grounds of his appeal to the Lord.

In verses 1–3 God is the real object of his trust, God's love and truth his real guidelines, in spite of his many sins. John Bunyan's Pilgrim, often erring and often stumbling on his way to the Celestial City, would have said the same.

In verses 4–5 David distances himself from the one assembly, and in verses 6–8 associates himself with the other. He does so deliberately and literally; a man is known by the company he keeps. We are not to 'love the world', says John, and we are to 'love our brothers', and that is how it is known 'that we have passed from death to life'.[209]

In verses 9–11 David is asking for rescue and for mercy, lest he share the fate of the wicked. Where the word 'blamelessness' would suggest that he doesn't need to make such a plea, the word 'integrity' recognizes that he does need to. And having made it, and been answered, he finds himself (v. 12) secure in the love of the Lord and the fellowship of his people.

Psalm 27

Two key words here are *confident* (vv. 3, 13) and *seek* (vv. 4a, 8).[210] The four sections of the psalm crystallize around them, in a chiastic pattern like those which we found in Psalms 6 and 7: confidence/ seeking // seeking/confidence.[211]

Psalm 27 is well placed in this part of Book I. We could imagine David, now king, looking back once more to his shepherd days, with the glimpses of Psalm 23 that we have here – paths of righteousness, the valley of the shadow (in which *the LORD is my light*), awareness of enemies, desire for the house of the Lord. This last also recalls Psalm 24 and the Lord's presence in the tent prepared for him by David in Jerusalem.[212] The new strain of humility and penitence that we heard in Psalm 25 is echoed here too, and Psalm 26:8 ('I love the house where you live, O LORD') could be the heading for the whole second section of our present psalm.

---

[209] 1 John 2:15; 3:14.
[210] *Seek* in v. 4c (RSV *inquire*) is a different word.
[211] See pp. 1.32, 1.35.   [212] 2 Sam. 6:17.

1. Confidence (vv. 1–3)

Enemies of one kind or another have come on the scene repeatedly from the very beginning of the David psalms. The threat has escalated: here in Psalm 27 what was once persecution is now war (v. 3). This is one of the pointers to its being another psalm of the great rebellion, when David is no longer an outlaw, but a ruler.

Verses 1–3 indicate not only his higher position, but also his greater confidence. And these are not mere words. What lies behind them is the experience gained while David was being hunted by Saul. None of us enjoys learning the hard way, but that is what turns theory into reality.

Nor do they represent an elementary lesson, to be left behind as the pupil progresses. In this very psalm there will be a further and more demanding test. 'You have been faithful with a few things; I will put you in charge of many things.'[213]

2. Seeking: focused on God (vv. 4–6)

In Old Testament days it was, as we have seen,[214] God's wish that his friends should find him 'At Home' in a particular place, in an actual tent or house. They rightly regarded this as a high privilege (though we today have an even greater one).[215] Yet David, who loved God's house so much (26:8), here pictured it in no fewer than five different shapes. As well as the general word *house*, he saw it as a temple or palace such as his son Solomon would one day build; as the tent that he himself, like Moses, had set up; as a humbler structure, a 'dwelling' or shelter, as erected at the feast of Tabernacles (or by a shepherd boy in the Bethlehem fields?); and even as the rock, his wilderness fortress and not a structure at all, which he bracketed with the rest as a place to which God had welcomed him as his host.

David's array of metaphors is a further pointer to this being a psalm of his mature years; he is looking back over his varied experience. It is also an indication that one who greatly valued the cultus of the Jerusalem shrine knew nevertheless that God could be sought and found anywhere. I can remember years ago walking alone through a great city in the small hours of the morning, and a word from God which said, not 'I am with you' (which would have been comfort enough), but 'Son, *you* are always with *me*'.[216] He was already there; he lived there – always had done.

David's twofold desire, *to behold* and *to inquire* (v. 4 NRSV), to know ever more intimately the beauty of the Lord's Person and the wonder of his will, combines as the *one thing* he wants above all others.

[213] Matt. 25:21, 23.   [214] See Pss. 15, 16, pp. 1.54–57.   [215] Matt. 18:20; 1 Cor. 3:16.
[216] Cf. Luke 15:31.

3. Seeking: stressed by circumstances (vv. 7–12)

The translations of verse 8 vary; the Hebrew is difficult. But the gist of it, the desire to seek God, is similar to that of verse 4. It is the spirit in which David expresses it which is different. Halfway through the psalm delight has given way to alarm.

Big trouble is brewing, and David does the right thing and turns to God. It has been his experience, as it has no doubt been ours, that time spent with God on such occasions is always well spent. Sometimes the trouble then simply evaporates. Sometimes it remains exactly what it was, but we find we have a new courage and clarity in facing it.

But sometimes nothing changes. Then we, like David, are thrown back on the great facts about God that we have known all along. (Perhaps that has been the object of the exercise.) Again we confess that we are sinners, who deserve nothing, and we turn to God as our Saviour (vv. 9–10). Again we claim guidance, in the sense in which Psalm 25 has spoken of it, and we admit our helplessness in the face of attacks like Absalom's smear campaign (vv. 11–12).[217]

The confidence of verses 1–6 has not fallen apart. The buoyant tone of that part of the psalm has changed, certainly. Now that David has as it were turned round to have a good look at those who *rise up against* him, he speaks if not in panic then at least in agitation. But he is in this third section speaking *to the Lord*: that is the great thing.

4. Confidence (vv. 13–14)

No, his confidence is still intact. It is a trust in a God whose goodness is to be experienced here, in this world; that is the force of verse 13. Some have taken *the land of the living* to mean the next world; but while there are indeed pointers in the Psalter to the hope of resurrection and an after-life,[218] this is not one of them; David expects to see answered prayer here and now, or at any rate here and sooner-or-later. 'The mills of God grind slowly,'[219] and it is no surprise that saints of great vision should sometimes pray prayers whose answers do not arrive till after they have gone to glory, but they see plenty of *the goodness of the LORD* before they go. They are the kind of people who know all about the alert, tip-toe expectancy which is what Scripture means by *wait for the LORD*, and which gives his hard-pressed people heart and strength.

[217] 2 Sam. 15:1–6.   [218] See Pss. 16, 17, pp. 1.58, 1.61.
[219] Henry Wadsworth Longfellow, 'Retribution'.

Psalm 28

Having reached this psalm by way of its twenty-seven predecessors, we can see how much of it is illuminated by what we have read in them. We shall first look at these reflected lights, and then see what Psalm 28 itself as a whole has to show us.

1. What we have seen elsewhere

There is in verse 1 a fear of death, or of an experience like death, which we met in 6:5; that is, a fear of a situation in which David (assuming again that he is the author) can get neither a hearing nor an answer from God. The title of *Rock*, in the same verse, we found in 18:2, 31, and 46, and the theme of God's house or holy place (v. 2) has figured in most psalms from 23:6 onwards; 27:5, indeed, brought the two ideas together.

The wicked of verse 3 have appeared often, usually as David's enemies, and as recently as 27:12 the Psalter has shown him praying not to be handed over to them. The prayer here is that he should not be reckoned *with* them. The polarizing, the taking of sides, and the eagerness that it should be known which side he is taking, we considered in 26:4–8; what we have here is a restatement in different words of 26:9.

Repay them for their deeds (v. 4) raises again the issue of the vindictive tone of some of the psalms, which was touched on in 17:13. We shall have cause to think hard about this in connection with later psalms. Verse 5 is a portrait of the wicked man of 10:4, 11, and 14:1–3, and him we shall consider further in a moment.

On a different tack, verse 6 answers to verse 2 as an inclusio or chiasmus (as in 6:2–3 and 8:1, 9), and helps to make the poem's structure clear:

> Prayer (v. 1),
> *Hear my cry* (v. 2),
>   centre section (vv. 3–5),
> *He has heard my cry* (v. 6),
> praise (vv. 7–9).

Verse 7, where in the closing praise the Lord is David's *strength and shield*, answers to verse 1, where in the opening prayer he is David's *Rock*.

The last two verses open out from the singular to the plural, as 25:22 did. David has been speaking as an individual; but he never loses sight of the fact that just as he distances himself from the company of the wicked, so there is another company with which he identifies (26:4–8 again). God's blessings are never for him alone but for all God's people.

Two final titles look both back and forward. We have already seen in 2:2, 6, the king as God's anointed (here v. 8), and in 23:1 the Lord as the shepherd (here v. 9). These two will ultimately converge, of course, in the God-Man, Christ the Lord.[220]

2. *What we see here*

In spite of all these connections with earlier psalms, Psalm 28 is not a mere 'thing of shreds and patches'. Its distinctive message is what its middle section says about the wicked. David speaks both passionately and dispassionately. With verses 3–5 as its centre of gravity the psalm is a dispassionate portrayal of the evil of the human heart, especially that of an individual whose vision is blurred and conscience blunted by the peer pressure of bad company. Yet it is at the same time passionate, in the sense that first David's prayer, then his praise, for rescue from such evil, are so deeply felt – in the one instance almost panic (vv. 1–2), in the other almost ecstasy (vv. 6–7).

He rightly fears the *power* of the wicked not only when they are on top, but even when they go under, and involve others in their ruin (v. 3a). Of the various circumstances suggested for this psalm perhaps the likeliest is here again the great rebellion; civil war is a hugely damaging thing for both sides. We need to be aware how high the stakes are when we pray, 'Deliver us from evil.'[221]

The *method* of the wicked is dissimulation (v. 3b) – not simply hypocrisy, but every kind of falsehood: wherever perception does not tally with fact. Just as according to Scripture Satan is the great Destroyer, which tells us his object, so he is also the great Liar, which tells us his technique.[222] Most of us need to be a good deal more alert to his lies, and to our own gullibility as victims of them, than we are.

The *repaying* of the wicked (v. 4) we can notice only briefly here; we have touched on it in Psalm 17 and shall meet it head on in Psalm 35. For the moment we should observe first that David is asking God to take responsibility for it, and secondly that the tone of his prayer, set by the opening verses, is not vindictive but pleading. To say that the Hitlers and Stalins, the Amins and Pol Pots, of history ought somehow to have the enormity of their crimes eventually brought home to them, expresses not vindictiveness but outraged justice; and who but God can bring about the righting of such a wrong?

---

[220] Both David's Son and David's Lord – Ps. 110:1; Matt. 22:41–46. More of that in its proper place.

[221] Matt. 6:13 mg.   [222] Rev. 9:11 mg.; John 8:44. See p. 1.29, n. 30.

The *motivation* of the wicked (v. 5) is the self-centredness which, as noted above, makes the 'practical atheist' of Psalm 10, and the 'fool' of Psalm 14, tick. Whether it is power or gain or notoriety that he lusts after, for God and the works of God he cares nothing. Since he does not recognize God as the maker of the world in which he, the practical atheist, operates, he will have no grounds for complaint when one day that world is unmade around him.

Psalm 29

John Oxenham, imagining the 'hidden years' of Jesus' early life, has a younger lad tell of a ramble in the country with the carpenter's son. On the way home to Nazareth,

> I saw a great black cloud sweeping in from the West and darkening all the sky … The thunder was clapping all about us … long before we began to climb the hill.
>
> But the boy seemed actually to like it, for he began singing at the top of his voice … 'It is the Glory of God that thundereth … Eloi! Eloi! Eloi!' … With his arms thrown up towards the terrible black sky … he sang amid the thunder claps, and his voice was steady as a trumpet, and he knew no fear.[223]

It is the twenty-ninth Psalm, of course, which the novelist has put into the mouth of the boy Jesus. Whatever our view of such fiction,[224] this song well suits the imagined circumstances.

1. The movement of the psalm

Like some other psalms we have considered, this one has a main central section framed between a short introduction and a short conclusion. More than in any other so far, we notice its repetitions: the word *Ascribe* three times in verses 1–2, *The LORD* four times in verses 10–11, and *The voice of the LORD* seven times in verses 3–9. Repetitive does not mean boring. Far from making the poetry mark time, these reiterated phrases drive it vigorously forward.

The movement of verses 3–9 is that of a thunderstorm which rolls in from the Mediterranean to the cedar-clad slopes of Lebanon and Mount Hermon (Sirion) in the north, turns to travel down the whole length of Israel, and sweeps away into the southern desert of Kadesh. Lightning, like the axe of a heavenly woodsman, *hews out flames* (v. 7 NASB); wind, as it *twists* and *strips* the trees, makes the hills

---

[223] John Oxenham, *The Hidden Years* (London: RBC, 1946), pp. 21–23.
[224] See p. 1.175.

themselves seem to heave and sway,[225] though even the treeless desert is shaken by it.

There is a movement also in the psalm as a whole, from heaven (vv. 1–2) where praise is given to God by his angels, to earth (vv. 10–11) where peace is given by God to his people. The temple in verse 9 is not a building, but simply 'where God dwells'. At the outset it seems that that is heaven. There the *mighty ones* – we may assume they are angels, and Job 38:7 and Psalm 89:6 will back us up[226] – praise him, declaring what they know him to be and bowing in obedience to him. That is what *ascribe* and *worship* mean, and that is where true praise begins: if mind and will are engaged, heart and emotion will surely follow.

Yet God is just as really present here on earth. Here, where he presided *over the flood* (*the* flood, Noah's flood), he presides still, and earth is as much his temple as heaven is.

The observation of Delitzsch on the psalm's opening and closing verses is too good to miss: '*Gloria in excelsis* is its beginning, and *pax in terris* is its end.'[227] Thus Psalm 29 too points forward to the Lord Jesus, at whose coming the angels sang, 'Glory to God in the highest, and on earth peace.'[228]

2. A nature psalm

From boyhood David, like Jesus, would have recognized the glory of God in the wonders of creation. As in due course he would write of the vastness of the night sky in Psalm 8 and of the tyrannous heat of noonday in Psalm 19, so in Psalm 29 he would describe the clamour of the thunder. He would see here in the storm, as there in the starlight and the sunlight, something of 'God's invisible qualities … understood from what has been made'.[229]

One later tradition in Israel linked this psalm with the feast of Tabernacles, another with the feast of Weeks (Pentecost). The former certainly celebrated among other things the water and light which God provides for his people's welfare. But the latter recalled water and light in a rather different form, for it was connected with God's coming to his people on Mount Sinai, in the time of Moses, amid

---

[225] Visible movement (in the case of the desert, that of sand, stones, tumbleweed) seems more likely than the imagined movement of immovable mountains; though see 114:4, and Weiser, pp. 263–264. Cf. A. E. Housman: 'On Wenlock Edge the wood's in trouble; *His forest fleece the Wrekin heaves*; The gale, it plies the saplings double, And thick on Severn snow the leaves' (*A Shropshire Lad*, xxxi).

[226] 'Sons of God' (two very similar Hebrew phrases) are the 'mighty ones', 'angels', or 'heavenly beings' in these passages.

[227] Delitzsch, vol. 1, p. 373. I join other recent writers in being unable to resist quoting this comment, made well over a century ago.

[228] Luke 2:14.   [229] Rom. 1:20.

thunder and lightning.[230] So also later God would make himself seen and heard in the days of Elijah, first at Mount Carmel[231] and then at Mount Horeb.[232]

The Elijah story in particular shows us in what sense Psalm 29 may be called a 'nature psalm'. For the Baal whom pagans in and around Israel worshipped was specifically a thunder god. 'We believe that that noise is the voice of Baal,' they would have said, 'you believe it's the voice of Yahweh, same god with different names probably, and anyway everyone's entitled to his own opinion.' So what, if anything, is distinctive about Yahweh the God of Israel?

What happened at Carmel was not just that God answered prayer and Baal didn't. God sent the fire from heaven, and then the rainstorm which broke the drought; but those three years of pitiless sun had come from him also. He was behind all these events. Baal, by contrast, was *in* the thunder and lightning. He *was* the thunder and lightning. If there was no fire and rain, and the drought continued, it meant that he must be away, or asleep.

What happened next, at Horeb, spelled this out for Elijah. The Lord passed by, with a wind, an earthquake, and a fire, but he was not *in* any of them. He was above and behind them, their Maker and Controller.

Myriads of our contemporaries, ranging from the most mystical of New Agers to the most hard-nosed of economists, believe that a particular thing – a crystal, a market – can have a life and power of its own. You manipulate it if you can, or endure it if you can't. In Bible terms, they worship and serve 'created things rather than the Creator'.[233] From their point of view, Baal lives!

But the nature psalms will not allow this. They teach us to distinguish between the world and the God who made it; to admire the one, certainly, but to focus our respect and worship on the other.

3. A *church psalm*

There is a further thought in the mind of the author, which relates to what was in the mind of the compilers. Why did they place this psalm where it is, and not in the vicinity of the eighth or the nineteenth? Its open-air exhilaration is quite different from the tone of most of its neighbours here in the third quarter of Book I.

But one feature it does have in common with them. Some of them have spoken of God's house, the holy place (23:6; 24:3; 27:4). In others the individual *I* becomes the plural *we*, God's people, the holy assembly (20:5; 22:25; 25:22). The two concepts, house and people, come together in 26:6–12. Our present psalm follows exactly the pattern of its predecessor by ending with two verses that celebrate

---

[230] Exod. 20:18.   [231] 1 Kgs. 18:38, 45.   [232] 1 Kgs. 19:11–12.   [233] Rom. 1:25.

102

the Lord as the strength and blessing not of the psalmist only but of all his people (28:8–9; 29:10–11). The common theme is, in a word, the church.

David with his limited view of the next world sees the church primarily as the assembly here on earth. But he does know of the 'angels in joyful assembly' in heaven.[234] With these two gatherings in mind, he seems to be going back to the beginning of the Bible story for both his introduction and his conclusion – to the making of the world out of nothing, and to its remaking after the flood.

When God 'laid the earth's foundation ... all the angels shouted for joy';[235] perhaps they are the reason for the mysterious plural 'Let *us* make' in Genesis 1:26. Their assembly sings the *Gloria in excelsis*. When God presided over the greatest natural disaster ever (he *sat enthroned over the flood*),[236] he was both destroying the wicked and preserving his own people, as the New Testament makes plain.[237] Their assembly rejoices in the *Pax in terris*. The real Thunder God is not some third-rate Baal, but the Judge of the world and the Saviour of the church. By the voice of the storm Psalm 29 calls his people to recognize, praise, and obey him as such.

Psalm 30

We have found several psalms in which the psalmist has been in trouble, and some in which he has been rescued from it. In a few (6; 16; 18; 22) the trouble appears to have threatened his life. We need go no further than its first three verses to see that Psalm 30 is one of these.

1. The structure of the psalm
The remarkable baroque church of Vierzehnheiligen, the 'fourteen saints', in Germany, seems at first glance to be a rectangular building, with straight walls and straight rows of columns. A second glance shows that its floor plan is actually a series of intersecting ovals and circles. It is more complex than you thought. So with this psalm. Like Psalm 29, and others we have noticed, it begins and ends in praise, with a longer explanatory middle section. But there is more to it than meets the eye.

It has five sections rather than three. According to verses 1–3, the psalmist has been healed of an illness. He praises God not just for the experience, but for what it teaches him of God's character – his *holy name*, as he puts it in verses 4–5, where he calls God's people to join him in praise. In terms of the psalm we have just been reading, he with his words will 'ascribe to the LORD the glory due

[234] Heb. 12:22.   [235] Job 38:4–7. See n. 226 above.   [236] V. 10 mg.
[237] Luke 17:26–27; 1 Pet. 3:20–21.

to his name', and they with theirs will 'worship the LORD in the splendour of his holiness' (29:2).

'To participate meaningfully ... they must know more about the psalmist's deliverance,'[238] so in verses 6–7 he goes back behind his illness to explain why it happened. All is within God's plan, as we shall see. Verses 8–10 record his plea to God for mercy and healing, and verses 11–12 the praise that followed, bringing the psalm full circle.

2. A deliverance psalm

It tells us much about God and the way he works in the life of the believer. His healing work in particular teaches us about his saving work in general. He is God the Deliverer.

Leaving aside for the moment Bible passages which may relate to who wrote the psalm, and when, one passage that is very like it is the prayer of King Hezekiah in Isaiah 38. He too has been suffering from a near-fatal illness, and praises God for his rescue from 'the pit of destruction', from death and the grave,[239] as the psalmist does here in the first section or stanza (vv. 1–3).

The second draws contrasts: not only the believer's weeping and rejoicing, but what lies behind them, God's anger and favour (v. 5). Jesus teaches very plainly on at least two occasions that suffering is not necessarily a consequence of sin.[240] But it may be. The psalmist is under no illusions: his own misery is the result of God's anger. Hezekiah's lines spell out the same truth in detail: 'He broke all my bones' and 'made an end of me ... He himself has done this.'[241]

And is this the work of God the Saviour? How can we suppose such a thing? The third stanza tells us. The psalmist's 'slide toward the pit'[242] began when his confidence in God became self-confidence. His words in verse 6 are perilously close to those of the wicked and arrogant man of 10:6. What is so bad about them is that they flout the fundamental terms of God's covenant with his people. Deuteronomy states these clearly: either you remember God, and recognize that all you have is a gift of his grace (8:10–18), or you forget him, and perish (30:15–20).

The fourth stanza, again like Hezekiah's psalm, is partly a bold reasoning with God. What would be the 'gain' – what good would it do God! – to snuff out one of his own worshippers? (for the psalmist, as we have seen, cannot imagine the 'new song' of the church triumphant in heaven,[243] any more than Hezekiah can).[244] More important than the reasoning is the fact that the stanza as a

---

[238] Craigie, p. 254.   [239] Is. 38:17–18.   [240] Luke 13:1–5; John 9:1–3.
[241] Is. 38:13, 15.   [242] Craigie, p. 254.   [243] Rev. 14:3. See p. 1.33.
[244] Is. 38:18–20.

whole is a cry for mercy, not an argument. But both writers know that to have been so close to death is certainly a gain for *them*: 'Surely it was for my benefit that I suffered such anguish.'[245]

The benefit is, of course, as the last stanza says, that the lesson of humility has been learnt: *I will give you thanks for ever* (v. 12) – not yet thinking of the next life, as we realize, but certainly for all the rest of this one.

3. A church psalm

Psalm 30 belongs in this part of Book I not only in length, style, and structure, but also in being a community psalm and not just an individual one.

This is not primarily because its heading looks like a reference to a church service. *Temple* is misleading – the word is simply 'house'. When we ask, 'Which house?' we are raising the questions of authorship and occasion, the who and the when.

The heading might refer to any one of six events. David had a house built for him when he moved to Jerusalem (*secure* on his *mountain*, vv. 6–7? and with his enemies confounded, v. 1?).[246] Later there were *dancing* and *joy* (v. 11) when he set up the Lord's house there also, in the shape of a new tent for the ark.[247] In due course he chose the site of the temple, an occasion marked by a plague sent by God,[248] and a pointer to a new thought: that the writer of the psalm might be speaking not individually, but for the nation, with its sin, its punishment, and its deliverance. That temple was duly built and dedicated by Solomon,[249] an event full of the *rejoicing* of verse 5. Centuries afterwards it was destroyed and then rebuilt and rededicated,[250] and *you healed me* (v. 2) might mean God restoring his people after the exile. Later still the second temple was cleansed and reopened after the Greek king Antiochus had desecrated it amid terrible persecution. The surviving remnant of the nation might well have cried then, *You healed me ... You turned my wailing into dancing* (vv. 2, 11).

There is no reason why the psalm should not have been composed by David and used on any or all of these occasions. It is in itself a song for the church, because the psalmist invites the saints to join him in celebrating the name of the Lord.

That great and meaningful name includes all that we have already seen of God's plan and method in the individual's life, and we may add a further point from the second stanza, where the church too is bidden to praise him. Verse 5a may mean not that God's anger is brief and his favour life*long*, but that his anger is destructive and his

[245] Is. 38:17. [246] 2 Sam. 5:6–12. [247] 2 Sam. 6:16–17. [248] 1 Chr. 21:1 – 22:1.
[249] 2 Chr. 5:1 – 7:10. [250] Ezra 6:13–16.

favour life-*giving*.[251] 'I have come that they may have life, and have it to the full,' says Jesus.[252] In New Testament terms it actually lasts more than a lifetime! It is 'eternal glory ... out of all proportion'.[253] The church needs to recapture this truth. What Kirkpatrick finely says of the weeping of God's people is true also of that just but merciful anger of God which causes them to weep: it 'is but the passing wayfarer, who only tarries for the night; with dawn ... joy comes to take its place'.[254]

Psalm 31

Much of the territory covered here is by now familiar. Several times we have seen the theme of trouble and a cry for help, followed by God's answer and the psalmist's thankfulness. In a number of psalms the individual has invited others to join him in prayer and praise. In a dozen places, especially from Psalm 23 onwards, we have noted words and phrases which are now repeated in Psalm 31.[255] Though longer than most in the latter part of Book I, this psalm is of a piece with its companions.

We should not on that account imagine them to be mere mosaics, of whose fragments this is a further (and rather undistinguished) rearrangement. Three points worth considering may catch our attention.

1. Three intriguing features

The many phrases common to this and earlier psalms are not just formulae, as some would describe them. Still less are they pious clichés. Rather, the psalms collected here speak a common language of faith and experience. An excellent way to discover that language is to follow up the marginal references in the 1885 Revised Version; unlike the notes in many newer editions of the Bible, they are a guide to a goldmine.[256]

Yet the wording of Psalm 31 ranges from these 'commonplaces' to phrases singular enough to be quoted years, or centuries, afterwards. Examples are *in the secret of thy presence* and *the strife of tongues* (v. 20 AV);[257] the passage quoted at the beginning of Psalm 71 (vv. 1–3 here); that quoted in Jonah 2:8 (v. 6); several which are paralleled in Jeremiah (vv. 10–17, especially *terror on every side*,

---

[251] Craigie, p. 250; VanGemeren, pp. 260–261.   [252] John 10:10.

[253] 2 Cor. 4:17 JB.   [254] Kirkpatrick, p. 153.

[255] For pre-echoes of this psalm, see, e.g., 4:6; 6:2, 7; 9:15; 18:2; 23:3; 25:5, 15, 22; 26:5, 11; 27:5; 28:2, 4, 6; 30:4, 6.

[256] This system of references appeared first, with an explanatory preface, in the 1898 edition. It is a rare find today, but enormously valuable.

[257] The first phrase was adapted for the well-known hymn by Ellen Goreh.

v. 13);[258] and most notably, that which Jesus made his own at the moment of death, *Into your hands I commit my spirit* (v. 5).[259]

A second intriguing feature is that suggested authors and occasions for the psalm range from David threatened by Saul with a siege in Keilah, at the very beginning of the monarchy, to Jeremiah involved in the siege of Jerusalem, at the very end of it 450 years later.[260]

A third feature is the wide variety of suggestions about the shape of the poem, ranging from a straightforward sequence (describing the psalmist's experiences in the order in which they happened) to a complex and irregular chiastic structure (pivoting on the lament in vv. 9–13). It seems to me that without being over-ingenious, it is, like Psalm 30, not quite as straightforward as it may seem. As 30:1–5 was the simple statement of the psalmist's experience (the apparent 'rectangle' at Vierzehnheiligen), and 30:6–12 the more detailed narrative of what had actually happened (the 'circles and ovals'), so 31:1–8 is an outline of prayer and praise, which 31:9–22 then repeats and amplifies. Then in 31:23–24 the singular 'I' becomes the plural *you*, so that the psalm ends like several of its predecessors with the Lord praised by *all his saints*.

2. The shape of the psalmist's experience (vv. 1–8)

Verses 1–5 are the psalmist's prayer, and verse 6 shows it is a prayer of faith. It is a prayer for rescue from a *trap* (v. 4). Much as we might like to know at once what sort of trap (and as we have seen, the end of the psalm is going to explain it to us), there is value in not knowing. As with the New Testament example of Paul's 'thorn in [his] flesh',[261] it enables all of us to put ourselves in the writer's position, and to say, 'That could be me.' In this case the unspecified trap could be for the reader any threatening circumstances from which there seems no escape, whether the literal enclosure of prison walls, or bureaucracies, or sufferings, or even duties. Another set of word links is provided by the covenant language which takes us back to God's revealing of himself at the exodus: his *righteousness* (v. 1), his *name* (v. 3), his promise to *redeem* or rescue (v. 5). Slavery in Egypt, and the life of the unsaved sinner which that represents, are equally *traps* of this kind.

Verses 7–8 are the psalmist's praise for answered prayer. He is still thinking in terms of entrapment and deliverance, for behind the words *anguish* and *spacious* is the contrast between 'narrow' and 'broad', even between 'closed' and 'open', which we came across in Psalm 18:5–6, 19.[262] He who *saw* and *knew* the psalmist's trouble is

[258]Jer. 17:18; 20:10; 22:28.   [259] Cf. Luke 23:46; cf. also Ps. 22:1 and Matt. 27:46. [260] V. 21; cf. 1 Sam. 23:7–8; Jer., *passim*.   [261] 2 Cor. 12:7.   [262] See pp. 1.62–64.

the Lord who had seen and known Israel's in Egypt,[263] and who now, as then, brings out of a tight place those who cry to him.

3. The detail of the psalmist's experience (vv. 9–24)

It is not that he has been rescued from his predicament and *set ... in a spacious place* (v. 8) and then finds himself again *in distress* (v. 9). Rather, he now goes back over the whole experience, begins this time at the very beginning, and gives a fuller account of the ups and downs of his prayer life through this traumatic period. His actual prayer (vv. 14–18) and his praise (vv. 19–22) are preceded by a description of his plight (vv. 9–13) and followed by a call to his people (vv. 23–24).

Verses 9–13, still without explaining what the trap is, tell us what it feels like to be in it. The effects on mind and body (vv. 9–10) are a misery that many will recognize. The effects on relationships (vv. 11–13) are equally destructive, for it seems that everyone is either opposing the psalmist or abandoning him. Both in Saul's time and in Absalom's, David had to cope with slander and conspiracy; so did Jeremiah in his day.

This is the plight the psalmist was in, and the background to the prayer with which the psalm began. Verses 14–18 are now a restatement of that prayer. Notice the parallel between verses 5–6 and verses 14–15: *Into your hands I commit my spirit ... I trust in the LORD; I trust in you, O LORD ... My times are in your hands.* Notice the insistence that this is a prayer of faith, now starting from that fact (v. 14) instead of working towards it (v. 6). Notice exodus language here also, the shining face and the covenant love of verse 16.[264]

Verses 19–22 reiterate the praise of verses 7–8: there, for having been brought out of a tight place (*anguish*) into a spacious one; here, for having been brought into the Lord's presence out of *a besieged city.* Now we know what the *trap* was!

The historical link, as we saw at the outset, may be with David's experience or with Jeremiah's. But the mass of connections between this and other psalms, and between these psalms and other parts of Scripture, encourage us to cultivate a repeat of the patterns in our own experience. When in verses 23–24 the psalmist associates himself with all others *who hope in the LORD*, he means those who use the past (its language, its thought-forms, its habits of prayer) as he does, and who therefore can look to the future (its promise, its certainty) as he does.

---

[263] Cf. Exod. 3:7 NRSV.
[264] Cf. Num. 6:25; Exod. 20:6; 34:7; and see on Ps. 17:7 above (p. 1.61).

Psalm 32

Augustine, who like his master Paul was keenly aware of his own desires both to be a saint and to be a sinner,[265] cherished this psalm. Great divine that he was, he knew it to be as central to Christian theology as it is to Christian experience. As well as relating to neighbouring psalms, it ties together in a significant knot important threads from earlier ones. The first five verses give new depth to these themes, as they probe to the heart of the human predicament. The following six verses give them new breadth, repeatedly applying them to all God's people.

Like Psalm 51, this one has traditionally been linked with David's adultery with Bathsheba and his murder of her husband Uriah, recounted in 2 Samuel 11 – 12. Of the two psalms, 51 could well be David's immediate outpouring of contrition after the exposure of his sin, and 32 a considered later reworking of the subject, from which others might benefit. This one is called a *maskil*; we cannot be sure what the word means, but it seems to have to do with teaching or understanding. Such a meaning does not suit many of the *maskils*, but it fits well enough here.

1. A new depth (vv. 1–5)

The wisdom theme of verses 1–2 (vv. 8–10 speak in a similar tone) harks back to Psalm 1, and beyond that to books like Proverbs and Ecclesiastes. The first words of the Psalter celebrated the happiness of the righteous. This further great beatitude, which the psalmist wrote 'with his heart's blood',[266] looks deeper. It says, in effect, 'Happy are those who recognize that they are *not* righteous, and who know what to do about it.' It was a maxim of Augustine's that the beginning of knowledge is to know yourself to be a sinner.[267] Four words here hold up the mirror to that inner self. Transgression, which is rebellion; sin, or going astray; iniquity, or twisting the truth; deceit, which aims to disguise the other three – these are the characteristics of every human heart.[268]

The affliction theme of verse 3 has figured often in Book I. David has spoken of it regularly in personal, not theoretical, terms, and usually in connection with the ill will of his enemies. Here however he tells us that his misery is due to his own *keeping silent*: a cryptic clue, until we realize that it has to do with the deceit of verse 2. For how is the many-sided unrighteousness of verses 1–2 to be dealt with? We were told there that it is the Lord who will forgive David's

---

[265] Cf. Rom. 7:15–23; Gal. 5:17.   [266] Weiser, p. 283.

[267] *Intelligentia prima est ut te noris peccatorem.*

[268] AV/RV are more consistent in vv. 1–5 than any of the popular newer translations. It is not clear why NIV translates the same word as *iniquity* in v. 5 and as *sin* in v. 2.

transgressions, cover his sins, and not count his iniquity against him. But it is up to him himself to do something about his deceit. For that is his own unwillingness to admit how bad he is, his 'unrepentant silence'.[269] The only answer to it – simple, but not easy – is the one we shall find in verse 5: something that he, not the Lord, must do.

The discipline theme of verse 4 recalls Psalms 29 and 30, and the contrast between the God of Israel and the gods of Canaan. The Baals and their modern equivalents have to be placated if you are poor, or manipulated if you are powerful; otherwise they will hit you as soon as look at you, out of pique or temper, or because you haven't used the right formula or paid the right price, or indeed for no reason at all. The difference between them and the true God is not that he is never angry with his people, but that when he is, it is out of a concern for their long-term welfare. It is with this in mind that he sends not only the blessings of sunshine and shower but also the afflictions of drought and storm. This too is the wisdom of Proverbs: 'Do not resent his rebuke, because the LORD disciplines those he loves' (3:11–12).

The rescue theme of verse 5 has appeared as often as the affliction theme of verse 3. Now however the hints of Psalm 6 and the explicit words of Psalm 30[270] come into the spotlight: it is from *sin* in all its aspects, more than from anything else, that we need to be rescued. All four terms from the beginning of the psalm are taken up here, for transgression, sin, and iniquity are all dealt with the moment that deceit gives place to confession. When we stop trying to cover up our unrighteousness (v. 5), God really covers it (v. 1). So when Paul quotes the opening words of Psalm 32 in Romans 4:6–8, he says that David is speaking of that greatest of all gospel blessings, 'the blessedness of the man to whom God credits righteousness apart from works'.

2. A new breadth (vv. 6–11)

As poetry, the second half of the psalm is as closely woven as the first half was. There, beginning and end were bound together by four repeated words (God would *cover* David's *transgression*, *sin*, and *iniquity*, when David stopped *covering* his *transgression*, *sin*, and *iniquity*), though within the unity was the variety of a different word order. Here too beginning and end are bound together in a similar way. The relationship between verses 6–7 and verse 10 is not obvious, because the NIV translation varies what the original repeats,[271] but in fact *godly* corresponds to *unfailing love*, and *mighty* to *many*. The echo effect of these repetitions was meant to be

---

[269] Craigie, p. 266.   [270] See pp. 1.32, 1.104.
[271] A reprehensible practice; but you can't have everything.

something like this: If we are *loyal* to him, then amid *many* waters his protection will *surround* us; instead of the *many* woes of the wicked, we shall find him *loyal* to us, and he will *surround* us.

As liturgy, the second half opens out what could otherwise have been a very individual utterance into a piece entirely appropriate for public use. As with Psalms 20, 21, and 22, guesses have been made as to who might have said what on occasions when the congregation and its leaders joined in this psalm.[272] Some believe that in the original poem it was the psalmist speaking throughout, addressing himself to God till the end of verse 7 and to his people after that. Verse 8, *I will ... teach you in the way*, would then parallel the verses in the companion psalm where he had said to God, 'blot out all my iniquity ... Then I will teach transgressors your way' (51:9, 13). But *you* is singular in verse 8 and plural in verse 9, so perhaps the one represents God's word to the forgiven David, and the other is David's passing it on to his people. In either case, that word tells us that forgiveness requires repentance, and that repentance means a heart and mind devoted to following God's way from now on.

The three *selahs* give the psalm an elegant structure, dividing it into a longer and a shorter section in the first part, then a shorter and a longer in the second. If *selah* means a break for a scripture reading, the obvious passage would be 2 Samuel 11 – 12, in three sections: first David's sin, then his exposure, confession, and forgiveness, and finally the consequences. The centre point of the reading ties in exactly with that of the psalm. In the one, 'David said to Nathan, "I have sinned against the LORD." Nathan replied, "The LORD has taken away your sin".' In the other, *I said, 'I will confess my transgressions to the LORD' – and you forgave the guilt of my sin.*[273] In both, the immediacy of forgiveness is striking, and Augustine (to quote him once more) has a comment equally striking: 'The word is scarcely in his mouth, before the wound is healed.'[274]

It is the plurals, and the assumption that one man's poem may properly be used in a gathering of many people, that open up a new breadth in its second half. Verses 6–7 were Charles Wesley's starting point for the hymn 'Jesu, lover of my soul', very personal lines which he nevertheless intended for the use of 'everyone who is godly'.[275] The *songs of deliverance* in verse 7 likewise suggest many singers. The plural *you* of verse 9 we have already noted; and the

[272] See pp. 1.74ff., 1.79. [273] 2 Sam. 12:13; Ps. 32:5.
[274] *Vox nondum est in ore et vulnus sanatur.*
[275] The nineteenth-century hymn writer John Ellerton 'believed that there was a line to be drawn ... between "inward" hymns and "congregational" hymns ... "Jesu, lover of my soul", he thought, "stood absolutely *upon* the line"' (Watson, p. 400).

psalm ends, like so many before it, with a call to *all ... who are upright in heart* (v. 11).

Suppose a congregation hearing the apostolic words 'If we confess our sins, he ... will forgive us our sins'.[276] Suppose it then joining in this psalm: *I said, 'I will confess my transgressions to the LORD' – and you forgave the guilt of my sin.* Suppose it singing with the spirit but also with the mind,[277] and actually doing what it said it was doing. What would be more likely to bring a formal liturgy vividly to life? We are not talking about conversion, which of course may be sudden for some but is gradual for others. We are talking about confession, which when it is a true abandoning of deceit, an uncovering of sin (at least to God, whether or not the rest of the assembly sees it), calls forth for all of us the instant forgiveness of God.

Psalm 33

The first verse of this psalm is very similar to the last verse of the previous one. Perhaps the two were once linked in some way, since there is no *of David* heading such as we might have expected here.

Psalm 32 went deep, exposing the fundamental problem of sin, and then broadened out to offer to everyone the answer to it. Psalm 33 likewise sets that same profound problem and its answer in a broad context – the broadest possible: the gospel as it relates to the whole of space and time.

It begins with three verses calling God's people to praise him.[278] It ends with three verses expressing their trust and confidence in him. The sixteen verses between look as though they might fall easily into two, four, or eight equal sections. But the sequence of thought suggests a division which is slightly less regular, without I hope seeming too baroque.

1. The word, the work, and the covenant love of the Lord (vv. 4–5)[279]

A more exact translation than the NIV would identify in verses 4a, 4b, and 5b these three great expressions of the power of God. The psalmist will be showing in verses 6–19 what they bring about in our world. Here first in a short introduction to this main part of the psalm he makes it very plain, by bracketing the Lord's word and work with his covenant love, that that power is not *mere* power.

---

[276] 1 John 1:9.   [277] Cf. 1 Cor. 14:15.

[278] With freshness, skill, and fervour (v. 3): 'Three qualities rarely found together in religious music', observes Kidner drily. We may chuckle or wince over our experiences of the seven other possible permutations of these qualities.

[279] Note the nouns in the NRSV's rendering of these verses. See p. 1.61.

Everything God does is *right and true*, and *faithful* to his own character. *Righteousness and justice* underpin it all. In a world where so much is evidently not right, we may not always see how this can be. But the truth is that none of the areas of human study touched on in Psalm 33 – science, history, geography, politics – can ever be properly understood apart from this moral framework. Good and evil are woven into the fabric of the universe, and those who explore and exploit it ignore that fact at their peril.

2. His creation at the beginning (vv. 6–9)

The wording of verses 7 (mg.) and 8, with its paradoxical picture of the *deep* piled in a *heap* and the nations awestruck by what they see, recalls Israel's song at the crossing of the Red Sea.[280] But the psalmist is of course going back beyond Exodus to Genesis. God can control the sea, and the sky too, because it is he who created them.

Earlier psalms have taken for granted that he made the sky (8:3) and the earth and sea (24:1–2); here at last the great fact is actually stated. The psalmist is concerned to say not how the process worked out, the 'how' of scientific curiosity, but simply how it was set in motion: God *spoke, and it came to be*. Whatever scientists discover about the beginning of things, this is what lay behind it.

The New Testament will give capitals to the Word and the Breath of verse 6, and tell us of the Son and the Spirit, one with the Father from all eternity. But the statement of Genesis 1:2–3 is as definite as an Old Testament statement can be: 'The Spirit of God was hovering … and God said …'

3. His purpose through the ages (vv. 10–12)

As God stood behind the creation of the world, so he stands behind its history. The universe follows its own rules, and humanity follows its own desires, yet it is God who writes the play, just as it is he who sets the scene. As in their personal lives, so also on the world stage, godless people pursue their godless plans. But the Lord overrules them so as to forward his own plans. In the end theirs come to nothing and his *stand firm for ever*.

In the previous section, the *unfailing love* of which *the earth is full* (v. 5) could be seen in God's providence in creation and the dependability of nature. In this section, it can be seen in his choosing out of the nations one nation which will align itself with his purposes instead of theirs (v. 12). Blessed is that nation – the next of the Psalter's beatitudes, after 1:1, 2:12, and 32:1–2 – and blessed are the millions who through it, and through its greatest Son, have found the forgiveness of sins and an eternal inheritance.

[280] Cf. Exod. 15:8, 14–15.

4. His control of the present (vv. 13–15)
God's original creation of the universe and his ongoing concern with history form a pattern repeated in every person in every age. It is as true today as it ever has been, that *he who forms the hearts of all ... considers everything they do*. It stands to reason that he who has made not only the countless multitudes of the human race, but the complex body and mind of each one of them, is also, from his heavenly vantage point, totally aware at every moment of their every thought and deed.

These are not yet the *eyes* of compassion and care of which verse 18 will speak. This is the Lord who *looks down, sees, watches, considers* his friends and his foes equally, and who acts upon what he sees a great deal more than they might like.

5. His promise for the future (vv. 16–19)
When Psalm 33 speaks of the God who made the universe and who has overseen human history right up to the present time, it looks back to Genesis and the story of creation. But in speaking of his covenant love (v. 5), his mastery of the sea's turmoil (v. 7), and his choosing of a people for himself (v. 12), it is looking back also to Exodus and the story of redemption. The picture of Israel's rescue from slavery, of Egypt's king thwarted and its warriors and horses overwhelmed,[281] is the classic biblical portrait of God the Redeemer. The eyes of this God still watch over his people, and all their hope for the days ahead may confidently be placed in him. Their deliverance from death (v. 19) takes on a whole new dimension with 'the appearing of our Saviour, Christ Jesus, who has destroyed death and has brought life and immortality to light through the gospel'.[282]

It is at this point (v. 18) that God's *unfailing love* reappears, as the *hope* of his people. The last three verses of the psalm, our personal response, will speak of his love yet again, and of our hope not once but twice more. By the end we shall have realized something of the wonder of a sentence near the beginning, in verse 5. Even grander than the cry of the seraphim in Isaiah 6:3, that 'the whole earth is full of his glory', is the psalmist's perception that that glory comes into focus in God's grace and mercy, and that *the earth is full of his unfailing love*.

Psalm 34

The what and the when of Psalm 34 are not quite straightforward.

As to what it is, those who classify the psalms according to the way they may have been used would call it 'an individual thanksgiving' (though for public rather than private use). But that

[281] Exod. 14:21 – 15:12.   [282] 2 Tim. 1:10.

really labels only its first part. It changes gear halfway through, and the second half is in the style of the wisdom books, as though Psalm 33 and Psalm 1 had been stitched together.

As to when it was written, the heading points us to the events of 1 Samuel 21:10–15, when David in flight from Saul found that the court of Achish, the 'Abimelech' or king of Gath, was not the refuge he had hoped, and escaped only by a ruse. But for various reasons many critics think that connection unlikely.

However, the two halves *are* joined, indeed closely integrated (for this is another acrostic, like Pss. 9/10 and 25),[283] even if we cannot readily find a label for the resulting combination. And someone at some stage, considerably nearer to the world of the Old Testament than we are, reckoned that the text and the heading also belonged together in some sense. If the first users and the compilers of the Psalter did not find the connection odd, perhaps that was because it was real. The psalm 'has all the marks of relief and gratitude for a miraculous escape',[284] and there is no good reason why it should not be David's.

An acrostic psalm is not easy to break down into manageable sections. Its twenty-two verses tend to be, like a prime number, divisible by one, and not much else. But in this case it is possible to find divisions larger than single verses. There is as we have seen a definite break halfway. The first part celebrates the blessings of those who fear the Lord, and the second explains what that fear means. (First the singing, then the sermon!). Kidner suggests the headings 'Rejoice with me' and 'Learn from me'. Beyond that, the content suggests three smaller sections in each part.

1. The Lord to be praised (vv. 1–3)
Singular and plural alternate in the first half of 34, as in many other psalms, most recently 32.[285] *I will extol* … sings David, then *Let us exalt* … Verses 1–3 are counted and printed as three couplets (3 × 2), but the rhythm, so to speak, crosses the bar-lines, with two triplets (2 × 3): I will extol, praise, boast – let us rejoice, glorify, exalt. In music this is an intriguing pattern (*one*-two, *three*-four, *five*-six / *one*-two-three, *four*-five-six);[286] we might say it anticipates in a tiny way one of the joys of heaven, where endless praise will never be boring because we shall find endlessly new ways of expressing the same thing. We have already seen this suggested, possibly, by the 'new song' of 33:3.

---

[283] See pp. 1.40ff., 1.90. As in 25, *waw* is missing and an extra *pe* is added at the end.
[284] Kirkpatrick, p. 138.   [285] See p. 1.111.
[286] Lovers of Czech music (e.g. the well-known 'Zither Carol') will recognize the exhilarating rhythm of the *furiant*!

Apart from Psalm 23, so familiar as 'The Lord's my Shepherd' from the 1650 revision of the Scottish Psalter, this is the first one whose seventeenth-century metrical translation is still in common use. The famous 1696 'New Version' of it by Nahum Tate and Nicholas Brady, 'Through all the changing scenes of life', covers the first ten verses, and makes them readily memorable.

2. The Lord of one and all (vv. 4–7)

The four verses at the centre of this first half also alternate between the one and the many. We can imagine how they might have been sung congregationally, solo and tutti turn and turn about.

David's pretended madness before the Philistines was even more undignified than his dancing before the ark.[287] But it was effective in getting him out of a dangerous place, as both scriptures (1 Sam. and Pss.) tell us, and the psalm gives the reason: not the cleverness of David's acting, but the cry of his fearful heart. Assuming the choir's or congregation's response to the leader, we hear the one state the plain fact, that David was *answered* and *delivered* (v. 4), and the many fill out its implications: radiance instead of shame, delight in a God who does not let you down (v. 5).

Similarly, their response to verse 6, which is simply verse 4 in different words, fills out what is happening when *this poor man* is *heard* and *saved* by the Lord. As Tate and Brady put it, and as Scripture tells us repeatedly in its 300-odd references to angels, 'The hosts of God encamp around The dwellings of the just; Deliverance he affords to all Who on his succour trust.'

3. The Lord to be trusted (vv. 8–10)

The psalm's first part ends with a call to trust, as its opening verses were a call to praise. The encouragement to an initial *taste* of the Lord's goodness finds a New Testament echo in Hebrews 6:5 (where incidentally it is a taste of 'the word of God') and 1 Peter 2:3. The *fear* of God means of course reverence, unlike the *fears* of verse 4, which mean terrors. Tate and Brady play on the two meanings: 'Fear him, ye saints, and you will then Have nothing else to fear.'

Such trust never goes unrewarded. Even the lion, greatest of the beasts of prey, the most self-sufficient of animals, may sometimes go hungry; but those whose sufficiency is in God will find they *lack nothing. Those who seek the LORD lack no good thing.* Columba, whose life of Christian service spanned most of the sixth century, had been copying out the Psalms when he died on the Scottish island of Iona, and these were the last words he wrote. It is a fine testimony.

[287] See 2 Sam. 6:16.

4. What the Lord requires (vv. 11–14)

There seems little in this first section of the wisdom half of Psalm 34 that a well-meaning unbeliever might not commend. Until, that is, you take into account its biblical framework.

The style comes from Proverbs, a book which deals with the practicalities of living always with an eye to the Lord we revere. Being the great God he is, he will no doubt have considerably more to say to us than the 'Be good' of these verses. We for our part are in the position of 'children', learners, recognizing authority, admitting ignorance, relishing instruction, accepting discipline – a whole raft of unfashionable attitudes.

New Testament endorsements come from James and Peter, who echo and even quote this passage in setting forth God's requirements for Christian living.[288] An Old Testament summary of what the Lord requires of us comes from Micah: 'To act justly and to love mercy and to walk humbly with your God.'[289] A reminder of the divine principle of consequences, which many try to ignore, comes from Paul in Galatians 6:7: 'A man reaps what he sows.' In David's words, if you desire good, then do good.

5. What the Lord does (vv. 15–18)

So the previous section is largely about the way life is to be lived amid all the practicalities of this world. But it has indicated, and the present section makes plain, that there is One behind the scenes, very much in touch with what is going on. His eye sees far more of our situation than we are aware of ourselves, his ear nevertheless listens to our version of it, and his face is set against all who try to get their own way regardless of the damage and suffering caused in the process ('the LORD *looked down* from the pillar of fire and cloud at the Egyptian army and threw it into confusion').[290]

His care for his own people is expressed again in terms of hearing, delivering, and saving, together with a new thought, his closeness, a word which the Old Testament uses for a near relation as well as a near neighbour. These verses recognize a truth which the following section will spell out: it is possible, and even to be expected, that the righteous should sometimes have *troubles* and be *broken-hearted* and *crushed in spirit*, however much this may seem to contradict the belief, noted above, that the good you do should bring you the good you desire.

---

[288] Jas. 1:27; 2:8; 3:1–12; 4:1; 1 Pet. 1:13–16; 2:1, 11–12; and particularly 3:10–12.
[289] Mic. 6:8.   [290] Exod. 14:24.

6. What the Lord promises (vv. 19–22)

No, says David, speaking out of his own experience, *a righteous man may have many troubles*. The Lord promises deliverance from such things, but that is not the same as exemption from them, nor does it necessarily come when or how we want it. As Stephen, the first Christian martyr, could have testified as they stoned him to death,[291] the promise of verse 20 does not apply in every case; but perhaps it was David's testimony about *his* bones as he scrambled around the wilderness of Judah two steps ahead of his pursuers. For in the wisdom of God this saying of his converged with the ancient regulation concerning the Passover lamb ('Do not break any of the bones')[292] in the mind of John, as he stood at the cross. Soldiers broke the legs of the crucified thieves, to hasten their death, but Jesus was already dead, and so (John tells us) the Scripture was fulfilled.[293]

For Psalm 34, like so many of its fellows, speaks greater things than it knows. David was a prophet, as we have seen;[294] how far he understood the reach of his own words, we do not know. It is a fact, all the same, that not even the New Testament's most splendid visions of the future can show us essentially more than the final verses of our psalm: the wicked, destroyed by their own evil; the servants of God redeemed; those condemned, and these justified, for ever.

Psalm 35

This psalm echoes the language of the last one, which spoke (no doubt rather quaintly to our ears) of a 'poor man' crying out for deliverance, and finding that the Lord's eye was on him and that the angel of the Lord would protect 'all his bones'.[295] The difference is that 34 celebrates a rescue which in 35 has not yet happened. The psalmist is confident it will, though, and each of the three sections, verses 1–10, 11–18, and 19–28, ends by expressing that hope.

Before considering these sections briefly in turn, we shall try to come to terms with the major problem raised by the psalm as a whole.

1. A mixture of metaphors

As well as its reminiscences of 34, the language of 35 is full of metaphors. Or is that what they are? The psalmist describes his enemies as warriors, hunters, robbers, litigants, slanderers. Which words is he using literally and which metaphorically?

---

[291] Acts 7:54–60.   [292] Exod. 12:46.   [293] See John 19:36.   [294] See pp. 1.61, 1.82.
[295] Pss. 34:6–7, 15, 17, 20; 35:5–6, 10 (*all my bones* NRSV; see n. 39, p. 1.32), 17, 22. These are the only two psalms to use the term *angel of the Lord*.

This has a bearing on the question of date and authorship. If the situation is that of one of David's descendants defending his kingdom against attack by a former ally, as some think,[296] the warfare will be literal and the pit and the hunters' net metaphorical. If this is David himself on the run from Saul, the hunt is literal, and the law court metaphorical.

The earlier occasion is I think the more likely. In fact much of the psalm might reflect those early days: Saul's illness, David's flight; pursuit, slander, traps, betrayal, and more. As with so much of Book I, not least the psalm we have just read, there is no good reason why this one also should not belong to David's time, if not indeed to David's pen.

2. 'May ruin overtake them'

It confronts us with a major question, that of the so-called 'imprecatory psalms'. Imprecation, or cursing, is found a good many times in the Psalter; not cursing in the vulgar sense of bad language, but the serious invoking of supernatural power against one's enemies. It was touched on in our reading of Psalm 7, and we shall find conspicuous examples later, in Books II and V, but this is the first psalm where it looms large.[297]

In such psalms 'the spirit of hatred which strikes us in the face is like the heat from a furnace mouth'. So C. S. Lewis in his *Reflections on the Psalms* begins his chapter on 'The Cursings'.[298] The Church of England's Alternative Service Book of 1980 marked passages in thirteen of them which for this reason 'may be omitted', it said, in public worship. In one case (58) the entire psalm was so marked. Thus the editors discarded the requirement of the 1662 Prayer Book that 'the Psalter shall be *read through* once every Month'. Thankfully, their successors were less swayed by the spirit of the age, and *Common Worship*, published in 2000, contains no such editorial high-handedness.

In a way, even the omitting of a whole psalm is not so crass as the excising, here and there, of odd verses, which authors, compilers, and users over the centuries have understood to be integral parts of the psalms in which they appear. For, in Lewis's memorable words, 'the bad parts will not "come away clean"', being 'intertwined with the most exquisite things'.[299]

---

[296] Craigie, pp. 285–286.

[297] Shepherd and Wenham between them focus on the following eight psalms: 35, 58, 68, 69, 79, 109, 137, 139. Wenham (p. 163) refers to a study some years ago which concluded that on the grounds of their 'bloodthirsty threats and curses' no fewer than 84 psalms (out of 150!) were 'not fit for Christians to sing'!

[298] Lewis, p. 23.

[299] Lewis, p. 24. As always, Lewis writes brilliantly, and sets forth the question with

This is true on the larger scale also. Bigger questions open up before us. What are the rights and wrongs of cutting out sections, short or long, not only from this or that psalm, but from the Old Testament – indeed, from Scripture – as a whole? And if you decide the 'bad parts' have to stay in, what are you to make of them?

3. The bigger problem

The reaction of many people to words like *may ruin overtake them* (v. 8) is not only distaste, but some such remark as 'Typically Old Testament.' The cursings are thought to be of a piece with the rest of that primitive book, a portrayal of the bad old days of Jewish religion before sweetness and light came in with Christianity and the New Testament.

Well, yes and no. Yes, because the Old Testament does contain many other cursings, all the way from the Pentateuch (e.g. Deut. 27 – 28) to the Prophets (Is. 13, Jer. 18 – 19, Nah. 3, among others). No, because the Old Testament also contains stern warnings against vindictiveness and gloating, and teaches a very 'New Testament' ethic of love even for enemies (e.g. Prov. 24:17–18; 25:21–22).

More than that: as there is, to the surprise of the uninformed, 'Christian' love and forgiveness in the pre-Christian world, so there is (equally surprisingly) 'pre-Christian' wrath and denunciation in the Christian world. It is surely with a conscious echo of the cursings of Deuteronomy that Jesus sets 'woes' alongside his blessings in Luke 6:24–26, and Paul's anathemas simply follow his Master's lead.[300]

In other words, the real problem is how Old and New Testaments alike can approve *both* charity *and* ill will towards one's enemies. As I indicated above, the question is not, Wouldn't the Psalms make better sense if we left out all this cursing? but, What sense do they make if we keep it in?

To find an answer, we should ask a further question. Who, in the imprecatory psalms, is the object of these curses?

4. Who is being cursed?

Obviously, the psalmist is cursing his enemies. But it may never have occurred to us to ask who they are. If it has not, then of course we are likely to find his attitude offensive and spiteful. The psalms are largely personal poems, and we shall assume that the cursing psalms are simply expressing personal animosities.

---

clarity. But for once I think he misses the answer, and Shepherd and Wenham have got it.

[300] See also Luke 10:13–15; 11:39–52 (in particular); 17:1–2; 22:22; 1 Cor. 16:22; Gal. 1:8–9.

But when we see in so many other parts of Scripture cursings which are equally fierce and which cannot be so easily dismissed, we have to think again. And we find that from Moses in Deuteronomy to Paul in Galatians, indeed from the curse of Genesis 3:14–19 to that of Revelation 22:19, and supremely in the words of our Lord himself (Matt. 23 is even more sustained and terrifying than the Luke references just noted), all these imprecations have a similar object. They are directed against those who *reject what God has said*.

This sheds new light on Psalm 35. The one by whom, or for whom, it was written was using the covenant name of the God of Israel. He identified with the Lord, and with no other god. *Who is like you, O LORD?* (v. 10). So the conflict was between one who accepted the Lord's authority and others who rejected it. He was on the Lord's side, and his enemies were the Lord's enemies: *Contend, O LORD, with those who contend with me* (v. 1). That is why he could say that they were attacking him without cause (vv. 7, 19); true, it was over his distress that they were gloating (v. 26), but it was really the Lord with whom they were at odds.

If all this is about David and Saul, then the psalm not only reflects the long story of 1 Samuel 13 – 31 in some detail (right down to David's concern for Saul in his illness, and the groundlessness of Saul's hostility),[301] but also makes the theological point very clearly. God had spoken through his prophet Samuel to both Saul and David. Saul had disobeyed the word that had come to him,[302] and had refused to recognize the word that had come to David.[303] That was why he was rejected. Perhaps it was because of the scruples which stopped David from killing Saul, when he twice had the opportunity, that the psalm never names an individual, but always speaks of enemies in the plural, and anonymously. It is nevertheless with Saul's downfall that David's prayer is answered, and the cause of his doom, spelt out for him by the spirit of the dead Samuel, is exactly what lies behind every imprecation in Scripture: 'Because you did not obey the LORD … the LORD has done this to you.'[304] Not one disobedience, nor two, but a whole mindset which has turned against God, an inexorable wilful march to ruin.

5. Who is cursing?

It is the innocent victim who utters the curse, the one who is being persecuted *without cause*. As we need to ask just why Saul should

---

[301] 1 Sam. 16:14–23; 18:10–11; 19:9–10. Three of the Psalter's six uses of *ḥinnām*, 'for no reason' (1 Sam. 19:5), occur in this psalm.
[302] 1 Sam. 13:7–14; 15:13–29.   [303] 1 Sam. 23:15–17; 24:11, 20.
[304] 1 Sam. 28:18.

be cursed, we need equally to ask why David should be the one to curse him.

It is not being virtuous that gives him the right. He isn't, and that is not the point at issue. Nor is it really that he is innocent *as charged* – that whatever he may have done wrong in other respects, Saul's accusations against him are not true. (His friend Jonathan, Saul's son, has dared to tell his father so, to his face: 'he has not wronged you'.)[305] But that is not the point either.

No; something else is even more important. It is precisely where Saul was in the wrong that David is in the right. A thousand years afterwards God's own testimony to this man will ring out as clear as ever: 'I have found David son of Jesse a man after my own heart; he will do everything I want him to do.'[306] David's 'delight is in the law of the LORD', despite his lapses into sin; Saul is 'like chaff that the wind blows away', despite his spasms of remorse; it is the distinction laid down at the beginning of the Psalter, in Psalm 1, with its language echoed here in verses 5 and 28.

The story of David and Saul draws the lines more clearly for us than they would be drawn at most later stages in the history of Israel. Later, we should not have found the curses uttered by a man whom Scripture, as we have seen, calls a prophet as well as a king. Later, the notion might creep in that God was simply being required to fight for Israel against Aram, or Assyria, or whoever; whereas the conflict between Saul and David took place entirely within Israel, and the question had nothing to do with nationality, race, or even religion, but only with obedience and disobedience.

6. Six practical points

In view of all this, can we today use Psalm 35 and other scriptures like it without embarrassment, even with profit?

Let me make six suggestions.

First, even if David did feel vindictive towards his enemies, he would have been doing the right thing with his feelings: not taking the law into his own hands, but committing the matter to God in prayer. Both Testaments make this point: 'Do not take revenge … but leave room for God's wrath … "It is mine to avenge; I will repay," says the Lord.'[307] All the imprecatory psalms are prayers, in which God is being asked to do what only he, and not the psalmist, has the right and power to do.

In fact David is not being vengeful. There are such things as right anger and proper hatred. 'Be angry but do not sin'; 'Hate what is evil' – again the New Testament agrees with the Old.[308] In a world

---

[305] 1 Sam. 19:4.   [306] Acts 13:22; cf. 1 Sam. 13:14.
[307] Rom. 12:19, quoting Deut. 32:35.
[308] Eph. 4:26 NRSV, quoting Ps. 4:4; Rom. 12:9, quoting Amos 5:15.

where much really is hateful and where many things, and people, richly deserve our indignation, easy-going Christians could learn something from David's passion. There is plenty of moral outrage expressed today by hypocritical people in inappropriate directions, but not nearly enough of it where it is needed.

Thirdly, David is in illustrious company – Moses, Isaiah, Paul, Jesus – both in his prophetic status and in the object of his denunciations. There are, alas, those who have wilfully and finally rebelled against the loving plan of God, and these mouthpieces of the voice of God tell us plainly that such willing instruments of Satan not only are, but ought to be, doomed to destruction. 'Depart from me, you who are cursed, into the eternal fire prepared for the devil and his angels': not even David goes as far as the 'gentle Jesus' does in such an imprecation.[309] This too we must take seriously.

We need, furthermore, to recognize that whenever we pray, 'Your kingdom come', we are praying as David prayed, for the destruction of the existing kingdom. Quite literally, his reign could not begin until Saul was removed. Do we want the triumph of good? Then we want the defeat of evil. There will be much pain in the process, and we ourselves (like David) will not be exempt from it: 'We must go through many hardships to enter the kingdom of God.'[310] But by the same token we have to recognize that asking for the downfall of any wicked system is (to be realistic) asking for the downfall of those who persist in identifying with it. If our prayer is to be answered, they too are bound to suffer, for they too cannot be exempt from the implications of their choices.

Fifthly, the principle of retribution is an integral part of the rule of God. Those who fight against God will find God fighting against them. The net they hid for me will entangle them; they will fall into the pit they dug for me (vv. 7–8). One would not expect to find profound theology in the operas of Gilbert and Sullivan, but amid the buffoonery of *The Mikado* there is a terrifying depth to the words 'My object all sublime I shall achieve in time, To let the punishment fit the crime.' We do well to realize this – and, it may be added, to apply it to the wickedness of our own hearts.

Lastly, we should notice the way the New Testament quotes this psalm, added evidence that far from being passages which 'may be omitted', the cursings are integral to Scripture. The evil against which David prays has attacked him *without cause*. It is envious and sadistic, hurting and spoiling and destroying merely for the sake of it. Christ's ultimate object, and ours, is that the destroyers be destroyed. But in the meantime he accepts 'what is written in their

[309] Matt. 25:41. [310] Acts 14:22.

Law: "They hated me without reason,"' and warns his followers to expect the same treatment[311] – and, adds Peter, not to retaliate. How do you follow the Lord in combining non-retaliation with implacable opposition to evil? The challenge is not an easy one. But paradoxical though it may sound, 'to this you were called'.[312]

7. What the psalm says

These six points will help us to read Psalm 35 as the author would have wanted it read.

In the psalms strong feeling and elaborate form are, as we know, by no means mutually exclusive. In this case, however, there are no greater complexities in the structure of the poem than a simple division into three sections, each ending on a note of joyful confidence (vv. 9–10, 18, and 28).

In the first, David pleads for divine help, on the basis that the Lord's cause is his, and that therefore his enemies are the Lord's (vv. 1–3). If the cause is to prevail, the enemies must be destroyed, and their punishment will correspond to the evil they have done (vv. 4–8). The outcome, eagerly awaited, will be demonstrably the victory of good over evil (vv. 9–10).

In the second section, the facts of the case show that David is suffering undeservedly and Saul's party is acting maliciously (vv. 11–16). Again the wronged man appeals for help (v. 17), and again he anticipates the Lord's deliverance (v. 18).

In its final section, the psalm for the third time exposes David's enemies in their unrighteousness and cries to the Lord in his righteousness (vv. 22–25). Its prayer is that truth will be vindicated by the confounding of the one party and the praises of the other (vv. 26–27), and leads into the confident close of verse 28.

Psalm 36

Psalm 1's theme of the two ways, the way of the righteous and the way of the wicked, is never far from the minds of the compilers of this first David Collection. In these psalms, so many of which seem to reflect David's own experience, we see a man who often identifies himself quite unselfconsciously with the righteous, not out of conceit, but simply as one who is suffering at the hands of the wicked. He is being accused unjustly, or assailed by enemies, or deceived, or betrayed, or for one reason or another driven to call on God for help.

The collection so far comes to something of a climax with Psalm 35, which envisages in the most real and personal terms, and asks God for, a fulfilling of Psalm 1:6: 'the LORD watches over the way

---

[311] John 15:18–25, quoting v. 19.   [312] 1 Pet. 2:18–23.

of the righteous, but the way of the wicked will perish'. After it the compilers have placed a poem which is a kind of rewriting and expanding of that introductory one, in the light of all that has happened between.

1. The way of the wicked (vv. 1–4)
The order of the first psalm is reversed in the thirty-sixth, which deals with the wicked man first; and where 1 spoke of the end to which his way would take him, 36 speaks of the way itself.

The description of this, the way of life of the wicked, is a thoroughgoing condemnation of the human race in every age. There might now and then be an indignant plea of 'not guilty' to a particular charge: the ancient Greeks would claim to be wise, both sides during the wars of religion in Europe would claim to be rejecting what is wrong, our own age would claim to be for ever doing good. But all such claims are undercut by humanity's guilt in every other respect.

Significantly, its sinfulness begins with a lack of the *fear of God*. For once, fear means not reverence but terror; the wicked may make some show of revering God, but they will not see that he might be a frightening God, or that they might be facing future judgment.

The exact sense of the opening words of the psalm is disputed. Verse 1a may be describing an *oracle*, the kind of message spoken by God through his prophets, here spoken by *Sinfulness* personified. If it means, 'Concerning the wicked, Sinfulness speaks within *his* heart,'[313] it is the voice of the wicked man's own sinful nature, prompting all the outworkings of verses 1b–4. If it means 'Concerning the wicked, Sinfulness speaks within *my* heart,'[314] I am as it were overhearing what it says to him, no doubt because I too have a sinful nature which says the same kind of thing to me. There is something unrighteous in the hearts of the righteous which Psalm 1 did not mention. They may deplore it, but at least it should keep them from conceit and complacency, and teach them to be watchful and humble. This truth is opened up in their half of Psalm 36, to which we now turn.

2. The way of the righteous (vv. 5–9)
This part of the psalm does not at first look like an amplification of what Psalm 1 said about the way of the righteous. A more obvious counterpart to verses 1–4 would be Psalm 15, which is just such an

---

[313] RSV; from the LXX. (NRSV, following its inclusive-language policy, has 'their hearts'.)
[314] AV/RV/NIV; from the Heb.

amplification contrasting with what those verses say about the wicked. But verses 5–9 are not like that either. In fact they do not focus on the righteous man at all, but on his God.

They speak first of some of God's qualities, and of the greatness of those qualities. We might despair of reaching their oceanic depths, their mountainous (even celestial) heights, did we not realize that it is precisely these things – his love and faithfulness, his righteousness and justice – that he brings to bear upon us and our needs. The second mention of his covenant love relates it directly to his care for us and all his creatures. It may 'be too great to grasp' (v. 5), but it is 'too good to let slip' (v. 7).[315]

The cluster of metaphors illustrating this love and care points us to other psalms, as well as to remoter scriptures: God's wings in 17:8,[316] his house in 23:6,[317] his river in 46:4,[318] his fountain in 87:7,[319] his light in 27:1.[320]

What a God he is, to be pictured thus! But what does all this have to do with our heading 'The way of the righteous'?

3. The personal response (vv. 10–12)

The opposite of the way of the wicked is not primarily the way of morality, of trying to think wise thoughts and speak truthful words and do good deeds which will contrast with those of verse 3. Such things are by-products; they arise from a heart which has been set right because it has come to know the Lord. And that knowledge does not originate with man either. The whole previous paragraph, verses 5–9, is an ecstatic song of praise to a God who *gives*: 'every good and perfect gift is from above',[321] including this gift of knowing him. Verse 10 tells us that the upright in heart are those who have joyfully accepted it, in the spirit of 18:1, 'I love you, O LORD, my strength.' When we recall the words of 26:5, 12, 'I abhor the assembly of evildoers ... in the great assembly I will praise the LORD', we realize that verse 11 of this psalm evidences the same taking of sides: to identify with the God of verses 5–9 is to distance oneself from the wicked of verses 1–4. Verse 12 sums up the fate of the wicked, which has already been set forth comprehensively in 35:4–10 and concisely in 1:6b.

The 'oracle of sinfulness' makes itself heard in the hearts of the

[315] Kidner, p. 147.

[316] See also Ruth 2:12; Matt. 23:37.

[317] Surely in this context not the Jerusalem temple, but the whole earth; he provides for his creatures everywhere. See Ps. 104.

[318] See also Gen. 2:10 (interestingly, 'Eden' means 'delight'); Ezek. 47; Rev. 22:1–2.

[319] Though the Hebrew word is different. See also Is. 12:3; Rev. 21:6.

[320] See also Is. 10:17; John 1:4–9; 8:12; 9:5.

[321] Jas 1:17.

righteous as well as in the hearts of the wicked. And although it tempts them repeatedly to sin, it also reminds them constantly how helpless they are to lift themselves out of the one assembly into the other. They cease to rely on any goodness of their own to commend themselves to God. Instead they rejoice that his covenant love, his faithfulness, his righteousness, his justice, can do for them what they cannot do for themselves. The great words of verses 5–6 are great New Testament words too. 'By grace you have been saved, through faith'[322] was a truth as well known in David's time as in Paul's.

Psalm 37

Of all the psalms we have considered so far, 37 is second only to 18 in length. How can it best be broken down into sections of manageable size?

We have already noted some of the psalmist's poetic devices, such as inclusio and chiasmus. Another is the repeating at intervals of phrases which act as markers, rather as some modern hymns and songs have a repeated refrain or chorus. Here, for instance, people who either *inherit the land* or else are *cut off* figure five times, the two phrases mostly bracketed together. As we shall see, they help us to understand the psalm. As a marker dividing it into sections, however, they do not work very well. A simpler and more equal division, which also seems to accord with the way the psalmist's thought develops, turns on the words *the wicked plot* (v. 12), *the wicked borrow* (v. 21), and *the wicked lie in wait* (v. 32). This gives four sections, which we shall look at in turn, with some preliminary remarks and then a review at the end.

1. Another acrostic

The NIV, with many other modern translations, does in fact divide the forty verses into twenty-two stanzas, which even without its footnote would suggest to us that this psalm was the next of the Psalter's acrostics. Of the points we noted about poems of this kind when we first encountered them in Psalms 9/10, the one to remember here is that the ABC scheme – *aleph* beginning verse 1, *beth* verse 3, *gimel* verse 5, and so on – made them easy to memorize. In other words, it was a teaching aid. We notice too that this is one of the few psalms in the first David Collection in which the words 'O Lord' or 'O God' are nowhere to be found; instead, the psalmist is addressing his fellow-believers. This is not prayer or praise, but instruction and exhortation.

[322] Eph. 2:8.

What it teaches is thoroughly practical. It is in no way abstract or philosophical, though it does raise major theological issues.

Behind it lies the wisdom tradition. Its style is that of the book of Proverbs, and it repeatedly echoes the teaching of that book. Its opening verse reproduces Proverbs 24:19 almost word for word. Ahead of it lies the teaching of the New Testament, particularly the Beatitudes in the Sermon on the Mount, where Matthew 5:5 ('the meek … will inherit the earth') is in its turn a quotation of verse 11 here.

2. The 'two assemblies' again

Like the wisdom style, the idea of the assembly, or rather the two assemblies, goes back through many of the intervening psalms to the very first one. 'The man' of 1:1–3 does not stand alone; he belongs to 'the assembly of the righteous' which in 1:5 stands over against the (plural) wicked. In this respect also 37 reflects the world of Proverbs. As well as likenesses in many individual verses, we find in that book an entire chapter which especially in its last section (Prov. 10:27–32) is about the two kinds of person, and the contrast between them.

As in Psalm 1, so here the righteous are not at first called the righteous, but are described in terms of how they relate to God (1:1–3; 37:1–9). They are those whom the psalmist is instructing. After that he speaks of them as *the meek* (v. 11), and then as *the righteous*, *the upright*, and *the blameless*, which as we saw in Psalm 26 has to do not with sinlessness but with integrity.[323] The wicked by contrast are those who care nothing for God. They too have become familiar through the pages of the David Collection.

3. The success of the wicked (vv. 1–11)

The many imperatives in this section – do this, don't do that – are not meant to be taken as orders. (Our generation, like others before it, rebels against being told what to do.) Rather they are exhortations, reasoned and affectionate. They are concerned with the obvious fact that people can care nothing for God and yet 'succeed in their ways'. A provoking fact, for those who do care about God and don't seem to get on very well! What should be their reaction to it?

Not fretting and anger, says the psalmist. There is of course a righteous anger, as we saw in Psalm 35, and a place for it, when bad people get away with crime and profit from it too. But the point here is that we should not react to the wicked with their own weapons. We should not play their game. What we should do is to

---

[323] See p. 1.93.

'cultivate faithfulness' (as the phrase *enjoy safe pasture* in v. 3 might be translated). That is, we should act on the psalmist's positive urgings, which are all about identifying not with the wicked but with the righteous, the Lord's people, and developing our confidence in the Lord.

That attitude highlights one thing in particular of which we can be confident. Notice how often the word *will* occurs here. The trump card in the hand of the righteous is that they 'know who holds the future',[324] and he assures them that the flourishing of the wicked is only temporary. It is like grass, which in the climate of the Middle East is green in spring and withered by the end of summer. The *soon* of verse 2 may be relative, but the tenor of the whole section is that a just outcome is *certain*: *The meek will inherit the land*. That is their confidence.

4. The hostility of the wicked (vv. 12–20)
This second section reiterates in different words some of the teaching of the first. Again we are told that the flourishing of the wicked is like that of *the beauty of the fields*, spectacular but temporary, whereas the righteous can look forward to a permanent inheritance.

Verses 12–20 also take the theme a step further. Their opening words are, *The wicked plot against the righteous*. These are not simply two kinds of people eyeing each other with disapproval; one is actively hostile to the other. In the New Testament, 2 Peter 2:8 pictures the 'righteous man' (in this case Abraham's nephew Lot, living in the city of Sodom) 'tormented in his righteous soul by the lawless deeds he saw and heard', while 1 Peter 4:4 goes the next step, and pictures the wicked, who 'think it strange that you do not plunge with them into the same flood of dissipation … [heaping] abuse on you'.

Again the Lord is presented as one who holds the future. He knows all about the wicked and *their day*, that is, their coming judgment (vv. 12–15), and with the terrible laughter of Psalm 2 he will bring on them the fitting retribution of Psalm 35:7–8.[325] One positive lesson the cursing psalms teach us is that we should not even think of avenging ourselves in this way, not because the way itself is wrong but because we should get it wrong. It is the Lord's way; and if we leave it to him he will get it exactly right, and *their swords will pierce their own hearts*.

Equally, he knows the *days of the blameless* (vv. 16–19). Them he upholds and provides for, with a provision which may seem 'little'

---

[324] A. B. Smith and E. Clark, 'I do not know what lies ahead'.
[325] We saw this as far back as Pss. 7:15–16; 9:15–16.

in comparison with the *wealth* of the wicked, but which like the bread of Sinai and the water of Shiloah never fails.[326] It is precisely that unfailing confidence for the future that the godless lack.

5. The curse of the wicked (vv. 21–31)

The wicked borrow and do not repay, the NIV's literal translation of verse 21a, sounds like greed, or at least selfish thoughtlessness. However, some translations and commentaries take it to mean, 'The wicked *have to* borrow and *cannot* repay.' This is not in the text, but it is in the context, for it relates to the cursing and blessing in verse 22, which relate in their turn to the motto theme we noted at the outset: that of some who *will inherit the land* and others who *will be cut off*. They are mentioned several times in the psalm, and two of the mentions form an inclusio in this section (vv. 22 and 28–29).

Such language takes us into an unexpectedly stark landscape, 'remote from ... the more domestic horizon' of the wisdom books and of wisdom-type psalms like this one.[327] We are in the world of Joshua and the conquest, where the Canaanites are *cut off* and the Israelites *inherit* their land.[328] It is there that by Moses' direction the Lord's curses and blessings are pronounced,[329] and one of each is precisely what the psalmist is describing in verse 21. Deuteronomy 28 tells us that among God's promised blessings will be the ability to lend (v. 12), and among his threatened curses will be the need to borrow (vv. 43–44). So as the latter passage puts it, financially as well as in other ways the cursed 'will sink lower and lower' and the blessed 'will rise ... higher and higher'. We are encouraged to look beyond the anxieties of the present, as described in verses 12 and 14 in the previous section, to a time when what verse 16 called the *wealth of many wicked* will become poverty, and the *little that the righteous have* will become plenty.

But is that what really happens?

The psalmist thinks so, for he continues blithely to assure us that never in all his long life has he seen the righteous in financial need (vv. 25–26)! Brueggemann, discussing this psalm at length, suggests that such a statement would make sense in a 'very protected environment', a 'settled, stable, reliable, controllable' society; but for

---

[326] Cf. Exod. 16:35; Is. 8:6 (with Ps. 46:4?).

[327] Brueggemann, pp. 237–238.

[328] Cf., e.g., Deut. 12:29 (where 'dispossess' is the same word as *inherit* in Ps. 37), and other uses of the words *kāraṯ* ('cut off') and *yāraš* ('inherit') in Num., Deut., and Josh.

[329] We note of course that the heathen nations of Canaan have long since been under God's curse (Gen. 15:16; Deut. 9:5), and that in the curses of Deut. 27 – 28 it is Israel who is now being warned.

most people in most ages life is just not like that, and only the 'very young' will be sufficiently trusting, and the 'very devout' sufficiently other-worldly, to make anything of such an assurance.[330]

To this we must return. Meanwhile there is another assurance, at any rate, that we need have no hesitation in accepting: that God will in the end deal as ruthlessly with every power of evil abroad in our world as he did with the accursed civilizations of Canaan.

6. The future of the wicked (vv. 32–40)

The final section draws the threads together. Verses 32–33 remind us of the hostility of the wicked towards the righteous (like v. 14): it will come to nothing. Verse 34 recalls the righteous waiting patiently for the Lord (like v. 7): he will exalt them. Verses 35–36 speak again of the flourishing of the wicked (like v. 2): they will wither. Verse 10 has said the same, and all these passages point back to the beginning of the Psalter, to Psalm 1:6, which sums them up: 'the LORD watches over the way of the righteous, but the way of the wicked will perish'. The many uses of the word *will* in this psalm are put in another way in its last couplet but one, verses 37–38: *there is a future for the man of peace ... but ... the future of the wicked will be cut off.*

Does the psalmist mean an immediate future within the lifetime of himself and his readers? Or is he pointing to the fortunes of their *posterity* (NIV mg.), in generations yet unborn? Or has he in mind the kind of future which is occasionally glimpsed in the Old Testament, the life of the world to come?

The when and the how of his confident forecasts we shall consider in a moment, in reviewing the psalm as a whole. We should first note the connection between all he says about the future and what he says in verses 25–26 about the past: *I was young and now I am old, yet I have never seen the righteous forsaken or their children begging bread.* Before you ask what that sentence means, think what it implies: an appeal to experience, to the facts of the past. This is an outlook altogether at odds with that of much of modern society. Entire systems of thought and education, entire cultures, are today turning their backs on the past. Even in secular matters they care little for tradition, know practically nothing of history, and reject the authority of age and experience. People need not go to Scripture to find this frighteningly widespread way of thinking condemned: as certain also of their own prophets have said, 'Those who will not learn from history are doomed to repeat it.' But the Old Testament too grounds its warnings and promises for the future in its record of the past; and the New Testament's future hope

[330] Brueggemann, pp. 239–240.

likewise is based squarely on past fact. The confidence of verses 39–40 is meaningless otherwise.

7. The vexed question of how and when

It was perhaps a tongue-in-cheek comment of Brueggemann's that verses 25–26 make sense only to the 'very protected', the 'very young', or the 'very devout'. These are, all the same, three suggestive pointers to an understanding of Psalm 37. In a comfortable, law-abiding, caring, 'protected' society, its assurances could be taken at face value. During the peaceful interludes in the time of the judges or the reigns of efficient, godly kings, the promises of the psalm meant for Israel exactly what they said, with the cutting off of the wicked and an enjoyment of the inherited land.

To the 'devout', the psalm would be as true in bad times as in good. They might be accused of spiritualizing away the concreteness of the promises, when things were difficult and they were obviously not enjoying their inheritance in the land in any literal sense. Not so, they would retort – they were enjoying 'an abundance which might be material or spiritual, as God saw fit'.[331] As in due course the hope of heaven came into focus, they would say that it was only a matter of time, and they were perfectly happy with spiritual blessings now in view of the 'solid joys and lasting treasure'[332] that they would have later.

As for the 'very young', that which a child in a loving home takes for granted about its parents' care is a picture of the truest faith of all. It may seem an unsophisticated, simplistic view of things, like (we might say) the outlook of Psalm 37 and Proverbs and Job's friends. It gets shot to pieces by the hard facts of real life and the hard questions raised, for example, by Job himself, and by all whose suffering belies such easy assurances. Yet in the end the child's confidence turns out to have been right after all. 'The kingdom of heaven belongs to such as these.'[333]

In the end. That too is a Proverbs phrase, a wisdom phrase. This is a psalm about waiting and patience and hope and the long view. The way the apostolic church used this psalm is instructive. In the NRSV, verse 5 reads, *Commit your way to the LORD; trust in him, and he will act.* Both Paul and Peter echo it, and both in precisely this way. 'The one who calls you is faithful, and he will act,' is the literal rendering of 1 Thessalonians 5:24,[334] and what Paul has just been

---

[331] Kidner, p. 151. Kidner points to examples in both Old Testament (Ps. 73:26; Hab. 3:17–18) and New (Matt. 4:4; 2 Cor. 6:10; Phil. 4:12).

[332] John Newton, 'Glorious things of thee are spoken'.   [333] Matt. 19:14.

[334] Exactly as in Ps. 37:5, the verb is absolute – not 'he will do *this*' or 'he will do *it*', but simply 'he will *do*'.

saying is, 'May your whole spirit, soul and body be kept blameless *at the coming of our Lord Jesus Christ.*' 'Cast all your anxiety on him,' says 1 Peter 5:7, 'because he cares for you'; and what Peter is saying in the surrounding verses is, 'Humble yourselves ... under God's mighty hand, that he may lift you up *in due time*' (v. 6); and 'the God of all grace, who called you *to his eternal glory* in Christ, after you have suffered a little while, will himself restore you' (v. 10). He will put everything right in the end.

In what sense is this psalm meant to be taken literally, when it speaks of the inheriting of the land? Many Jews, and Christians too, would say that it had to do with a particular territory in the Middle East, and really came true with the setting up of the state of Israel in 1948. Any fulfilment other than that, however 'spiritual' (they would say), is less than its true meaning.

But consider again the most direct quotation from it in the New Testament: 'Blessed are the meek, for they will inherit the *earth*.'[335] The same Hebrew word means both 'land' and 'earth', and so does its Greek equivalent. When Jesus quotes Psalm 37:11 in the Sermon on the Mount, translators take it for granted that he does mean the earth and not just the land. For we are well aware that in the end the inheritance of his people will be a universal one. And what is true of the 'how' will also be true of the 'when'. Amid the 'solid joys' of heaven we shall perhaps be able to look back, and realize with hindsight that in every respect that matters the wisdom of this psalm did come true at the right time and in the best way. We shall by then have come into possession of a whole new world.

Psalm 38

It might seem a nice irony on the part of those who arranged the psalms to set 38 alongside 37. At first glance, the outlook of the earlier one looks like the wisdom of Job's friends (it is sinners who suffer, the Lord protects the righteous); while the theme of this one looks like the cry of Job himself (complaining about the misery the Lord has brought on him).

As we have seen, however, there is more to Psalm 37 than the simplistic notions of Eliphaz, Bildad, and Zophar, and in the same way the psalmist's cry in Psalm 38 is in important respects very different from Job's, though the two use similar language about their sufferings.[336]

As the cry of a believer in pain, the closing verses of our present psalm hark back to 22.[337] Its opening verse echoes that of 6, which

[335] Matt. 5:5.   [336] Cf. Job 6:4; 7:5; 16:12–13; 19:13–20; 30:10, 12.
[337] Ps. 38:21–22 echoes Ps. 22:1, 11, 19.

is a closer parallel, in that its author (unlike the author of 22) recognizes God's anger against him on account of his sin. Both of those earlier psalms were set to music and used in liturgy; the heading of this one, *to bring to remembrance* (AV), may also have to do with cultic use, though it may mean simply a personal plea like that of the thief on the cross, 'Jesus, remember me.' The psalmist would have agreed with him: 'We are getting what our deeds deserve.'[338]

The twenty-two verses do not in this case mean an acrostic, and no broader division into stanzas or sections catches the eye. Four times, however, the psalmist addresses God, saying in effect, 'Lord, you hurt me' (vv. 1–2), 'Lord, you know me' (v. 9), 'Lord, you hear me' (v. 15), and 'Lord, you save me' (vv. 21–22), and these brief sentences indicate the flow of his thought, without marking any rigid poetic structure.[339]

1. 'Lord, you hurt me' (vv. 1–2)

Complex things are going on in the psalmist's inner world, but what onlookers would first be aware of would be his physical illness (vv. 5–8). His *wounds* in verse 11 are the sores caused by the kind of skin complaint often, though wrongly, called 'leprosy',[340] but to judge by his own description of his symptoms 'the patient has almost every disease in the book'![341]

He himself is aware that behind them lies his own *sinful folly* (v. 5). As we have been reminded,[342] Jesus warns us against assuming that suffering and disability must be the result of sin, but they certainly can be. 'It would be as wrong to think that this is never so, as that it is always so.'[343] On the principle, Job agreed with his friends; what he did not accept was that it applied in his case.

As we trace the sequence of cause and effect back through the psalm, we find the psalmist recognizing God's part in it. Because of his sin, God was angry; because of God's anger, the psalmist's health suffered (v. 3). Whatever the illness was, he felt it piercing him like sharp arrows and crushing him like a heavy hand (v. 2), and both the pain and the depression came from God.

At the very outset he reveals the special insight from which we can learn. There is an extra link in the chain. If it were simply 'I sin, so God is angry, so he makes me suffer,' that could mean that in his anger he wants to punish me. But the psalmist knows, and says

---

[338] Luke 23:41–42.

[339] With the 'O Lord' phrases as markers, the verses could be neatly divided 2 + 6 + 6 + 6 + 2, but the scheme does not seem natural or fit the content.

[340] 'Sore' in Lev. 13, particularly v. 3.

[341] Craigie, p. 303.   [342] See p. 1.104, n. 240.   [343] Kidner, p. 154.

plainly in verse 1, that this is not punishment; it is rebuke and discipline. These also he would rather not have; but they do show that he is in an altogether different relationship to God from that of the wicked. He is not a wicked man, but a righteous man who has sinned. In New Testament terms, such people have been justified through faith; and the gospel makes it clear that for those who cast themselves on God's mercy, his punishing anger has at the cross of Calvary been deflected from them on to another. What may still come their way is not that, but God's disciplining anger, which has a positive and loving purpose.

2. 'Lord, you know me' (v. 9)

C. S. Lewis once famously said that 'God whispers to us in our pleasures, speaks in our conscience, but shouts in our pains: it is His megaphone to rouse a deaf world.'[344] We know from the first thing the psalmist says to God (v. 1) that he does not enjoy such harsh treatment, but the second thing he says (v. 9) shows that it has at any rate roused him. He is quite prepared to accept that it comes from God, for its unpleasant but valuable effect is to strip away all posing and pretence and to expose him as he really is.

The consequences of this disciplinary illness ripple outwards. They begin with what we might understand as physical symptoms, both particular (palpitations) and general (debility), and these naturally surround the sufferer with an air of gloom (v. 10). The malady in which he would appreciate some help is the very thing which keeps away the people from whom he has a right to expect it – people who should be bound to him by ties of affection, interest, or relationship, as the wording of verse 11 implies. Beyond that, people who actively dislike him take advantage of his plight to forward their own schemes at his expense (v. 12).

But the worst thing is that his misery, and therefore his shame (since the misery is due to his own sin), is laid bare before the Lord. 'Think how all-seeing God thy ways And all thy secret thoughts surveys.'[345] The worst thing, and yet at the same time the best thing; because once he accepts that neither his *sighing* nor anything else about him is *hidden from* the eye of God, the way is open for things to be put right.

3. 'Lord, you hear me' (v. 15)

Two small changes in the NIV's wording in verses 13–16 show that now the psalmist is talking not about the problem but about the answer. It is not that he cannot reply when people say hurtful things

[344] C. S. Lewis, *The Problem of Pain* (London: Bles, 1940), p. 81.
[345] Thomas Ken, 'Awake, my soul, and with the sun'.

about him (v. 14), but that he *does not*; and *the reason* (v. 15 should begin with the word 'for') is that he is waiting on God. In other words, I give *no sharp answer in return*, he says, *for I put my trust in you, Yahweh, and leave you to answer for me* (JB). He does not like the idea of people being rude about him (v. 16), but much more important is that they should not be rude about God.

So he is confident that his prayer will be heard and answered, and that God will uphold his own honour. *For* (yet again, now in v. 17) this whole experience has opened his eyes to see the way things really are. That is the gist of verses 17–20. He recognizes now that he is always prone to sin, as Bunyan understood when he named a devout *Pilgrim's Progress* character Mr Ready-to-Halt, from the AV of verse 17. He is learning both to confess his sin, and to be distressed about it, and that continually, as the tenses of the verbs show (v. 18). He accepts that there will always be those who will want to make things difficult for him, and that their accusations are not in themselves sufficient reason for him to feel guilty (v. 19). And he grasps that since the divine anger is acting not to punish him but to rebuke and discipline him (unpleasant though that may be, as v. 1 has said), he must be one of those who, deep down, *pursue what is good* (v. 20) – who in their 'inner being … delight in God's law'.[346] Out of his pain comes reassurance: he belongs not with the wicked, but with the righteous, who may commit sins and suffer for it, but who know where to find forgiveness.

4. 'Lord, you save me' (vv. 21–22)
One final reassurance for the sinful, suffering, but penitent believer is implicit in the prayer with which the psalm ends.

He has addressed the three earlier prayers to Yahweh (LORD, vv. 1 and 15), to Adonai (*Lord*, vv. 9 and 15),[347] and to Elohim (*God*, v. 15). In verses 21–22 he brings the three names together again and adds what is virtually a fourth: *my salvation* (AV), *my Saviour* (NIV).

We can think of the psalmist in New Testament terms, as a believer and a justified sinner, because of what he here calls the one to whom he prays. He begins by addressing him as Yahweh, the name by which the Lord reveals himself when he comes to make Israel his own at the time of the exodus: *O LORD, do not forsake me*. The thought that such a one might forsake him is almost a contradiction in terms, for the covenant that Yahweh makes with his people is one of loving and unbreakable loyalty, and to forsake them is exactly what he cannot do. So is the prayer pointless? Not at all.

[346] Rom. 7:22.
[347] The 1984 NIV has misprinted 'Lord' as 'LORD' in vv. 9 and 22.

It is the kind of prayer which picks up what God has promised and throws it back to him: in the words of David quoted earlier, 'Do as you have said.'[348] Its value lies not in getting the Lord to do what I want, but in learning to want what the Lord is going to do.

Secondly, he prays: *Be not far from me, O my God.* There was only ever one Yahweh, but 'there be gods many',[349] and when the psalmist speaks of *my God*, he means his God over against all the others. (This God is also, of course, the only real one, but that is not the point at issue.) Gods in Bible times were local gods, of this or that country, or of the sea or the battlefield or the farm. The powers that people worship in our own times likewise belong to particular areas of life: the gods of economics, of self-fulfilment, of nationalism, of political correctness, and so forth. It is assumed that the territory of the Christians' god is church organizations, just as the territory of the Israelites' god was thought to be the hills rather than the valleys. If in the latter case Israel's armies could be lured to the lowlands they would be far from his protection;[350] and in the same way today he is not expected to stray beyond his boundaries.

In fact, of course, the God of the Bible is a universal God. 'He is not far from each one of us,' says the New Testament; 'Where can I flee from your presence?' asks the Old.[351] *Be not far from me, O my God* (v. 21b) is therefore the same kind of prayer as *O LORD, do not forsake me* (v. 21a), because *far from me* is exactly what *my God*, the Everywhere God, cannot be. I am asking him to be what he is anyway. Again, the object of such prayer is to mould my own thinking, not to manipulate God's.

And the same is true of the third prayer, *Come quickly to help me, O Lord my Saviour.* Here the word *Lord* is not Yahweh but Adonai, the master, the ruler, the sovereign. The psalmist brackets this title of power with the title of salvation, and puts the gospel in a nutshell: you know God's real greatness only when you have seen him bring all his power to bear on the saving of a world of sinners. Three times in the final chapter of the Bible Jesus, our Lord and Saviour, says, 'I come quickly,' and three times the response is, 'Come.'[352] Do as you have said; and what we know you will do finally at the end of time, we ask you to do in whatever lesser way is right meanwhile, for every suffering but trusting sinner who cries out to you as the psalmist did.

[348] 1 Sam. 7:25 JB. See p. 1.66.   [349] 1 Cor. 8:5 AV.
[350] 1 Kgs. 20:23.   [351] Acts 17:27; Ps. 139:7.
[352] Rev. 22:7, 12, 17, 20 AV.

Psalm 39

What Psalm 39 is about, and why it should appear where it does in the Psalter, are not obvious at the outset. Little by little, however, we realize that it inhabits the same world as Psalm 38. The silence and the anguish of verses 1–2 (38:8, 13–14), and the *scourge* of verse 10 (translated 'wounds' in 38:11) which verses 9–11 say comes from the hand of God as a rebuke for sin and a discipline (38:1–3), these link the two. Further similarities link both of them with Psalm 37 also: a psalmist whose hope is, remarkably, fixed on this same God, stern though he is (37:7; 38:15; 39:7), and plotters and scorners who are his real enemies (37:12; 38:16; 39:8).

Yet each of the three psalms makes out of these elements a whole which is quite distinctive, and unlike the other two. It is, so to speak, not its neighbours but its relatives who will shed light on the distinctiveness of our present psalm – not neighbouring psalms, but related books. We noticed the family resemblance between Psalm 37 and Proverbs, and that between Psalm 38 and Job. We are still among the wisdom books; Psalm 39 is the Ecclesiastes of the group.[353] Three times the word which dominates that book figures in this psalm – *hebel*, 'vanity' or 'meaninglessness', here translated *breath* or *in vain* (vv. 5, 6, 11). If the *selah* which in each place follows the word *breath* indicates a break for a Scripture reading,[354] Ecclesiastes 2:17–26 and 5:10–15 would be two very suitable passages.

1. Loyalty says 'Be silent' (vv. 1–3)

There was something the psalmist was aching to say, but would not say in the presence of unbelievers.

What was it? Not necessarily, of course, what he eventually did say, in private, to God, from verse 4 onwards. Had he perhaps been going to complain about the prosperity of the wicked, touched on in Psalm 37? Or about the suffering of the righteous, the theme of Psalm 38? For all their similarities, we are not justified in taking it for granted that topics from either of the two previous psalms will have been carried over into this one. All we really have to go on is what comes out in due course in verses 4–13.

What is clear from verses 1–3, though, is that whatever the burden on his heart may be, the attitude of the psalmist's mind is an admirable one. He has faith; he has questions; and he has loyalty.

First, his faith. He is not comfortable in himself, nor is he exactly comfortable with the Lord – *I am overcome by the blow of your*

---

[353] Job is in fact linked with all three. Ps. 37 however echoes not him but his friends. *Anguish* (39:2) is the 'suffering' and 'pain' of Job 2:13, 16:6.

[354] See pp. 1.35–36.

hand, he will say in verse 10. But in spite of the muzzled mouth and the hot heart, it is naturally and automatically to the Lord that he turns when he can hold back no longer.

Secondly, he sees no contradiction in having both faith and questions. To have faith does not mean you have no more questions. To have questions does not mean your faith has failed. It is childish to imagine that a tide moving one way will never be accompanied by waves moving the other way.

Thirdly, what these verses chiefly show is the psalmist's loyalty to his Lord. Why will he not blurt out his theological problems before an unsympathetic audience? Surely because he does not want to provoke *the scorn of fools* (v. 8) not only against himself but against God. David – let us take *of* him to mean 'by' him – had by his sin in the matter of Bathsheba and Uriah 'made the enemies of the LORD show utter contempt';[355] he would not want in the present case to take even a step towards another betrayal of his Lord.

2. *Perplexity says 'Speak' (vv. 4–6)*
Perhaps these verses do after all represent what the psalmist had been bottling up; and perhaps it might be paraphrased as follows. 'Lord, I wouldn't say this in public, but ... You tell me the prosperity of the wicked is short-lived,[356] but isn't my life equally fleeting? And what comfort is it to know that they will soon be gone, if their short life has been full of prosperity, while mine will be just as short, and full of misery? Lord, may I address to you at this point an Old Testament reading (Eccles. 2:12–16, or Job 7:17–21), and an Epistle (Jas. 4:13–14), and a Gospel reading (Luke 12:13–21), and ask you what I am supposed to make of all this?'

These questions lead to a further one, or rather, revert to an earlier one. Rebuke and discipline (v. 11, as in 38:1)[357] are the object of the exercise; but to what end? If all the psalmist's short life is to be taken up with the shaping of the vessel, when is the finished article going to be put to use? And that of course leads in turn to one of the greatest questions of all, that of life after death. It was raised as far back as Psalm 6, the only previous occasion where the 'rebuke and discipline' pairing has appeared. 'How long, O LORD, how long?' says the psalmist there (6:3). It is all very well your treating me like this, but if it's to go on till I die, 'Who praises you from his grave?' (6:5).

To this further question we shall return. For the moment the author of Psalm 39 seems chiefly perplexed by the seeming heavy-handedness of God. 'What is man that you make so much of him,

---

[355] 2 Sam. 12:14.   [356] Ps. 37:35–36.
[357] Though the word for 'rebuke' is different.

that you give him so much attention … ? Will you never look away from me, or let me alone even for an instant? … Why have you made me your target?' says the Job reading mentioned above. If my life is so fleeting and fragile, and I am so small in the overall scheme of things, are your disciplinary dealings with me anything more than mere sadism? 'Who breaks a butterfly upon a wheel?'[358]

3. Submission says 'Be silent' (vv. 7–9)

I was silent (v. 9) does not refer to the silence of verses 1–2; the psalmist has here fallen silent a second time. The JB conveys the meaning of this verse well, including the fact that (as in 37:5) the verb *do* has no object: *I am dumb, I speak no more, since you yourself have been at work.*

It was out of loyalty – dare we say, even confusion or embarrassment? – that in the presence of the wicked the psalmist would not say what he was burning to say. Now it is in submission to God that he shuts his mouth, accepting without any more complaint that what has been happening to him has come from God.

The faith touched on in verses 1–3 is here made explicit. It is faith in the sense of trust. The psalmist's questions have not been answered, but what he does know about the Person outweighs what he doesn't know about the problems: as in our New Testament times a believer might sing, 'I may not know the answer, but I know the Answer Man.' The psalmist has grasped the paradoxical truth that 'only the Lord's favour can deliver us from the Lord's disfavour'.[359] He knows that it is the God who has hurt him who alone can heal him. And since the hurt is the result of his own sin, the healing will come when the sin is confessed and forgiven. Hence the prayer of verses 7–8.

4. Humility says 'Speak' (vv. 10–13)

In the spirit of humble trust which is as it were 'silent' before God, the psalmist feels able to speak to him once more.

He accepts the two facts, first that his sin is quite properly followed by the Lord's *rebuke and discipline*, and secondly that his life is brief and its earthly trappings perishable (v. 11). Not now complaining, I think, but submissive, he asks for the discipline to be lightened (v. 10); is he saying that he has learnt his lesson?

The two final verses are wonderfully revealing. Why would he like to enjoy just a little of the rest of this brief life free from the pains of discipline? Because, to quote the very last words of the psalm, so far as he can see there will be *no more* opportunity

[358] Alexander Pope, *Epistle to Dr Arbuthnot*, l. 308.
[359] Motyer, p. 510 (on Ps. 38).

afterwards for the kind of worship, the praise and the service, with which he is at present familiar. If Proverbs 3:11–12 (quoted in Heb. 12:5–6) would be an apt *selah* reading reflecting the *rebuke and discipline* of verse 11, Job 10:20–22 would relate equally aptly to the dismal outlook of verse 13.

Yet the very words with which the psalmist bewails the transience of life carry a freight of hope which he seems not to realize. *I dwell with you as an alien, a stranger, as all my fathers were.* It sounds bleak. But aliens and strangers were a special object of God's care. Israel learned to show them the same care, since the Israelites had themselves been aliens and strangers in the land of Egypt.[360] Even after they had inherited the land of Canaan, as Psalm 37 put it, they were in a sense still aliens and strangers there.[361] Their ancestor Abraham had been one;[362] David was still one, even when he ruled the land.[363]

Such language is quoted more than once in the New Testament, and the apostolic writers bring out what was always implicit in it. 'All these people … admitted that they were aliens and strangers on earth. People who say such things show that they are looking for a country of their own' – not Chaldea, not Egypt, not even Israel, but 'a better country – a heavenly one'.[364] So we return to the question of life after death. The very concept of the alien and the stranger held within itself another of the Old Testament pointers to the New Testament hope of heaven. The fact of all these people having no real home here implied that in the mind of their loving Lord they would eventually have a proper home somewhere better. Tents for the present, one day a city, says Hebrews 11:9–10. Did they see that prospect clearly, and therefore look forward to it eagerly? Do we? We have far less excuse if we fail to do so.

Psalm 40

Threads from the last half dozen psalms are drawn together here. The waiting and the cry of verse 1, the blessed man of verse 4 whose trust is in the Lord, the law in the heart and the praises in the assembly of verses 8–9, have all figured earlier in this part of Book I, from Psalm 34 onwards. Much of verses 12–13 we recall from Psalm 38, much of verses 14–17 from Psalm 35. Both the exalted Lord of verse 16 and the poor and needy people of verse 17 have appeared twice before. Psalm 40 weaves these familiar themes into a striking new pattern, of far-reaching significance.

There is a sharp change of tone at or after verse 11. In fact the final five verses are reproduced in Book II as a separate psalm (70).

---

[360] Deut. 10:17–19. [361] Lev. 25:23. [362] Gen. 23:4.
[363] 1 Chr. 29:15. [364] Heb. 11:13–16. See also Eph. 2:19; 1 Pet. 2:11.

But the combination of praise for the past and alarm about the future is not artificial. If this psalm is, as many think, a 'royal' one, so that it is the king who speaks in and to (and perhaps for) the 'great assembly', some watershed in his or his people's fortunes would account very well for the Janus-like two-way look, first backward then forward.

Such subject matter lends itself readily to the chiastic way of thinking that we have noted often in the psalmists' poetry. A possible division of this kind gives six roughly equal sections, ABC/CBA, which may be set out in a diagram similar to that which helped to clarify the shape of Psalm 28:

> Looking backward (vv. 1–3);
> looking upward (vv. 4–5);
> looking inward (vv. 6–8);
> looking outward (vv. 9–11);
> looking around (vv. 12–15);
> looking forward (vv. 16–17).

We shall consider each in turn, and then go back to the third of them, which is the core of the psalm.

1. Looking backward (vv. 1–3)

The waiting of 37:7, 38:15, and 39:7 has been rewarded. This tiptoe expectancy (as distinct from finger-tapping impatience or yawning boredom) is the vital thing that the Lord looks for in his people, since it shows a positive, active trust. The old Latin title of Psalm 40, *Expectans expectavi*, indicates both its eagerness, and the Hebrew that lies behind the words *waited patiently*, namely a doubling of the verb: 'Expectantly I expected the Lord to act.'

The *horrible pit* and the *miry clay* (AV) were the literal experience of Jeremiah,[365] and the *new song* and the awe-struck witnesses were that of Moses.[366] For an Israelite king who used this psalm they would be metaphors. He and his people had been through the kind of misery that Jeremiah would go through, and had emerged with the kind of jubilation that Moses had known. The song is always new; the picture language of verses 1–3 expresses today as freshly as ever what, looking back, we see God has done for us.

2. Looking upward (vv. 4–5)

Every experience of the Lord's grace in the past should lead us to look up to him with trust for the present and the future. This section

---

[365] Jer. 38:6.   [366] Exod. 15:1–2, 14–16.

puts into words the reliance we should place in him (v. 4) and the confidence he gives to us (v. 5).

The reliance is a deliberate looking up to God instead of a search for popular and fallible sources of help. In the days of the psalmist, the latter might mean a look to Egypt – not now the enemy, as in Moses' time, but a possible friend. In the phrase *the proud ... those who lapse into falsehood* (v. 4 NASB), *proud* is *rāhāb*, a name often given to Egypt, not least when in the days of Isaiah she promises Israel military help and then breaks her word.[367] The confidence which the Lord gives to his people, by contrast, is based on what he has not only said but done, repeatedly, as far back as anyone can remember. In fact *wonders* were exactly what he did in Egypt in the days when she was the great enemy.[368] The numberless proofs of his goodness and faithfulness are to be set against the psalmist's numberless troubles and sins in verse 12 in the fifth section. Perhaps they were also in the mind of John when he wrote of the deeds of Jesus at the end of his Gospel: 'If every one of them were written down, I suppose that even the whole world would not have room for the books that would be written.'[369]

3. Looking inward (vv. 6–8)

The psalmist who can thus look back to the deeds of God in the past, and up to the greatness of God in the present, is one who can look into his own heart and there find the attitude which God will bless.

Ahead of this passage lies the remarkable quotation of it in Hebrews 10, which we shall consider later. But behind it surely lie the events of 1 Samuel 15. Saul, first king of Israel, went through the motions of offering God sacrifice, while insulting God with the disobedience of his heart. For this he received Samuel's stinging rebuke: 'To obey is better than to sacrifice ... You have rejected the word of the LORD, he has rejected you as king.'[370] For this he forfeited the throne.

Against the background of such a fearful warning, David and every subsequent Israelite king knew perfectly well that in the heart attitude of Psalm 40:6–8 lay their only guarantee of blessing. It was God himself, of course, who had imposed on Israel the system of sacrifice; but sacrifice *per se* was not what he wanted – he was looking for the inward grace of which sacrifice was the outward sign. An applicant who is obviously unfit for a job is liable to have his sheaf of certificates and testimonials rejected; it is not papers that the employer wants (although he has in fact asked for them), it is the abilities which the papers are supposed to represent.

[367] Is. 30:7.　　[368] Exod. 15:11.　　[369] John 21:25.　　[370] 1 Sam. 15:22–23.

Into each half of this section is inserted a brief sentence as it were in brackets. The first (*but my ears you have pierced*) has to do not with the making of a hole in the lobe of the ear, the mark of the willing slave in Exodus 21:5–6, but with the opening of the earhole itself, to enable the psalmist to listen and heed: 'The Sovereign LORD has opened my ears, and I have not been rebellious.'[371] The second (*it is written about me in the scroll*) means that God's law explains how people are to live, and the psalmist intends to be the kind of person there described. In the case of David and his successors, there is a very specific law for the king, in Deuteronomy 17:14–20; but it includes within it the rest of the law also. This, he claims, is within his heart. He has not only the duty to know it, but the desire to obey it.

4. Looking outward (vv. 9–11)

Law in the last section, and righteousness in this one, are both in the psalmist's heart, and are obviously related ideas. What is said about them is not as contradictory as it may seem. A heart that hides God's law (v. 8) means the desire for God's way of thinking to govern one's own life. A heart that does *not* hide God's righteousness (v. 10) means the desire for God's way of acting to be known to one's fellows. As the psalmist has a duty to practise personal faith and obedience, he has equally a responsibility to the community to which he belongs, and here shows how he wants his people too to be blessed.

To clarify this section, we should read verse 11 not as a prayer but as a statement, like the rest,[372] and should also note that *seal* and *withhold* represent the same Hebrew word. The three verses are thus bound together. Among his people, the *great assembly*, the psalmist is saying in effect: 'With regard to them, I do not withhold/seal my lips, but show your love and truth; with regard to me, you do not seal/withhold your mercy, but show your love and truth.'

What he says that he will do, we have already seen being done in 36:5–6. The proclaiming of the Lord's righteousness, faithfulness, salvation, love, truth, and mercy bring both glory to the Lord and blessing to his people, for these things are more than abstract qualities. They have been expressed in concrete events, and it is by the telling of such stories, true stories of the wonders God has done (40:5), that now as then he is made known and his people are taught and encouraged.

Western culture has been fortunate to have had a long tradition of storytelling of this kind. For hundreds of years, and to millions of people, most of them in no real sense God's people, the acts of

---

[371] Is. 50:5.   [372] See NASB, NEB.

his righteousness have been proclaimed through literature, art, and music, and indeed through the basic texts of education. It is our generation which is losing sight of this heritage, along with so much else of the past. As we look outward and see such ignorance of it even within the assembly of the church, are we not challenged to make known afresh by every available means the tale of the deeds of God?

5. Looking around (vv. 12–15)

Even if the rest of the psalm was once a separate poem, it follows on very naturally from verses 1–11 for a psalmist (a king?) who has one great deliverance behind him and now looks like needing another.

Corresponding to the look upward to God in the second section, this fifth section is a look around at the enemy. There, the blessings of God were *many*, indeed *too many to declare* (v. 5); here, it is the surrounding troubles which are *without number*. Even the sins hatched in the psalmist's heart have outward consequences that are now overtaking him.

Of recent psalms, 38 has close parallels to much in these verses. We do not here see trouble in the form of illness, or with the purpose of discipline, as we do there; but the effect on the psalmist is similar – 'My guilt has overwhelmed me', 'My heart pounds, my strength fails me; even the light has gone from my eyes', 'Those who seek my life … talk of my ruin', 'Come quickly to help me' (38:4, 10, 12, 22).

It is 35, however, which foreshadows the second half of this section, with its prayers for the defeat of the enemy. That is where we last heard those who seek the psalmist's life and plot his ruin, who say gloatingly 'Aha! Aha!', and who he prays may 'be put to shame and confusion' (35:4, 21, 26). The rights and wrongs of such prayers we have already considered at length in that place.

6. Looking forward (vv. 16–17)

The positive forward look which ends Psalm 40 is one of confidence, in spite of the new menace that has arisen. It corresponds to the backward look of thanksgiving in verses 1–3. Again the pattern of Psalm 35 is evident: *May all who seek to take my life* (v. 14; cf. 35:26) is followed now by *May all who seek you* (v. 16; cf. 35:27), and in each psalm the last verse but one cries, '*The LORD be exalted!*'

Verse 17 is perhaps more positive than it seems in the NIV: *As for me, I am poor and needy, but the Lord takes thought for me* (NRSV). Even if the psalmist is praying, 'May the Lord think of me,' his concern about his own safety is put in perspective by his having first been concerned about the Lord's glory, *The LORD be exalted*. It is

145

with this last word that the ancient Hebrew creed, the *Yigdal Yahweh*, opens, its sung version familiar in the Christianized eighteenth-century translation by Thomas Olivers, 'The God of Abraham praise'. Abraham himself figures hardly at all in Psalms (only in 47 and 105). But innumerable descendants of his would testify, with him, that to exalt the Lord is the surest way to find blessing for oneself.

7. 'When Christ came into the world'

We return to verses 6–8, the heart of this psalm. As we have seen, there is no more fitting background for it than the events of 1 Samuel 13 – 16. Samuel had already told Saul, the first time he offered sacrifice with a disobedient heart, that he would be replaced by a man after God's own heart (13:14). The second time it happened, the Lord (who 'looks at the heart', 16:7) revealed David to be the chosen replacement. David and all his successors would have to grasp one way or another that 'to obey is better than sacrifice' (15:22).

In the New Testament, Acts 13:22–23 links David with Jesus in precisely these terms: 'After removing Saul, [God] made David their king. He testified concerning him: "I have found David son of Jesse a man after my own heart; he will do everything I want him to do." From this man's descendants God has brought to Israel the Saviour Jesus' – i.e., one who stands in the Davidic tradition of obedience. And Hebrews 10:5 does not hesitate to make the link quite explicit – 'When *Christ* came into the world, *he* said' (as the psalmist had said so long before), '"Sacrifice and offering you did not desire"' – and proceeds to quote all three verses from our psalm.

So what does Hebrews say the words mean when we read them as the words of Christ?

First, the two little sentences in parentheses 'unfold the mystery of the *incarnation*'; they are the Psalms/Hebrews equivalent of John 1. Each of them now has a deeper meaning. *My ears you have pierced* became in the LXX *A body you prepared for me*, for when the ear is truly opened to the word of God he will mobilize the whole body to obey it. *It is written about me in the scroll* meant that the duties of God's servant king were laid down for him in the Book of the Law. Thus far, David could have said both these things. But in Hebrews, the first is in the fullest sense about a body specially prepared, that in which the Son of God would become incarnate; and the second tells us that the entire Old Testament outlines the way of the chosen King, not so much for his guidance as for our illumination.

Then the statement as a whole sets before us the breathtaking irony of *redemption*. Christ's obedience was so perfect that for the only time in history the sacrifices for sin were in very truth not required – yet it took him himself to the place of sacrifice: he became 'obedient to the point of death, even death on a cross'.[373]

In a nutshell, the principle is 'Not animal sacrifice but self-giving obedience.' To see its application today we must pursue it a little further. What did it mean, and what does it mean? What exactly was, and is, God's requirement?

The Old Testament understood him to require not primarily animal sacrifice as such, but the death of the self that it represented, together with a conscious total commitment of which no animal is capable (*I desire to do your will, O my God*). The former might be a legal obligation, but the latter was a moral necessity.

Today's world, insofar as it has any notion of a God with requirements, takes him to require, not blood sacrifice at all, but obedience instead, a civilized replacement for ideas which were primitive and barbaric.

The New Testament agrees that he no longer requires blood sacrifice. But its reason is quite different. This is the great argument of Hebrews 10. The old system of animal sacrifice was done away for good when it was replaced by the obedience of Christ ('He sets aside the first to establish the second,' v. 9); but that was an obedience which led to the most fearful blood sacrifice of all. New Testament Christians rejoiced to be free of the old sacrificial system, not because it was primitive and bloodthirsty, but because it had been an interminable burden, and (worse) one which never actually took away sins (v. 11). Christ, however, 'offered for all time one sacrifice for sins' (v. 12), and thereby 'made perfect for ever those who are being made holy' (v. 14).

But it has to be said that for many, inside as well as outside the churches, this is not the welcome relief we might have thought. For there is nothing more deeply ingrained in the human heart than the desire to get into God's good books by offering sacrifices, even by offering obedience, *of one's own*. Psalm 40:6–8, understood in Christian terms, sounds the death knell for all attempts to make oneself right with God and fit for heaven. Out of every such *slimy pit, out of the mud and mire*, he will lift the soul that abandons these hopeless efforts and instead looks eagerly for the blessings that flow from the obedience and sacrifice of Christ. *Expectans expectavi.*

Psalm 41

The threads are drawn together one more time in the final psalm of the first David Collection. Again there is sin that needs forgiving, as

[373] Phil. 2:8 NASB.

in 32 and 38, and sickness that needs healing, as in 6 and 38. Again there is the malice of enemies; again a cry for help gives place to new confidence; and the opening words of this psalm echo those of the very first one, 'Blessed is the man who ...'

1. Psalm 41: is it a poem?

Yes, it is. It has a simple structure, in which we can easily recognize the now familiar chiasmus. Verse 13 is not part of it, being a doxology designed to round off Book I as a whole, but the rest follows a clear ABCBA pattern. Verses 1–3 correspond to verses 11–12. The beginning of the psalm declares the kind of person God will bless, the ending testifies that God has blessed him. The opening promise is that the Lord *will not surrender him to ... his foes*, and *will sustain him*.[374] The closing testimony is that *my enemy does not triumph over me* and that *you uphold me*.

Verse 4 corresponds to verse 10. Each is a prayer for mercy and healing, though verse 10 has the further hope of a chance to pay out the psalmist's enemies – a sentiment with a smell of cordite about it, to which we shall have to return.

Verses 5–9 show that he is even more distressed by the malice of these people than by his own illness. It may be true, as they are saying, that a *vile disease* has attacked him, but they *imagine the worst*, either about its cause or about its outcome, and spread damaging rumours to that effect.

2. Psalm 41: is it a liturgy?

It could be; though such a combination of troubles would scarcely happen very often, and the liturgical use of the psalm could not have been frequent. Still, the *director of music* figures in the heading, and on occasions when he did direct it to be used, we might picture a 'worship leader' or priest declaring verses 1–3, and the sick person himself reciting verses 4–10. The commentators tend to label such passages 'laments', though they are normally expressions not of sorrow but of distress; 'complaints' would be a better word, even if in this case a punning one.

After that, some suggest, a response from God would be looked for, in a prophetic word from another person present, either from Scripture or given extempore. The previous speaker would then respond in his turn with the words of verses 11–12.

The hypothetical word from God was not actually needed. The psalmist surely knew already what God says to one who, like him, sets forth his need, admits his sin, and asks for mercy. Instantly the

---

[374] V. 3b is literally, 'he will turn, or change, his bed for him' – a nice touch of practical care!

joy and praise of verses 11–12 can be his, as we saw in Psalm 32:5.[375]

However, it is always good to be reminded of that truth, which is at the heart of the gospel. The priest might have uttered some Old Testament equivalent of the Absolution in the Prayer Book's service of Morning and Evening Prayer: 'Almighty God ... hath given power and commandment to his Ministers, to declare and pronounce to his people, being penitent, the Absolution and Remission of their sins: He pardoneth and absolveth all them that truly repent and unfeignedly believe his holy Gospel.' What a privilege for Old Testament priests, and for New Testament preachers – not just those often called 'priests' today, for this is gospel *preaching*.[376] Modernize the words of the Absolution by all means, but when the Church of England fillets this proclamation of the good news, replaces it by a prayer, or still worse, discards it altogether, it does so to its own shame and loss.

3. Psalm 41: is it what had happened to David?

The events described here must have happened to someone (it is scarcely fiction), and that someone could well be David. Although we know of no illness of his to which this psalm, like 6 and 38, might be referring, we do know he had many enemies. The particular feature here is his betrayal by a foe who was a supposed friend, who *lifted up his heel* against him.[377] To David one of the most painful episodes of his career was the revolt of Absalom, his treacherous son; and there was at that time, notoriously, a treacherous friend also – Ahithophel, the renowned political adviser who deserted the king for the rebel prince: top of the league for acumen, bottom for loyalty.[378]

If Psalm 41 does relate to the great rebellion, we have to assume an illness of David's that 2 Samuel does not mention (unless it lies behind 15:1–4). But we also find light shed on the apparent vindictiveness of verse 10; for if this is David the king, it is in fact his duty to see that justice is done. While he is down, he is in no position to quell the rebellion and punish the traitors. If God will raise him up, he will be able to *repay them*. In the event, he was not able to be objective in his blinkered fondness for his dreadful son, and he came within an ace of failing in his kingly duty in the same way that Saul had done.[379] But for David as king, to *repay*

[375] See p. 1.110.

[376] Anglicanism has not yet come to terms with the inconsistency of authorizing deacons and readers to preach, but not to 'preach' the Absolution.

[377] Various suggestions as to what lies behind this metaphor include 'the kick of a horse, vicious and unexpected' (Bruce Milne, *The Message of John*, BST [Leicester: IVP, 1993], p. 200, on the quotation of v. 9 in John 13:18, with regard to Judas).

[378] 2 Sam. 15:12, 31; 16:15, 23.   [379] 2 Sam. 18:1 – 19:8; cf. 1 Sam. 15.

was the execution of public duty, and not the indulgence of personal malice.

4. Psalm 41: is it what would happen to Jesus?

Yes, because Jesus says it is (John 13:18). Not that David was aware of this, nor that everything he said here could have been said by Jesus; verse 4 obviously could not. But the general drift of the psalm, and verse 9 in particular, makes it a messianic prophecy. That means first, as D. A. Carson puts it, that 'David himself [is] a "type", a model, of "great David's greater Son", the promised Messiah'; secondly, that 'many of the broad themes of his life' (not all of them, let alone the details of it) 'were understood that way'; and thirdly, that the crucial fact of the Messiah's suffering corresponds to a 'similar strand in David's life'.[380] Such was the view of the apostolic church, based upon the teaching of Christ himself. As recently as Psalm 40:6–8, we have seen these principles working out.

In this connection, there is one other observation that turns out to have more to it than meets the eye. We saw that Psalm 37 is a showcase for the third Beatitude, 'Blessed are the meek, for they will inherit the earth' (Matt. 5:5). Psalm 41 is the Psalter's version of the fifth, 'Blessed are the merciful, for they will be shown mercy' (Matt. 5:7). If David has been compassionate towards others, he will find in his turn that God *delivers him in times of trouble*. As a model for us, he demonstrates that if we heed Mrs Doasyouwouldbedoneby, we shall discover that Mrs Bedonebyasyoudid is a friend, not an enemy.[381]

But this is a messianic psalm; David is also a model of Christ, and as such he highlights the fact that the same principles apply to his great descendant. If the meek inherit the earth, so does the meek Messiah, for (as C. S. Lewis says somewhere) he is subject to his own rules; and he inherits it in the fullest possible sense. Similarly, the one who brings mercy down from heaven is one who is himself raised from death by the mercy of God. We do not know what David understood by *set me in your presence for ever*; whether he 'was looking beyond this life ... or not, the answer would not disappoint him'.[382] But we do know that for the Messiah, *ever* means *ever*; and fittingly the first book of the Psalter ends with the praises of God being sung *from everlasting to everlasting*.

---

[380] D. A. Carson, *The Gospel according to John* (Leicester: IVP, 1991), p. 470 (on John 13:18).
[381] Charles Kingsley, *The Water Babies* (1863).
[382] Kidner, p. 163.

BOOK II
(Psalms 42 – 72)

The first Korah Collection and the first Asaph Psalm: Psalms 42 – 50

There were presumably methods and principles by which the compilers of the book of Psalms arranged its contents. They did not think it important to explain in any detail what these were. We do however have three clues to the Psalter's architecture, and all of them are noticeable as we arrive at this point. The first and most obvious is the basic division into five books which is built into the text itself; it is here with Psalm 42 that the second book begins.

Then we have the headings of the psalms. It has been questioned whether they are an accurate guide to authorship or background, but they can at the very least act as labels. Thus 42 is one of the many psalms collected by or for the 'director of music', one of the several *maskils* of which 32 was the first, and in particular one of the psalms 'of the Sons of Korah', about whom more in a moment.

Thirdly, the content of each psalm and its connections with the rest of Scripture help us to see also its connections with other psalms, and reasons why they may have been grouped as they were. We have only to read 42 and 43 to see why they belong together; other links will be less obvious but no less real.

The Korah label is particularly to be noted because it relates to the way the Psalter as a whole has been compiled. The psalms bearing it are grouped together as subsections of Books II and III. To appreciate what it means we need to recall some family history.

In the world of modern democracy there may seem no place for the hereditary principle. But to dismiss it out of hand is a great nonsense, and flies in the face of historical fact. We have only to think of the names of Plantagenet and Hapsburg, Bach and Wedgwood, Medici and Rothschild, Churchill and Kennedy, to realize that like it or not there is something in heredity. Famous dynasties of stage and screen, and obscure family businesses and family farms kept going over the generations, tell the same story.

For all its villains, for all its failures, and for all that no-one is ever either blessed or condemned automatically because of it, the principle is of immense importance throughout Bible history. The Sons of Korah are a case in point. Of Israel's original family, Levi and the tribe descended from him were chosen for a special destiny. From the descendants of his three sons, Gershon, Kohath, and Merari, came the nation's spiritual leadership. Of Kohath's line came Moses, his brother Aaron (and through him the hereditary priesthood), and their relative Korah, who rebelled against their leadership during the journey from Egypt to Canaan (Num. 16). Korah and his people died because of this, but at least one of his sons survived, and later generations of the family were installed as 'worship leaders' in Jerusalem by David.

With regard to the Psalter, three names stand out, one from each of the Levitical lines. Heman the Kohathite (a descendant of Korah), Asaph the Gershonite, and Ethan the Merarite were all 'put in charge of the music'.[383] Heman has a psalm attributed to him (88) and so does Ethan (89), while Asaph has an entire collection, the first of which is here in Book II (50). The Sons of Korah seem to have formed a guild of musicians, who composed or edited another collection, most of which is also here in Book II.

The spirit that prompted their ancestor to revolt had certainly been exorcized by the time their psalms appeared – a dozen of the most stirring songs in the book, unforgettable and utterly God-centred.

One other feature should be noted about the first Korah Collection. Together with the second David Collection and the Asaph Collection, in other words the whole of Book II and the greater part of Book III, it forms what is known as the 'Elohistic Psalter'. These forty-two psalms are so called because they regularly address their prayers and praises to Elohim (God) rather than to Yahweh (the Lord). The reasons we can only guess. Perhaps these collections were used in circles where Yahweh, the great Name, was already thought to be too holy for common use.[384]

In this also the combined Psalms 42 and 43 are representative of the whole group. In them the uses of Elohim outnumber those of Yahweh by twenty to one. But though we may miss the rich and complex resonances that belong to the latter, the great Name of

---

[383] 1 Chr. 6:31; see 6:31–46, and indeed the whole chapter.
[384] It became the custom for the consonants of the Name (YHWH) to be marked with the vowels of the word Adonai, to remind those who read aloud to say the latter word instead of the former. Early translators assumed, wrongly, that the consonants and vowels were meant to be combined, and that they represented a word 'Jehovah', which did not in fact exist.

Israel's God, nevertheless the Elohim of 42/43 is recognizably the same God, for he is Saviour, Life, Rock, Stronghold, Joy, and Delight.

Psalms 42 and 43

These are really a single psalm, bound together by several repeated phrases, including an entire verse which appears three times at regular intervals. Not surprisingly, no heading marks 43:1 as the start of a separate psalm. In fact we have here a poem in three stanzas, each ending with the same refrain: 42:1–5, 42:6–11, and 43:1–5.[385]

1. The Sons of Korah

This psalmist tells us that he *used to go with the multitude, leading the procession to the house of God* (42:4). We read in 2 Samuel 6 of David, whose name heads so many psalms in Book I, himself doing just that. The Sons of Korah, whose collection begins here, were appointed by David to an ongoing musical leadership of a similar sort.

The psalms that bear their name are as personal as those that bear his. Psalm 42/43 is almost as memorable and as well loved as Psalm 23, even if comparing people to deer or sheep sounds odd to today's secular city-dweller.

The Korah Collections do however have a flavour of their own. Though just as personal as that of the David Collections, it is not as individual. That is to say, we can profitably link many psalms in Book I with the very particular experiences of David, whereas there is no special interest in knowing when or why the author of 42/43 (for example) was away on *the heights of Hermon*. The difference is rather like that between Charles Wesley's 'And can it be that I should gain An interest in the Saviour's blood' and Isaac Watts's 'When I survey the wondrous cross'. When Wesley cries 'Died he for me, who caused his pain, For me, who him to death pursued?', you can hear the echo of his brother John's conversion testimony, three days after his own, in May 1738: 'An assurance was given me that He had taken away *my* sin, even *mine*, and saved *me* from the law of sin and death.' When Watts, on the other hand, writes 'His dying crimson like a robe Spreads o'er his body on the tree; Then am I dead to all the world, And all the world is dead to me,' the truth is no less deeply felt, but the hymn would gain nothing from being tied to a date or place in Watts's life.

---

[385] Ps. 42:5 may not be exactly the same as 42:11 and 43:5: its final *my God* may belong with 42:6.

2. A long way from home

So we do not know, and do not need to know, what our psalmist was doing in the far north of Israel. Was he simply travelling? Was he a hostage, a prisoner of war, an exile?[386] Whatever the reason, he was a long way from home. That meant a long way from God's home, too, the Jerusalem shrine where the ministry of the Sons of Korah was based.

Our psalmist will have recognized the paradox. He well knows both that God is everywhere, and at the same time that God is specially to be met with where his people meet. He is always in God's presence, and yet at the moment away from it. And there is a further paradox. The taunt of unbelievers, *Where is your God?* (42:3, 10) is his own question also, yet at the same time he knows the answer: God is here, for he is praying to him (42:1, 9; 43:1–4). The very words *Why have you forgotten/rejected me?* (42:9; 43:2) show that in the psalmist's mind God is remote enough for him to feel deserted, yet near enough for him to talk to.

'In the psalmist's mind': the crucial thing is the way he feels. It may even be simply 'in his mind' that he is away on the heights of Hermon. In other words, that far-off place where the din of great waterfalls is overwhelming could be stanza 2's metaphor for one aspect of his state of mind. By contrast, another aspect of it would be illustrated by stanza 1's picture of a region where the parched deer can find no streams at all.[387] That is the far south of Israel, as opposed to Hermon in the far north; the land ranged 'from Dan to Beersheba' not only in terms of distance[388] but in terms of variety of terrain. As for stanza 3's *ungodly nation*, the picture there is of an alien land beyond the boundaries of Israel altogether, whether it is Gentiles or unsympathetic Israelites who are being illustrated by it.

Like other psalms we shall come to in due course, 42/43 begins a sequence well suited for public use at one of Israel's great festivals. On such occasions people would travel considerable distances to Jerusalem. We read more than once of Jesus and his family doing so.[389] Here in 42/43, as in 84 and 120, an awareness of being a long way from one's spiritual home introduces a group of psalms which seem to have such a journey in mind.

Those however were religious events, and they belonged to Bible times. We may never find ourselves involved in pilgrimages of that kind. Our psalm takes on a much wider significance as an account

---

[386] See 2 Chr. 25:23–24; 28:5, 8; 36:17–20.

[387] Not that the creature is 'heated in the chase', as the 1696 New Version had it (Nahum Tate and Nicholas Brady, 'As pants the hart for cooling streams').

[388] Judg. 20:1, and many times thereafter.

[389] Luke 2:41; John 5:1; 7:2–10; 11:55; 12:12.

of the inner life of the believer. When we look at it in that way, its theme is surely *depression*. Roy Clements has a chapter,[390] and Martyn Lloyd-Jones an entire book,[391] which are based on it as a vivid and accurate account of that all too common experience.

3. Three frank confessions

'How are you?' is for once answered truthfully: 'I feel awful.' Goldingay sums up the feelings described in the three stanzas as 'parched', 'overwhelmed', 'misjudged'.[392] With a slightly different slant on the third, you could make a sermon with the headings 'Dry', 'Drowning', 'Disheartened'!

The drought of 42:1–5 is a long way from David's quiet waters in 23:2 or his river of delights in 36:8. 'Where is the blessedness I knew When first I saw the Lord? Where is the soul-refreshing view Of Jesus and his word?' complained William Cowper.[393] The metaphor of dryness, when everything seems 'weary, stale, flat, and unprofitable',[394] comes naturally to the depressed person. Christian people should never imagine that when they feel that way it must be their own fault, or the result of their sin, still less that they cannot be real Christians after all, 'because real Christians don't get depressed'. The cause may be physical or emotional or psychological, not spiritual at all. That does not make the symptoms any less real – including, as the psalmist says, the ironic fact that though his circumstances may be arid there is no shortage of tears.

The very different metaphor of drowning, in 42:6–11, speaks both of another symptom (everything seems to get on top of us), and of one possible cause (we may simply have taken on more than we can cope with). Although the headwaters of Jordan may be a series of impressive waterfalls, they are not exactly the *waves and breakers* of the ocean; even so they are an uncomfortable reminder of the *deep*, that symbol of chaos and disorder which the Hebrews always found unnerving. Jonah 2 expresses that prophet's feelings when he was literally in the depths of the sea, and this psalm is quoted in that chapter.[395] No wonder our psalmist cries out to God his Rock, something firm to cling to as he is swept off his feet and overwhelmed.

His prayer at the beginning of 43:1–5 is very like the frequent pleas for justice in the David psalms. But in the context, his enemies have been not so much attacking or even accusing him, as oppressing

---

[390] Roy Clements, *Songs of Experience* (Fearn: Christian Focus, 1993), pp. 11–32.
[391] D. Martyn Lloyd-Jones, *Spiritual Depression: Its Causes and Cure* (London: Pickering & Inglis, 1965).
[392] Goldingay, pp. 27ff.   [393] William Cowper, 'O for a closer walk with God'.
[394] William Shakespeare, *Hamlet*, I.ii.133.   [395] Jonah 2:3; Ps. 42:7.

him with their taunts (42:3, 9–10). *Ungodly* here means people who are lacking the love, the loyal or 'covenant' love, that we have seen so often as one of the great characteristics of the Lord and of his true people. These may be Gentiles, or they may be Israelites who ought to know better, but the point is that they have let him down. Everything they say is negative and unhelpful. He feels thoroughly disheartened.

4. Three practical suggestions

Cutting across the three stanzas, as it were, is a different threefold division of the poem. Goldingay again has useful headings: letting oneself go, making oneself think, pulling oneself together. First, we have seen how the psalmist is prepared to let go, to bring his depression out into the open, in every stanza. The opening verses of each do this; the refrain of each refers to his downcast and disturbed *soul*;[396] 42:10 complains of his suffering *bones* – nothing to do with arthritis, but meaning rather the man himself. He knows it is better to express his feelings to God than to bottle them up.

This is one good thing to do; but it is not enough. He must also make himself think. Certainly in the second and third stanzas, so probably in the first also, uninhibited speaking is followed by clear thinking. If so, then in stanza 1 the recollecting of earlier times is not mere nostalgia, adding to the psalmist's misery. Rather, it is a deliberate attempt to get something straight in his mind. To the question of 42:3 *Where is your God?*, the festivals recalled in 42:4 reply (a) 'Present among his gathered people,' and (b) 'Active today just as he was in the great days we were then commemorating.'

In stanza 2 the psalmist makes himself think beyond God's dealings with his people, to his dealings with him personally. 42:8 is another recalling of facts; the verbs are imperfects, and surely run parallel to those in 42:4 – the Lord *used to* direct his love to look after me.[397] Clear thinking reminds him that in the old days the Lord's care was his day-and-night experience (like his tears at the moment, 42:3). A God so constant cannot have changed.

In stanza 3 he reasons that God's light and God's truth can be his guides out of his present wretched isolation (43:3), just as in the previous stanza he has been reminding himself that God's love and God's song have been his companions in the past.

Having made himself think, he sets about pulling himself together, which is what the repeated refrain is about. He addresses his soul; that is, he talks to himself. To quote the seventeenth-century commentator John Trapp, 'David chideth David out of the dumps'.

---

[396] See on Ps. 6:2–3, p. 1.32.   [397] Anderson, p. 333; Kirkpatrick, p. 231.

'We are never helpless victims of our emotions,' says Clements.
'Don't let your feelings dictate to you; you do the dictating.'[398] Ask
yourself why you are downcast, he continues, and give yourself a
rational answer. Remind yourself that hope means a patient but
expectant waiting for God to act. Tell yourself that your day of
praise will certainly come, though in God's time, not yours.

Psalm 44

An individual voice is heard less often here than in many of the
psalms. The whole thing is addressed to God – *you* or *your* occurs
in practically every verse – but it is much more 'we', the
congregation, than 'I', the psalmist, who are talking to him. And it
soon becomes clear that this is more than a meeting; it is a big
occasion. *We* are not just an assembly: we who pray are the people
of Israel. 'I' am not just a poet or a cleric: I who speak to God am
the king of Israel. Such at any rate is the interpretation that makes
best sense of Psalm 44.

If verses 1–8 stood alone, they would be a liturgy designed to
celebrate some national victory. But almost as soon as we realize
who have come together for this special event, we see that it is by
no means a celebration. Verses 1–8 do not stand alone. Agonized
heart-searching follows them, and the rest of the psalm makes plain
that the atmosphere is one of distress, bafflement, even anger. We
have no idea what disaster gave rise to Psalm 44, though many
suggestions have been made. What matters is not its occasion, but
its content, which is extraordinary, indeed shocking.

1. What has God done? (vv. 1–3)

What God has done in the past is going to contrast sharply with
what he is doing now, in the time that the psalm describes. But that
is not yet our concern. For the moment there is much that the
modern church can learn from the awareness these Old Testament
people have of the great acts of God in times gone by.

What he did *in days long ago* here means particularly the bringing
of his people into the land he had promised them. That act cannot
of course be separated from the deliverance from Egypt and the
historic events of Sinai, though the conquest of Canaan is in the
forefront of Israel's mind now because of what has been happening
recently, as we shall see.[399] God's doings in the days of Moses and
Joshua are the facts on which her faith, her life, and her very

---

[398] Clements, p. 30.
[399] Goulder (*Korah*, p. 155) suggests that the conquest narratives in Joshua may have
provided readings at the *selah* following v. 8. There are many links between Ps. 44
and Josh. 24.

existence as a nation are founded, as his acts in Christ are likewise the foundations of the Christian church.

God was doing something else at the time of the exodus and the conquest. He was making it crystal clear to Israel that all the achievements of those momentous days were his and not hers. The founding fathers knew, and their descendants now singing Psalm 44 also know, that it was a divine arm and not a human one which had wrought these great things. For them as for us, all was based not only on fact but on grace.

Further, God had seen to it right from the beginning that the account of his deeds should be passed on from each generation to the next. 'Tell your children and grandchildren' (Exod. 10:2) is the first of many such instructions. Concerning a whole series of commemorations, observances, and monuments, sons were to ask 'What does this mean?' and fathers were to give the prescribed answer that would explain the sign. Oral tradition is thought of today as a primitive way of recording and teaching. But it has to be said that many related customs which are currently unfashionable – worship in the home, regular fellowship in the church, the memorizing of Scripture, catechizing, preaching, repetitive learning, and the teaching of sheer facts – seem to have produced a better grasp of the faith than more trendy methods do.

2. We are trusting (vv. 4–8)

The liturgy continues with the one and the many, the leader and the congregation, expressing their response to what God has done. We may imagine the voices of king and nation alternating in verses 4–7, and joining in verse 8.

The response is one of real faith. They not only believe what they are told happened in the past, they believe the same principles are true for them. They have been acting on those principles, and have found that God has indeed given them victories. The facts about God, his grace, the whole never-to-be-forgotten story, are as real to them as they were to their ancestors. His character, his being a God of this kind, is what is wrapped up in his covenant name; and though, like so many of the psalms of Book II, 44 does not actually utter the word Yahweh, it recognizes that that is the name of power (v. 5) and praise (v. 8).

There are no two ways about it, God's people are united in the conviction that they are in a right relationship with him. At this point in their history, whatever its actual date, they really are a believing, trusting nation. They represent what the Prayer Book calls 'the blessed company of all faithful people'. They are like the psalmist in the first David Collection who so often asserts his innocence; they are even more like the blameless Job (to whom we shall return).

It is important to insist on this conviction of theirs, because of the cry of outrage which is about to follow. When things go badly wrong not just for the individual believer but for an assembly of God's people, it is proper for them to come together to search their hearts for any sin among them which may have caused the disaster. So it was when one man's transgression brought defeat to the nation in the days of the conquest, to which the psalm has been referring.[400] But the whole point of Psalm 44 is that the assembly has presumably done that, and can find no reason for the events the next section is about to describe.

3. What is God doing? (vv. 9–16)

The word *but* that begins verse 9 wrenches the psalm violently out of the feel-good atmosphere of verses 1–8. It 'implies surprise', says Kirkpatrick,[401] suggesting 'and then' as a translation for it: 'You give us victory, and we praise your name – and then you reject us!'

Through verses 9–12 the 'distress … deepens with every line … rout, spoil, slaughter, scattering and slavery'.[402] Boldly and bitterly, the psalmist echoes one of the David psalms (30:9) in verse 12: it is not as though God were any better off when he had sold his people as slaves. Moreover, say verses 13–14, what will their unbelieving neighbours think of a God who can so let down those who have put their trust in him?

Of one thing the psalmist and his people are sure, and it is something many Christians today find hard to grasp. When Israel (to quote a modern witticism) snatched defeat from the jaws of victory, it was not that God had mismanaged the affair, nor even that he had permitted the disaster, but that he had actually made this terrible thing happen. One of the disadvantages of believing in a great God is that he faces you with hard questions!

What the psalmist and his people cannot see is the reason why. They know that there are circumstances in which their God is quite ready 'to uproot and tear down, to destroy and overthrow', as Jeremiah says,[403] and to do what Isaiah calls 'his strange work' and 'his alien task'.[404] But they have always understood – it is part of what they have *heard with [their] ears* from *days long ago* – that that is what he has in store for his *enemies*. They are not assuming that their Hebrew blood automatically makes them his friends. They are well aware that Israelites are just as liable to such punishments as their heathen neighbours if they too rebel against God.[405] But they

[400] See Josh. 7.   [401] Kirkpatrick, p. 238.   [402] Kidner, p. 169.
[403] Jer. 1:10.   [404] Is. 28:21.   [405] Deut. 28:7, 25.

know they haven't. The fourth stanza of the psalm spells out their protest.

4. We are obeying (vv. 17–22)

They are not disobedient rebels. In half a dozen verses they sum up the facts, as if challenging God to contradict them. The disaster has happened; God made it happen; they have not deserved it. They do not claim to be sinless. They do claim that if it is a punishment, they have not committed the kind of sins for which God has decreed such punishment.

There is no other psalm quite like this. It takes us back into the wisdom books, to the book of Job, though not as Psalm 38 did: there we found a reflection of Job's suffering, here we can almost hear him protesting that he does not deserve it. This fourth stanza recalls especially the great chapter 31, with which 'the words of Job are ended', and in which the long-suffering servant of God, 'bloody, but unbowed',[406] has uttered a whole series of challenging 'ifs', like verse 20 here; has claimed not to 'have turned from the path', as in verse 18 here; and has cried, 'Let the Almighty answer me'.[407]

As verses 17–21 point back to an earlier scripture, verse 22 points forward to a later one, the passage in Romans where Paul quotes it. Each appearance of the words is illuminated by the other. We may read Romans 8:36 ('For your sake we face death all day long') as an acceptance of suffering for Christ's sake. But in Psalm 44:22 the words have a different tone. They mean something more like *Because of you*,[408] and are practically an accusation: God, it's your fault. This 'statement of downright insolence'[409] is amplified in the hurt and angry words of the final stanza.

5. What will God do? (vv. 23–26)

The call to God to awake, rouse himself, and rise up, has a very respectable background in the tiny liturgy which he himself gave to Israel at Sinai. 'Whenever the ark set out, Moses said, "Rise up, O LORD! May your enemies be scattered."'[410] Much more disturbing is its reminder of Elijah's confrontation with the prophets of Baal, who tried to make their god answer them by 'vain repetitions' of just such a cry. 'Maybe he is sleeping and must be awakened,' jeered Elijah:[411] just what his own people now seem to think about their own great God.

What will God do? Will he answer?

He is not asleep – 'he who watches over Israel will neither slumber nor sleep'[412] – and yes, he will answer, in two ways.

---

[406] W. E. Henley, 'Invictus'. [407] See Job 31:7, 35, 40. [408] As in NRSV, NEB.
[409] Craigie, p. 335. [410] Num. 10:35. [411] 1 Kgs. 18:26–27. [412] Ps. 121:4.

The answer we find in Job may sound unsatisfactory. It is not that we have misunderstood the rules; the bad things that have happened really are the normal consequence of certain sins. It is not that we are deceiving ourselves; we really are innocent of those sins (though not of others). It is not that God has made a mistake; he really is still in control. It is simply that unaccountable things do happen in this world, and either he will not give, or else we could not grasp, the explanation of them.

The answer we find in Romans sheds light back on to Psalm 44:22, and beyond it to the apparent non-answer given to Job. Not *because of you* resentfully, but *for your sake* willingly, *we face death all day long*. We are prepared to endure sufferings, to cope with frustrations, to face with equanimity 'periods of blessing and barrenness, advance and retreat' which may bear no relation to our spiritual state, out of love for the Lord who has already proved his covenant love to us (v. 26). Kidner, from whom these words are quoted, finds in verse 22 an Old Testament glimpse of the fact that 'God's people are caught up in a war that is more than local', and that suffering may be not a punishment but 'a battle-scar ... the price of loyalty in a world which is at war with God'.[413] The great thing is that the Israel of this psalm, having *heard* all about God (v. 1), should also, like Job and especially like Paul, *see* something of the fuller picture of who he is and what he is doing.[414]

Psalm 45

What a contrast between the king in Psalm 44, depicted at one of his darkest moments, and the king in this psalm, shown at one of his most splendid! Christian readers can learn from both the gloom and the glory; 45, like 44, has a passage whose fuller meaning is opened up in a key New Testament scripture.

The two psalms are also linked coincidentally by a sidelong reference to a particular aspect of the culture of Bible times. That is, 44:1 has the singers' ears hearing what their fathers have told them; 45:1 has the poet's tongue reciting his verses. This is the oral tradition we have just noted. These opening lines also remind us that along with it Bible people valued equally *the pen of a skilful writer*. So did God, giving us his words through both media, with the vividness of speaking and the permanence of writing.

1. The king
To use the AV margin's quaint but delightful term, what 'bubbleth

[413] Kidner, pp. 168, 170.
[414] Job 42:5; Eph. 6:10–12.

up'[415] from the psalmist's heart is a set of verses for a king. There is no 'the', and we might call them simply 'king's verses', or even 'royal verses', since the second half of the poem is about the queen. However, an inclusio does top and tail the psalm with words addressed to the king: *therefore God has blessed you for ever* (v. 2 NRSV),[416] *therefore the nations will praise you for ever and ever* (v. 17).

A royal wedding is the theme. The traditional view, that it was the marriage of Solomon and the princess of Egypt (1 Kgs. 3:1), is as good as any and better than most. But again a Korah psalm has been composed for a particular occasion without our knowing which, or being at any disadvantage for not knowing. The poem no doubt provided a splendid anthem on many later occasions of the kind, and not only in biblical times.[417]

The first thing the psalmist notes is that the king is *the most handsome of men* (JB)! If he is Solomon, similar good looks are noted also in his father David and his half-brother Absalom,[418] and indeed in his bride (v. 11). Yet it is just when the handsome David first comes on the scene that we are warned 'Man looks at the outward appearance, but the LORD looks at the heart.'[419] So it is excellence in more important respects that the psalmist celebrates: the king's gracious speech, a *splendour and majesty* that consist in action *on behalf of truth, humility and righteousness*, and his resolve to maintain the reputation of the Lord's kingdom among the nations (vv. 2–5).

Of the honours paid to the king in verses 6–9, the most extraordinary is the one with which the section begins: *Your throne, O God, will last for ever and ever*. Some commentators suggest changes to the text so that it does not refer to the king as God. But the Hebrew is plain enough, and there are in fact scriptures 'in which the word "god" is legitimately used to refer to others than God himself'[420] – judges, angels, even the nation of Israel. So to speak thus of God's viceroy, who occupies God's throne in God's city and represents God's rule, is not quite so startling as it may seem at first.

---

[415] The stirring of the heart in 45:1 NIV.

[416] NRSV's *therefore* in v. 2 means not that the blessing resulted from the anointed lips, but the reverse: '*You can tell* the king is blessed, because he has anointed lips.' Hence the NIV's *since*. The same insertion makes sense of 1 Cor. 10:5: '*You can tell* God was displeased with them, because they died' (not 'God was displeased with them because they died'!); and of Luke 7:47: '*You can tell* she has been forgiven much, because she loves much.'

[417] Handel's fine setting graced the otherwise calamitous coronation of King George II and Queen Caroline in 1727.

[418] 1 Sam. 16:12; 17:42; 2 Sam. 14:25.   [419] 1 Sam. 16:7.

[420] D. A. Carson, *The Gospel according to John* (Leicester: IVP, 1991), p. 397. See the whole discussion there on John 10:34–36 / Ps. 82:6–7.

But there is more to this than meets the eye, as we shall find.

2. His ancestor and his descendant

'O king, live for ever!' was what Eastern monarchs expected to hear from their courtiers.[421] The thrice-repeated *for ever* in this psalm could be a formality of that sort, or it could be a genuine wish; it might have in view simply the king's lifetime, or the lifetimes of all his descendants too; it might even, as we have seen in earlier psalms, imply the New Testament's hope of eternity.

To use Lewis's phrase, this last is in fact its 'second meaning', whatever the psalmist understood his own first meaning to be. Before we consider how his words were going to be understood in New Testament days, we might recall that they had been meaningful from the earliest times. When man was first created, God 'made him ruler over the works of [his] hands', as one of the great David psalms has reminded us.[422] Man was intended to be 'the king of the earth',[423] with as enduring and illustrious a reign as the one here wished for the house of David, and with an empire vastly greater. In that sense the idea of a permanent kingship was built into God's world from the beginning, and had been planned from eternity past, as well as looking forward to the climax of history and beyond that to eternity future.

The forward look, however, rather than the backward look, is the special interest of verses 6–7, which are applied in Hebrews 1:8–9 to Christ. 'About the Son [God] says, "Your throne, O God, will last for ever and ever".' The New Testament passage is making three points. The main one is that God's Son has *a throne*, in contrast to the angels, who though they may be called sons of God[424] are in fact his servants: ministry is the angels' privilege, authority is the Son's. Then the nature of his rule is stated to be *eternal* and *righteous*; that is the special contribution of Psalm 45 to the Hebrews argument. Finally, though it is not the primary point, and indeed seems almost to be said merely in passing, the address to the king as a 'god' has the most astonishing second meaning of all. Everything said about the Davidic king in verses 2–9 is also said in the New Testament, in different words, about Jesus.[425] The royal line of David, which points back to its ancestor Adam, also points forward to its descendant Jesus, who really is in the fullest sense God as well as King.

---

[421] Dan. 2:4; 6:6, 21.
[422] Ps. 8:6, referring back to Gen. 1:26–28.
[423] See Erich Sauer, *The King of the Earth* (Exeter: Paternoster, 1962).
[424] See Job 1:6; 2:1; 38:7.
[425] See also such OT prophecies of Jesus as Is. 7:14; 9:6–7; Mic. 5:2.

3. The queen

Verse 9 is the hinge of the psalm. The last of eight verses addressed to the king, it introduces his *royal bride*, and leads in to six verses about her.

The first three are actually spoken to her, and sum up what is involved in the marriage relationship, while the other three describe the marriage ceremony. *Listen*, says the psalmist at the beginning of verses 10–12, briefly taking the tone of Proverbs, *consider*; for marriage 'is not by any to be enterprized', as the Prayer Book puts it, 'unadvisedly, lightly, or wantonly'. Consider, for example, that this new relationship will mean the severing of some old ones. Then understand how as a wife you will both be expected to give honour, and have the right to receive it.[426]

The procession (vv. 13–15) dramatizes the meaning of the marriage. The bride leaves her own quarters,[427] and with her bridesmaids enters the palace and is brought to the king. She is leaving her past life for a new one. If she is indeed the Egyptian princess of 1 Kings 3, what is happening here is just the opposite of what happened with Solomon's later marriages. He would be taking wives 'from nations about which the LORD had told the Israelites, "You must not intermarry with them, because they will surely turn your hearts after their gods."'[428] But in this case Solomon is still to the psalmist a wise man, and is not yet acting 'unadvisedly, lightly, or wantonly'. His foreign bride is a latter-day Ruth, that other foreigner who was prepared to forget her people and her father's house, and, so to speak, to *enter the palace of the king*.[429] This too has a momentous second meaning.

4. Her ancestor and her descendant

The queen, like the king, has a prototype in the first pages of the Bible. Genesis tells us that God created male and female (ch. 1), the man and the woman (ch. 2), Adam and Eve (ch. 3). It tells us further that in his eyes it is not good for man to be alone; woman is the proper and complementary partner for him, and her being brought to him is part of the marriage pattern. In every generation from then on the leaving of one's parents and the cleaving to one's spouse bring about a new and permanent relationship.

An actual example of human marriage is one thing we can see in the royal wedding of Psalm 45. It has a further dimension too. As

---

[426] *The Daughter of Tyre* (v. 12) almost certainly means the people or city of Tyre, Israel's wealthy neighbour and ally.

[427] *All glorious … within* does not refer to inward beauty (as in 1 Pet. 3:4), attractive though the suggestion is.

[428] See 1 Kgs. 11:1–6.   [429] See Ruth 1:15–18.

the authority of both Adam and the Davidic kings represented God's authority over his world, so the marriages of both represented God's relationship to his people. Several Old Testament prophets speak of this.[430] Not surprisingly, therefore, the New Testament takes it up and speaks of the church as the bride of Christ.[431] All that Genesis 2 says about the relation between the man and his wife, all that Psalm 45 says about the relation between the king and his bride, is a model for our understanding of both human marriage and the doctrine of the church, as the apostolic scriptures set them before us.

Psalm 46

A roundabout route into this splendid psalm is provided by the word *alamoth*, in the heading. What it means in itself (i.e. 'girls') is not in doubt, but what it means in its context is. David included in the arrangements for the Jerusalem sanctuary three groups of (male) musicians, one to play cymbals, another to play lyres 'according to *alamoth*', and the third to play harps 'according to *sheminith*'.[432] 'Girls' and 'eighth'? Perhaps a treble line and a bass line?

Goulder, following some of the old translations, suggests quite another meaning for the word: 'something hidden', and therefore 'depths'. This is one of many jigsaw pieces out of which he builds up a picture of the Korah psalms originating not in the Jerusalem shrine at all, but in a very different one. In 1 Kings 12 are described the break-up of Israel into two kingdoms, and the establishment of shrines in the north to rival Jerusalem. That sort of background would account, he thinks, for the mention of Mount Hermon and the 'deeps' and waterfalls of the upper Jordan in 42:6, of what he sees as Ahab's Tyrian bride and ivory palaces in 45:8, 12,[433] and of the mountains and streams here in 46:2–4.

Fascinating, if unlikely! The true *city of God* was surely always Jerusalem, especially as *the Most High* (v. 4) had been worshipped there as far back as the time of Abraham.[434] Once that city had become David's capital, the *God* who had been his fortress wherever he was, as we saw in 9:9 and 18:2, was *within her*. So also now for some later king, through a time of great trouble, God is there as a *present help*.

[430] See Jer. 3; Ezek. 16; Hos. 1 – 3.
[431] See 2 Cor. 11:2; Eph. 5:22–33; Rev. 21:2, 9ff. In view of this and the previous note, the pronoun 'she' seems appropriate for Israel (= the church = the Lord's bride). Convention too regards nations (like ships and locomotives!) as feminine.
[432] 1 Chr. 15:19–21. We have already met *sheminith* in Pss. 6 and 12.
[433] 1 Kgs. 16:31 (Ethbaal was king of Tyre and Sidon, the Phoenician 'twin cities'), 22:39.
[434] Gen. 14:18–24 (Salem = Jerusalem/Zion; cf. Ps. 76:2). It is difficult too to imagine Jerusalem, strongly disapproving of her northern imitators, ever using their song books, however well adapted.

1. Troubled earth, troubled life (vv. 1–3)

Although the Hebrews never felt at ease with deep waters, as a Korah psalm (42) and a David psalm (29) have already hinted, they did believe that the land had been established and the sea was controlled by God (24:1–2; 33:6–9). That was a fact of faith. At the same time earthquakes and floods were, directly or indirectly, a fact of observation. But God's people could say boldly, though the mountains might slide and the seas rage, *We will not fear.* They had proved his keeping power through turmoils even greater than these.

Our generation may understand better how the natural world works, but that only makes us more aware of its destructive power. Fears increase: yesterday it was the nuclear winter, today it is global warming, tomorrow it will be some newly discovered threat from our unquiet earth. Does faith increase to cope with them?

The basis of Israel's confidence is stated in the refrain of verses 7 and 11, which may originally have been sung after verse 3 also, making a three-stanza psalm like 42/43. We could amplify the end of stanza 1 like this:

> Let its waters roar and foam
> and the mountains quake with their surging!
> The Lord of hosts is with us,
> The God of Jacob is our fortress.

Line 1 of the refrain, about the Lord of hosts,[435] would be an apt rejoinder at this point. The *hosts* could be the 'hosts of heaven'; even if the natural world is controlled by heavenly powers, they in turn are controlled by the Lord. But what would be the point of line 2, about the God of Jacob?

The Bible gives us no indication that Jacob ever in all his 147 years experienced either flood or earthquake. His whole lifestyle was, outwardly at least, a quiet pastoral one, its tenor as level as most of its landscapes. But though he may never have gone up a mountain or down to the sea, his story is full of ups and downs of another kind. Genesis 25 – 50 depicts a family life seething with crises and dramas, deceptions and feuds, rebellion and heartache and colliding personalities that *roar and foam.* Condense it into 147 half-hour episodes, and you have the mother of all soap operas.

Not that Jacob's descendants were proud of the shabbiness of the story. But they were proud of the God who had taken hold of such a man and such a family, brought them under control, and used their turbulence and harnessed their energies for his own purposes.

---

[435] So AV/RV/NRSV, for NIV's LORD *Almighty.*

Readings from the account of that troubled life would slot in very suitably at the three *selahs*;[436] and the God who made something good out of it is with us also.

2. Troubled city, troubled church (vv. 4–7)

The natural disasters of verses 1–3 and the family upheavals alluded to in verses 7 and 11 are illustrations of the particular event which we assume gave rise to the psalm. As to when exactly *the city of God* was threatened but did *not fall*, the reigns of Jehoshaphat, Ahaz, and Hezekiah have all been proposed. Hezekiah's is the likeliest, when in the days of Isaiah an Assyrian invasion reached the walls of Jerusalem and then came to nothing. There are many similarities between the language of our psalmist and that of the prophet in the chapters leading up to Isaiah 36 and 37, which tell the story.

As with other Korah psalms, we do not really need to know. What the turmoils of the previous stanza illustrate is any such threat to the city of God. The collapse of the mountains and the uproar of the waters represent the uproar of nations and the collapse of kingdoms.[437] God is as much in control there, in the world of international politics, as he is everywhere else.

It is not only in Bible times that the relief of a besieged city has been perceived as God's coming to *help her at break of day*. Early one October morning in 1574, literal flood water was the salvation, not the destruction, of Leiden in the Netherlands, at last driving away its besiegers and bringing a fleet of rescuers. 'All repaired without delay to the great church ... The starving and heroic city, which had been so firm in its resistance to an earthly king, now bent itself in humble gratitude before the King of kings.'[438]

All the same, when a psalm about Old Testament Jerusalem speaks today it does not speak to any city as such, not to sixteenth-century Leiden, not to twenty-first-century London, not even to modern Jerusalem. From New Testament times onwards the city of God has been the 'heavenly Jerusalem', the spiritual reality described in Hebrews 12:22–24, the Mount Zion where Revelation 14:1 pictures the Lamb and his 144,000 followers: the church, the 'assembly' of Psalm 1. As in the psalmist's time stanza 1's natural disasters represented stanza 2's enemy nations, so now the nations in their turn represent every evil power mobilized against God, the 'kings' of Psalm 2. We see the church worldwide threatened here by

[436] Goulder, *Korah*, p. 155. With this suggestion I do think Goulder is on firm ground.

[437] V. 6 echoes vv. 2–3. Note the chiasmus, fall/roar // roar/fall.

[438] J. L. Motley, *The Rise of the Dutch Republic* (1856), IV.ii.

an earthquake of persecution, there by a flood of materialism. What confidence does she have of surviving these troubles?

Three further pictures from Old Testament times reassure the city of God in all ages. The only literal *streams* (v. 4) available to Jerusalem on its hilltop were those of the Gihon spring, just outside its east wall. Not much of a river, you might say; but the tunnel Hezekiah made brought them right into the city, and from that day to this it has never lacked a natural water supply.[439] Then the siege which took place during his reign ended when *at break of day* (v. 5) he and his people awoke to find the besieging Assyrian forces crippled and retreating,[440] just as in the most signal rescue of earlier times God's people had seen 'at daybreak ... the entire army of Pharaoh' overwhelmed in the sea.[441] And God points his people back to an earlier time still, when *his voice* (v. 6) first made the world.[442] What he has made, he can unmake; and if the world, then *a fortiori* the bad things in it.

These are God's assurances to the troubled church in all ages: his unfailing grace, the promise of a new day, and the certain doom of every evil power. It is through Christ that she is assured of these things, for it is to him that the remarkable paradox of verse 7 points, when it tells us that the Lord is both *with us* and *our fortress*. *With us* means that he is *within* the city, the church (v. 5); at the same time we take refuge in him; and the you-in-me, I-in-you, language must recall that of Jesus in John 15:4–5.

3. Troubled trouble-makers (vv. 8–11)

What verse 8 invites us to *come and see* is God's power to destroy. This is an idea neither welcome nor believable to those who haven't a clue about what the Bible teaches ('How many divisions has the Pope?' sneered Stalin). But it is inescapably there, and we should be glad it is. All over the world people of goodwill, with little power and few resources, pick away at the edges of evil, while others with enormous wealth and influence either will not or do not do anything about it. But God will; in fact God does, our psalm tells us. The warmonger, representing all such trouble-makers, duly finds himself *in trouble*, to devastating effect.

When and where, though?

The decimating of the Assyrian army before the gates of Jerusalem in 701 BC was only one of countless occasions in history when the forces of wickedness have themselves got into trouble. Perhaps that is one thing Psalm 46 has in mind. Certainly it looks forward also to a final and universal destruction of all that troubles

---

[439] 2 Kgs. 20:20; 2 Chr. 32:30.   [440] 2 Kgs. 19:35; Is. 37:36.   [441] Exod. 14:27–28.
[442] Gen. 1:3ff.

our world. The thrice-repeated *earth* must mean the earth, and not just the land, and the ending of war all over the earth must mean the ending of the deep evil that causes war, and the eventual doom of the many who do seem to get away with their crimes. An act of God on that scale and at that depth will take place only with the return of Christ at the end of our age.

So *Be still*, he commands; and though he might possibly be urging calmness on his own people, the entire poem has shown that they are already calmly confident, and it is time rather that the opposition, like the literal raging waters of Galilee in Mark 4:39, was told to stop its noise and recognize its Master.

His exaltation among the nations is as yet a future hope. Meanwhile we have been assured from the outset that he is in every sense a *present help* too. What he has been on so many occasions in years gone by, that he is for his people here and now.

Psalm 47

George Herbert's 'Antiphon (1)' reflects this psalm, both in the theme of its opening lines ('Let all the world in every corner sing, My God and King') and in the way it is set out in modern hymn books. The likenesses and unlikenesses of its two stanzas are simple, yet subtle and profound.[443] So it is with the ten couplets of Psalm 47. They divide equally, and the bare bones of the two stanzas are something like this:

> Clap, shout, with jubilation,
> Because Yahweh Elyon is king of all the earth:
>> Subduing the nations,
>> Choosing our inheritance,
> He is ascended amid the sound of trumpets.
>
> Sing, sing, with understanding,
> Because Elohim is king of all the earth:
>> Enthroned over the nations,
>> Surrounded by their nobles,
> He is exalted over the kings of the earth.

This outline omits some important points, which we shall take up in due course. It does highlight other key features. One is the basic structural balance of the poem. A second is that verse 2, like verse 7, should begin with 'For'; each gives a reason for the clapping and singing. Thirdly, verse 7 says 'Sing a *maskil*', a debated word we first

---

[443] See Watson, pp. 71–73.

came across in Psalm 32.[444] AV's *with understanding* may be right, and complements 'with jubilation' in verse 1. Fourthly, the English present participles 'subduing' and 'choosing' and past participles 'enthroned' and 'surrounded' are an attempt to convey something of the Hebrew tenses.[445] The verbs in stanza 1 are imperfects, not pinned to a particular occasion but expressing a recurrent pattern, while those in stanza 2 are perfects, expressing an act and the settled fact that results:[446] God has taken his throne, and now reigns; the nobles have assembled, and now gather around him.

The most important point missing from the scheme above should strike us forcibly in the very first verse. The nations, so often lined up in the psalmist's sights for judgment and punishment, are here called to applaud God, and that not compulsorily but with genuine joy. To this remarkable picture the end of the psalm will return.

As a whole, Psalm 47 is related to its neighbours, and like them to other scriptures also. We are not, I think, meant to identify it with any one period of Israel's history; it refers to several, and like so many of the Korah psalms has a timeless message.

1. A Hezekiah psalm

The events of 701 BC, as we have noted already, do seem to colour several psalms, including 47 as much as 46. God's title of *great King* (v. 2) was the one that Sennacherib of Assyria reckoned to be his.[447] Did he not rule *over all the earth*, as his arrogant messengers twice reminded the besieged Hezekiah?[448] 'Where is the king of Hamath, the king of Arpad, the king of the city of Sepharvaim, or of Hena or Ivvah?' asked his second letter. In our minds the question is probably one of genuine mystification! But Sennacherib would have read such a letter over with grim satisfaction, and his intended victims would have received it with terror. Subject peoples might have been forced to serve in his armies, but they all hated and feared him. So if the God of Israel showed himself to be a real *great King over all the earth*, not only Israel but the nations too would rejoice (vv. 1–2).

In an earlier message to Hezekiah through Isaiah God had warned the king against looking for military help from Egypt. He himself would 'come down' to 'shield Jerusalem'.[449] This coming down of his (by no means the only one, as we shall see) is the prelude to his going up in triumph (v. 5).

2. A David psalm

Whether or not Psalm 47 originates in the reign of Hezekiah, it

---

[444] See p. 1.109.   [445] See p. 1.68.   [446] Cf. Kirkpatrick, p. 261.
[447] Is. 36:4.   [448] Is. 36:18–20; 37:9–13.   [449] Is. 31:4–5.

recalls that of David, three centuries earlier. To 'ascend the hill of the LORD', as in Psalm 24:3, was a recognized aspect of worship at the Jerusalem sanctuary even before Solomon's temple was built. It may well have included as a ceremony at one of the great annual festivals – probably Tabernacles – a procession carrying the ark of the covenant into the holy place. That was what had happened at the original 'going up', when David first brought the ark to Jerusalem 'with shouts and the sound of trumpets' (v. 5 uses the same words as 2 Sam. 6:15).

That and other high points of his reign are the background to Psalm 18, which is as we saw reproduced in full in the 2 Samuel narrative (ch. 22). The subdued nations of this psalm (v. 3) figure also in that one (18:47), and so does God's coming down to fight for David (18:9), which precedes his going up again in triumph. Both defeated enemies and admiring allies are listed in another chapter of 2 Samuel (8). In Israel's occasional moments of glory, such as her brief imperial expansion under David and Solomon, as well as in her frequent times of stress, such as the Assyrian invasion during Hezekiah's reign, her God shows himself King over all the earth.

3. A Moses/Joshua psalm
Our psalmist seems to be harking back to a remoter time also. Verses 1–4 recall Israel's *cries of joy* when God brought his people out of Egypt. Exodus 15 contains the first of Moses' two great songs, which foresees how the nations will be in a very subdued, not to say terrified, frame of mind when Israel is brought into her inheritance, the promised land of Canaan.[450] Forty years later, as that prophecy is about to come true, Moses' second great song (Deut. 32) speaks of 'the Most High' as the God who (as here in v. 2) is *the great King over all the earth*, disposing all nations according to his sovereign will.[451] And eight chapters after that, Israel's first claim in Canaan is staked as her armies bring down the walls of Jericho with the *shouts* and the *sounding of trumpets* which we find here in verse 5.[452] In those days too God's people knew that he had 'come down ... to bring them up'.[453]

Here, in other words, is a Korah psalm which (like more than one of the David psalms) joyously takes hold of some of the greatest events of Israel's history, and proclaims that God is still the same kind of God and acts in the same kind of way.

4. An Abraham psalm
The specific divine action that our psalm celebrates is one we can easily miss in reading the Old Testament. It goes back even beyond

[450] Exod. 15:13–17.   [451] Deut. 32:7–9.   [452] Josh. 6:20.   [453] Exod. 3:8.

Moses, to the time of Abraham, and there we find it stated very clearly. In fact not until the New Testament will it be so clear again – except perhaps in half a dozen out-of-the-way scriptures like Psalm 47![454]

God's title of *Most High* first appears in those early chapters of Genesis. Abraham recognized one even greater than himself in the mysterious king of Salem, Melchizedek, who was priest of God Most High.[455] A *Canaanite* worshipper of the one true God? Yes; and alongside this strange meeting, we note Abraham's encounters with God himself, who three times told him that all nations would be blessed through him.[456]

For that is the truth behind Psalm 47. Most of the biblical background to the psalm as we have considered it relates to its first stanza, and its first verse does indeed have the unexpected picture of the nations defeated yet rejoicing in their Conqueror. But the last verse of the second stanza is the jewel in the crown. The NIV is surely right in translating it *The nobles of the nations assemble as the people of the God of Abraham*. Abraham's God has met them, overcome their enmity, won their admiration, and called forth their faith. God has done this; that is why *he is greatly exalted*. Not till Romans 4:11 and Galatians 3:7–9 will it be explained in Christian terms. But throughout Old Testament times we can trace the line of blessing – Jethro, Rahab, Ruth, the king of Tyre, the queen of Sheba, Naaman, perhaps even Nebuchadnezzar and Cyrus:[457] a few of the many outsiders who saw God in his people so clearly that they too came to acknowledge him. Do we, God's people today, hear the challenge?

Psalm 48

Musical settings of this 'song of Zion' still have people singing about *the north side*, or *the sides of the north*,[458] without any notion of the meaning of the words. They do mean something; so does the poem as a whole. It is another of the fine Korah psalms, with obvious likenesses to 46 and 47 in particular.

1. An ingenious poem

Acrostics, which we first met in Psalms 9 and 10, may have seemed an artificial kind of poetry; in a different way, this psalm could seem even more so. Some have suggested that the cardinal points, north,

---

[454] E.g. Ps. 87:4; Is. 19:25; 66:20; Hos. 2:23.
[455] Gen. 14:18–20; Heb. 7:1–10.   [456] Gen. 12:3; 18:18; 22:18.
[457] Exod. 18:1–12; Josh. 2:1–14; 6:25; Ruth 1:16–17; 2 Chr. 2:11–12; 9:5–8; 2 Kgs. 5:15; Dan. 3:28 – 4:37; Ezra 1:1–4.
[458] V. 2, Prayer Book version and AV.

east, south, and west, provide the framework for it.[459] *Zaphon* (v. 2) does mean 'north', though NIV is right to translate it as a place name.[460] *East* (v. 7) was also the Hebrews' word for 'in front', as they began reckoning their compass directions by facing the sunrise; and with east in front of them, not surprisingly their word for 'south' was *right hand* (v. 10). Then the word root which gives both *east* and one sense of 'before' (i.e. in terms of place, 'in front'), also gives the other sense of 'before' (i.e. in terms of time, 'previously'); while in the same way another word means both 'behind' (place) and 'after' (time). So those coming up 'behind' them were *the generation following* (v. 13 AV). In brief, the psalm divides into four stanzas, verses 1–3 (north: left hand), verses 4–7 (east: in front), verses 9–11 (south: right hand), verses 12–14 (west: behind); 'before' also means the past, and 'behind' means the future; and verse 8 stands at the centre as a summary of the whole.[461]

Too clever by half, I hear you say! Yet there are at least two relevant facts which the Psalter has already revealed about its authors. They believe that a God who is so good to them deserves their best efforts, including all their skill and ingenuity, in the praises they make for him. And they delight in what Lewis calls 'plays upon words ... plays upon thoughts, paradoxes, fancies, anecdotes ... such eloquence, such melody (song could have added nothing to it), such toppling structures of double meaning, such sky-rockets of metaphor and allusion ... the counterpoint of the mind, the mastery of doubled and trebled vision'.[462] We ought not to despise the poetic style of another age, especially a style that God has chosen to use, merely because our own culture encourages us to think it unnatural.

2. A dramatic liturgy

However that may be, these matters of style concern what the psalm is made of, rather than what it is about or what it is for. The weave of the cloth is one thing, the purpose of the garment is another. To the latter we turn now; and a cluster of dramatic events seems to provide both the inspiration and the object of Psalm 48.

[459] Goldingay, pp. 110–113, following M. Palmer, 'The Cardinal Points in Ps. 48', in *Biblica* 46.3 (1965), pp. 357–358.

[460] This is grist to Goulder's mill, his thesis being (as we have seen, p. 1.165) that the Korah psalms did originate in the sanctuary at Dan, in the far north of Israel towards Mount Hermon.

[461] To think of the past being in front of us and the future behind us seems the wrong way round, but it is very logical! The past is what happened 'before', and so it lies 'before' us: we know what it contains. The future is what is coming 'after' us, and we can't see it.

[462] C. S. Lewis, *That Hideous Strength* (London: Lane/Bodley Head, 1945), pp. 397–398, describing the descent into our 'silent planet' of 'the lord of Meaning himself, the herald, the messenger ... the angel ... whom men call Mercury'.

Verses 1–3, bringing together the names of Zion and Zaphon, the North Mountain, recall Psalms 42 and 43, whose author was up in the vicinity of Hermon looking longingly towards Jerusalem. As we saw, those psalms could well have been the starting point of a sequence of pilgrimage songs for one of the great festivals, when 'many went up from the country to Jerusalem'.[463] It would always have been a dramatic sight on such occasions to see the huge crowds converging on *the city of our God*. Even from the remote Syrian border they would journey,[464] scorning to make do with the heretical local shrine at Dan,[465] let alone the holy place at Zaphon where the pagan god Baal was supposed to live, the Mount Olympus of the Canaanites. No, the real *Zaphon* was Zion;[466] they would meet the true God where he chose to be met, as Deuteronomy 12 told them insistently. Just as Gihon was not much of a river (46:4), Zion was not much of a mountain, compared with the heights of the north; but it was God's mountain, and that made it *beautiful in its loftiness*.

Furthermore, Jerusalem had found his presence *in her citadels* (v. 3) proved by a particular event, dramatic in a different sense (vv. 4–7). The land had been invaded and its capital threatened. As in Psalms 46 and 47, the kings who *joined forces* were probably Sennacherib the Assyrian and his vassals,[467] attacking Israel in the days of Hezekiah. But then, as indeed on other occasions, God had rescued his city and destroyed its enemies, like the wild east wind which can wreck even great ocean-going ships.[468]

Verses 9–11 bring us, perhaps, to drama of a third kind. Joy among God's people and praise *to the ends of the earth* arise from what the NIV calls meditation on God's covenant love, which has defended and delivered his city. Here, to meditate means to picture; the word appears in the verse Bunyan quotes on the title page of *The Pilgrim's Progress*, 'I have used similitudes' (Hos. 12:10 AV). 'Most … take this as happening purely in the mind … but NEB sees here a dramatic ritual, and translates it "we re-enact the story of …".'[469]

Whether or not we are back with the concept of cultic drama which first came to our notice in Psalm 22,[470] verses 12–14 do seem

---

[463] John 11:55.   [464] 2 Chr. 30:1–13.   [465] See n. 460 above.

[466] There is neither 'like' (NIV) nor 'on' (AV/RV) in v. 2. However, NIV's *the utmost heights of Zaphon* does make a great deal more sense than AV/RV's *the sides of the north*.

[467] Is. 10:8.

[468] Tarshish (v. 7) is almost certainly a place name. Where it was is uncertain (Spain? Sardinia?), but the phrase *ships of Tarshish* always denotes large vessels designed for long voyages.

[469] Kidner, p. 180. '*Re-presented*', suggests Goldingay; 'the great acts of God … dramatized' (p. 117).

[470] See pp. 1.79–80.

to describe a festival procession literally wending its way round the city walls, 'beating the bounds'. *Count her towers*, urges the psalmist, *view her citadels*, our assailants have come and gone and you can see that God's city is still intact.

3. An imaginative song

Now it is true that the rituals of Old Testament religion were highly dramatic, and that such colourful liturgies can be moving, impressive, and memorable. They were, however, clearly defined and relatively limited, being based on God's dealings with his people at the time of the exodus. It is pure conjecture that Israel would have felt free to turn later events also into cultic dramas, and to invent such liturgies on the grand scale. Behind the assumption that she did so lies the idea that this is a more effective way to convey and to realize truth than speaking, singing, listening, and meditating are.

But as the child said, 'I like radio more than television, because the pictures are better.' If we understand verse 9 to mean picturing *in our minds* God's covenant love in action, it will bring into play that much undervalued gift, imagination. We shall not use our imagination to fill in gaps in the Bible story, to picture what God has chosen not to tell us. We shall use it rather to picture what God has told us: not what isn't there, but what is there. Bishop How recognized its limitations, but also its value:

> I sometimes think about the cross,
> And shut my eyes, and try to see
> The cruel nails, and crown of thorns,
> And Jesus crucified for me.
>
> Yet even could I see him die,
> I could but see a little part
> Of that great love, which like a fire
> Is always burning in his heart.[471]

So shut your eyes and look! See, says stanza 1, the world is controlled not by the statesmen and the billionaires, away on their Olympian heights at the top of the world, but by our God, here on Zion in the midst of his people. See, says stanza 2, all who join forces against the people of God are in the end themselves shattered like ships in an east wind; the pages of history, which lie open before us (the east!), will tell us so, if we take the trouble to read them. See, says stanza 3, here in God's temple – that is, among his people – is the heart of the world's joy, for his 'southern' hand is the right hand

[471] W. Walsham How, 'It is a thing most wonderful'.

of power and justice, and shall prevail. See, says stanza 4, what many have done literally in a small Middle Eastern city, and all may do in their imagination in the universal City of God of which Hebrews 12:22 speaks: a walk round the walls of Zion, which reassures us that the church is indestructible, and gives us a message to pass on with conviction to those coming up behind us, the next generation.

As we have heard, so have we seen, says the summarizing verse 8: we have seen it repeated in our experience, maybe; but also we have done our best to see it vividly in our mind's eye. And it is on what *we have heard* in Scripture, not on a range of attractive extras, that we meditate.

Psalm 49

This intriguing psalm, less straightforward than it may seem, completes the first Korah Collection. As in 37 in the first David Collection, we find in 49 something of the style and the themes of the Old Testament's wisdom books.

After four introductory verses, it is divided into two equal sections, each ending with a proverb-like refrain; in effect verse 20 repeats verse 12, though with one major difference, as we shall see.

1. From the centre of the world to the ends of the earth (vv. 1–4)
These lines, which might come straight from the book of Proverbs, are not addressed to God as praise or prayer, as so many psalms are. Instead, we who sing or say them are telling ourselves, and others, truths *from* God – things which the psalmist first receives and then passes on (v. 4). Like so much in the wisdom books, they are for humanity in general, and for every individual; that is both the significance of the words translated *low and high*, and the obvious point of verses 1–2.

The word with which the previous psalm ends ('our guide even unto *death*', 48:14 AV) is also the theme of this one. But the phrase *all you peoples* may point to a more important link between 49 and its predecessors. If like the second Korah Collection (84 – 88) and the Songs of Ascents (120 – 134) this group is a sequence of pilgrimage psalms,[472] it begins, as they do, a long way from home (42/43), finds its way to the city of God (46, 48), and once there can look out again to the wider world (47, 49:1). Certainly when you listen to what this present psalm says about death, a message which recalls Ecclesiastes more than Proverbs, you realize that it speaks to everyone, to the ends of the earth. You don't have to belong to the people of God in order to grasp its relevance. But you do have to

[472] See p. 1.154.

belong to them, to be as it were at the theological centre of the world, to be able to proclaim it.

2. *Looking towards death (vv. 5–12)*

In the mind of the Christian reader, the words *redeem* and *ransom* in this psalm are bound to connect at once with Christ. But it will be helpful to shelve for the moment these New Testament assumptions, and to look at verse 7 with secular eyes. There will be rich people who know all about the ransoming of a kidnapped child, and poor people who know all about the redeeming of a pawned watch. Though the one may involve a great deal of money and the other comparatively little, the principle is the same. Goulder has in mind the ransom of prisoners of war when he suggests as Scripture readings at the two *selahs* excerpts from Judges 7 and 8. The Midianite kings captured by Gideon might have expected to be ransomed (the story emphasizes their wealth),[473] but when God's enemies are under his curse *no man can redeem the life of another … no payment is ever enough*, and the royal captives perish.[474]

But we do not need a Bible story to make the plainer point for us. Zebah and Zalmunna might or might not have hoped that they could buy off the vengeance of Gideon, but no-one can buy his way out of death itself. This, although the translations differ slightly,[475] is the gist of verses 7–9. Verses 10–11 also have two possible meanings, though again they make the same general point. *Those who trust in their wealth* (v. 6) either have nothing but *their tombs* as a permanent possession when they come to die, or else have as *their inward thought* that at any rate their houses will endure – quite mistakenly, of course, since houses, like their owners, eventually crumble to dust.[476] Either way, these verses are well illustrated by God's words to the rich man in Jesus' famous parable: 'You fool! This very night your life will be demanded from you. Then who will get what you have prepared for yourself?'[477] To the inquisitive query 'How much did he leave?' they give the tart reply 'Everything.'

All this is actually meant as an encouragement! When the psalmist says that death comes to everyone, he is reminding us that that

---

[473] Judg. 8:21, 24–26.
[474] Judg. 8:21. Cf. also Josh. 6:17, 21; 1 Sam. 15:3, 7–33. On the other hand, there were cases in which the Law did allow a death penalty to be commuted to the payment of a fine (Exod. 21:28–30).
[475] *Redeem … another* (NIV), *truly … ransom himself* (RSV), *alas! … ransom himself* (NEB), represent three different Hebrew readings.
[476] *Tombs/graves*: NIV, NRSV, all the ancient versions, VanGemeren, Weiser; *inward thought*: NIV mg., AV, the Hebrew text, Goulder, Motyer.
[477] Luke 12:20.

includes people who have risen to the top in this world, using power and wealth to wicked ends, and causing suffering to others. Even so, the refrain of verse 12 does apply to all of us. Again, the translations vary. *Does not endure* means 'has no place to stay, no lodging'. You may have plenty of money now, but it will not buy you a home in the after-life: a tomb, no doubt, but not somewhere to *live*. Verse 12b adds the thought, paralleled in verse 20b,[478] that one who has riches now but will have no lodging then is no better than an animal. This we shall take up again at the end of the psalm.

3. *Looking beyond death (vv. 13–20)*

Once more the wicked (disconcertingly spoken of here as the self-reliant) are in view. We have seen what happens to their wealth when they die, and it is repeated in this section in different words: they *will take nothing with* them. But afterwards, what will happen to them themselves?

Verse 14 is another difficult passage, as the differences between the translations will show. *Death will feed on them* is a sufficiently horrid metaphor; this is one of the few places in the Bible where Death is spoken of as if it were a person. An even more unpleasant picture is that of the NRSV, *Death shall be their shepherd* – a hideous parody of what Revelation 7:17 is going to say about those who put their trust in the Lamb of God: he 'will be their shepherd' and 'will lead them to springs of living water'.

It was towards a New Testament promise like this one that the psalmist's confidence in verse 15 was pointing: *God will redeem my life from the grave; he will surely take me to himself.* It is inadequate to say, as some commentators do, that those words merely express the vain hope of the rich and powerful unbeliever.[479] However incomplete the Old Testament's perception of life after death, our psalmist believes that a ransom price too high for any human being to pay, in order to buy himself out of Death's clutches (v. 8), is not too high for God; and that once the price is paid, and he has (in whatever sense) escaped Death, he will be with God.

Verse 15 comes true in its fullest sense with the coming of the gospel. But already the two refrains of the psalm, verses 12 and 20, are vivid statements in Old Testament terms of what the divine wisdom has to say about death. We might paraphrase the latter like this: 'No better than the beasts that perish is the man who has everything except a spiritual understanding'; and the former, even more striking, like this: 'No better than the beasts that perish is the man who has everything except a final lodging.' They who know

---

[478] The verses are not identical, as might appear from the NRSV.
[479] So Craigie, p. 360.

that God has paid the price to guarantee them a final lodging are blessed indeed.

Two further observations, one from verses 12 and 20, the other from the psalm as a whole. The two refrains say something about the distinction between man and the rest of the animal kingdom. Man can have a kind of present understanding and future 'lodging' which the beasts do not have; and when he has these things, man does not perish, whereas the beasts do. This seems to be the fundamental difference. Whether for sentimental or for scientific reasons, some today are eager to blur that difference. Genesis 1:28 does not give the right to abuse any other living creatures to humans who despise them. Nor does the Bible equate their status, in this world or the next, with that of those who idolize them.[480] But what we can say is that to regard animals, even the highest of them, as practically human, or humans as merely animal, is to think unbiblically about both.

More importantly, although Psalm 49 (like others before it) touches in such a tantalizing way on the question of death and what comes after, it does at least hint at the full-blown New Testament teaching which is ours today.

There used to be in the Methodist Hymn Book a wonderfully Christianized version of this psalm, a celebration of the immense desirability of the life of the world to come. God's people do not sing much today about the glories of heaven, more's the pity. Once upon a time they did! Here is Charles Wesley at his most magnificent – you may here and there need a dictionary for the sense, but the sounds take care of themselves:

> How weak the thoughts, and vain,
> Of self-deluding men;
> Men who, fix'd to earth alone,
> Think their houses shall endure,
> Fondly call their lands their own,
> To their distant heirs secure.

God's people, in contrast, have 'a building from God, an eternal house in heaven, not built by human hands':[481]

---

[480] On the place of animals in the *palingenesia*, or 'renewal of all things' (Matt. 19:28), see C. S. Lewis, *The Problem of Pain* (London: Bles, 1940), ch. 9; John Wesley, *Sermon 65* ('The Great Deliverance', on Rom. 8:19–22 – creation 'liberated from its bondage to decay' when 'the sons of God [are] revealed'). John Oxenham imagines the young Jesus having a pet dog which dies, yet comes trotting beside its Master at one of his resurrection appearances in Galilee (*The Hidden Years* [see n. 223 above], pp. 108–110, 237) – a relationship re-created.

[481] 2 Cor. 5:1.

High on Immanuel's land
We see the fabric stand;
From a tott'ring world remove
To our steadfast mansion there:
Our inheritance above
Cannot pass from heir to heir.

Those amaranthine bowers
(Unalienably ours)
Bloom, our infinite reward,
Rise, our permanent abode;
From the founded world prepared;
Purchased by the blood of God.[482]

Psalm 50

Nearly all the Asaph Psalms are found in Book III of the Psalter, but the compilers placed the first of them here in Book II, and it forms an apt conclusion for the first Korah Collection. Psalm 50 is in some ways similar to Psalm 49. It has an introduction which might be given the same title as that suggested for 49:1–4. Here too the body of the psalm comprises two roughly equal sections. Its message however is quite distinctive.

1. From the centre of the world to the ends of the earth (vv. 1–6)

Verse 2 sums up these introductory verses: *From Zion ... God shines.* Zion, the holy mountain where God's house is, has been the focus of the pilgrims' thoughts since their journey began at the beginning of the Korah psalms (42/43). Mount Sinai in the far south, where God met his people after the exodus, is no longer such a focus; Mount Hermon in the far north ('the utmost heights of Zaphon', 48:2) never has been. Mount Zion is, as we noted in connection with 49:1–4, the theological centre of the world.[483] There the Mighty One (El) who is both the true God of all (Elohim) and the covenant Lord of Israel (Yahweh) meets his people.

And from there he shines. He shows his glory as a God who speaks, who *will not be silent,* and as a God who judges – two strong emphases of the Asaph psalms, as we shall see, and indications, along with the fire and tempest of verse 3, that though Israel is no longer *at* Sinai, her God is still the speaking, judging, God *of* Sinai.

---

[482] See Manning, pp. 55ff.
[483] With the coming of the NT gospel all three, and the Samaritans' Mount Gerizim as well, are abandoned in favour of the spiritual reality which lay behind them (John 4:19–24) and which, though it is still called 'Mount Zion', is in fact 'the heavenly Jerusalem' (Heb. 12:22).

From the centre of the world his voice goes out to its farthest limits, summoning earth and heaven alike to his judgment seat. If in recent psalms we have heard echoes of the wisdom writers, now we hear the prophetic voice of Isaiah (1:2ff.) and Micah (6:1ff.). So are the nations of the world at last being called to account? Are they in the dock? They are not. Israel is confounded to find that the psalmist, like the prophets, sees the world not as the defendant but as the jury; it is she, the church, who stands in the dock.[484] This exposition's whole approach to the Psalter, reading it steadily through in order and trying, in the main, not to spoil the plot by peeping in advance at what happens next,[485] helps also in details like this one: it is not until the very last words of verse 4 that we realize who is to be judged.

Is it really his *consecrated ones*, his *saints* (AV), who are the accused? Yes; their status does not exempt them. The word 'expresses the relation in which Jehovah has placed the nation towards himself, without necessarily implying that its character corresponds to its calling'.[486] The Judge is about to show whether those who are labelled 'holy' are holy in fact.

It is a solemn end to the sequence of pilgrimage psalms, which has expressed yearning for Zion (42/43), then joy in Zion (46, 48), then outreach from Zion (47, 49), but which concludes with a call to humility and renewed repentance, rather than with any sense of triumph.

We might envisage Scripture readings from Deuteronomy 31 and 32 at the *selah*. God's care for Israel during her desert journey (32:10–14) is the theme of the feast of Tabernacles, and 31:9–11 requires a special reading of the Law at that festival once every seven years. Both chapters are grimly realistic about how easy it is for the church of God to lose its first love for him.

2. Formalism in the church (vv. 7–15)

God speaks first to *testify against* his people in respect of their attitude to him. He is concerned with what many call 'religion', the religious observances which are best described by the word 'cultus'.[487] For God's people nowadays that almost invariably means church services, 'forms of worship' whether formal or informal. The most obvious feature of Israel's cultus never appears in ours: as

---

[484] She is still worse confounded if she has herself invited him: *Let our God come ...* (v. 3 JB; see also NASB).

[485] See p. 1.10.

[486] Kirkpatrick, p. 279. A helpful comment on Paul's startling use of 'sanctified' and 'holy' in respect of unbelievers (and children!) in 1 Cor. 7:14.

[487] See on Ps. 16, p. 1.56.

Lewis says, reminding us of what it had in common with other religions of antiquity, 'we should not have enjoyed the ancient rituals. Every temple in the world, the elegant Parthenon at Athens and the holy Temple at Jerusalem, was a sacred slaughterhouse,'[488] and reeked of blood. Old Testament people took for granted that the incessant sacrificing of animals was at the heart of their religion, just as we take it for granted that a mixture of sermons, sacraments, prayers and praises, all in a liturgical framework (acknowledged or not!), is what our cultus consists of.

God has no fault to find with these forms of worship as such (v. 8). What he does rebuke is the misunderstanding which can so often lie behind them. It may seem incredible that a people to whom he had so clearly made himself known should imagine that he actually needed their offerings, or that by bringing them they were doing him a favour or buying his goodwill. Yet the same motives, ludicrous as soon as you think about them, lie behind much Christian 'religion' today. I don't rebuke you for your offerings, says our God to his church, whether your tastes run to motets and medievalism, or to drum kits and dance. I don't in fact *need* them, any more than I needed Israel's bulls and goats, which were already mine anyway. So with what you Christians offer me; for already 'before the saphire-colour'd throne ... the bright Seraphim in burning row Their loud up-lifted Angel trumpets blow, And the Cherubick host in thousand quires Touch their immortal Harps of golden wires'.[489] But by all means bring me these offerings of yours (inferior though the best of them are), if they express a true devotion to me (v. 14) and a total dependence on me (v. 15). Otherwise they are mere formalism, and you have plainly misunderstood – indeed broken – the first four of my Ten Commandments.

3. Hypocrisy in the church (vv. 16–23)

The seventh, eighth, and ninth commandments are explicitly mentioned (vv. 18–19), and the rest of the second table of the law is implied, in this scathing indictment not of pagans and unbelievers but of the wicked who recite God's laws and take his covenant on their lips (v. 16). These are people who in our day are known as Christians, but for whom religion and morality are two separate areas of life, with the former as God's real sphere of interest; the latter, in their view, he takes no more seriously than they do (v. 21a).

Jesus directed his harshest condemnations, the fearful twenty-third chapter of Matthew, against such people: those who knew and

[488] Lewis, p. 42.   [489] John Milton, 'At a Solemn Musick', ll. 7–13.

even taught God's law, and who in a 'religious' sense lived by it. To use a phrase from that chapter, it always seems odd that some should strain out the gnat of the psalmists' cursings, yet swallow the camel of our Lord's denunciations: 'You snakes! You brood of vipers! How will you escape being condemned to hell?'[490]

And what was wrong with these people? They were hypocrites. The word means play-actors, who in classical drama wore masks. The face seen by spectators was not the real person. God of course does know what each of us is really like, and whether our moral life tallies with our religious pretensions. This second address of God to his erring people ends very much as the first did: By all means bring these offerings of yours, provided your life honours me and gives me a place in which to demonstrate my salvation.

4. 'Two men come tumbling over the Wall'

It is Kirkpatrick who calls the two kinds of person addressed here 'the formalist' and 'the hypocrite'. Were John Bunyan's words in the back of his mind? Bunyan's Pilgrim met these two early in the course of his Progress. He was making his way up a walled track, to which the only legitimate access was the one by which he himself had entered. It had brought him to the cross, where the burden of his sin had been taken from him and he had become a new man. But then 'he espied two men come tumbling over the Wall', not genuine pilgrims at all; 'the name of the one was Formalist, and the name of the other Hypocrisy'. Soon the Christian has to face the climbing of the hill Difficulty. To avoid it, one of his fellow-travellers turns left and is lost in the wood Danger (Formalist, who keeps up appearances only as long as it is safe and easy to do so?); the other turns right and perishes among the dark mountains of Destruction (Hypocrisy, who has gone the way of sinners and so shares their fate?).

Kidner puts it well: 'the mechanically pious folk of verses 7–15 needed reminding that God is spiritual, the hardened characters of 16–21 must face the fact that he is moral'.[491]

An assortment of dates has been suggested for Psalm 50, including the reigns of David, Jehoshaphat, Hezekiah, and Josiah, all of them times when there was a good deal of 'churchgoing' but not necessarily the inner attitude which God looks for. A David psalm has already made this point (40:6–8), and both that one and this one recall the words of Samuel: 'To obey is better than sacrifice.'[492] Our own generation needs reminding, especially when it sees encouraging growth in its church life, of another of the Lord's words to Samuel: 'Man looks at the outward appearance, but the LORD looks at the

---

[490] Matt. 23:24, 33.   [491] Kidner, p. 187.   [492] 1 Sam. 15:22.

heart.'[493] Beyond all the religion, is there a spiritual response to his grace, and a moral response to his truth?

The second David Collection and the first Solomon Psalm: Psalms 51 – 72

Of the next twenty-two psalms, the remaining two-thirds of Book II, eighteen have the name of David in their headings, and of the eighteen there are eight linked by the word 'when' to specific incidents in David's life. There were a handful of psalms introduced by such phrases in Book I (the first was 3, 'When he fled from his son Absalom'), and there will be one more in Book V (142, 'When he was in the cave'). These explicit links with events recorded in the books of Samuel are, as we saw when considering 42/43,[494] one of the features which give the David Psalms a different feel from that of the Korah Psalms.

For a variety of reasons, a good many modern commentators take it that such psalms were composed neither by David nor on the occasions described in their headings. Rather than being the great king's personal reaction to personal experience, they are thought to have been written considerably later, anonymously, for cultic use, with the headings added in due course to connect the liturgy of the present with the events of the past. The question has been touched on earlier;[495] suffice to say that there is generally no compelling reason why David, whether at the time or afterwards, should not have put into poetry his feelings on those occasions, and why the resulting poems should not have been arranged for liturgical use in after years. It seems more likely and more natural for the psalmists to have worked forward from life to liturgy, starting with real events and turning them into songs, than to have worked back from liturgy to life, starting with a book of songs composed for the cultus and then finding historical settings for them.

It may be that the first Asaph Psalm (50), which we have taken to be a solemn ending to a joyful sequence of Korah Psalms, was intended rather as an introduction to this second David Collection. Or perhaps the whole of Book II was compiled for use in circumstances which we can now only guess, but which might well have been one of the great festivals at Jerusalem. Goulder has a detailed reconstruction of a possible liturgy for the feast of Tabernacles, with the Korah Psalms of Book II (42 – 49), those of Book III (84 – 88), and all the psalms of Book IV (90 – 106), running parallel through the festival week. In his scheme, the Asaph/David/

---

[493] 1 Sam. 16:7.   [494] See p. 1.153.   [495] See Ps. 3, p. 1.26.

Solomon Psalms 50 – 72 would be concentrated 'on the last and greatest day of the Feast',[496] and related to a sequence of Scripture readings covering the period from David's victorious campaign in 2 Samuel 10 to Solomon's accession in 1 Kings 2.[497]

At all events, one-third of the way through Book II we come to the first of these David Psalms, a confession of sin unmatched in Scripture, both like and unlike the first of the Korah Psalms. The lament of 42/43 is for those who feel themselves separated from God by distance; that of 51 is for those who know themselves separated from God by sin.

Psalm 51

'Among the outpourings of the human heart agonized by the consciousness of sin, this Psalm stands pre-eminent.'[498] It must surely be rooted in the events of 2 Samuel 11: David's coveting and then theft of another man's wife, his adultery with her, his murder of her husband, and his conspiracy with his chief of staff to cover up the facts – five of the Ten Commandments broken in one sordid and cynical enterprise, and that by a man who had perhaps already given a hostage to fortune in the words 'I desire to do your will, O my God; your law is within my heart.'[499]

Only the living word of God through his prophet Nathan could bring this sinner to repentance. No Bible story describes the heart's convicting quite like 2 Samuel 12, no Bible prayer expresses the lips' confessing quite like Psalm 51.

There is little agreement about the structure of the psalm. One possibility would be to divide it according to the sense and the grammar of its verbs. Following the NIV, in verses 1–2 they are imperatives – not a happy term, since it sounds like God being told what to do, when in fact he is being pleaded with: 'Cleanse me, forgive me.' The verbs in verses 3–6 are statements (indicatives), as the psalmist recognizes the facts, the way things are. Verses 7–9 are again pleas for forgiveness. We might see in this half of the poem a straightforward ABA outline, the literary shape we have come to know as chiasmus.

After confession comes restoration (vv. 10–19). This half of the psalm has a different shape. Verses 10–13 are six prayers and a promise, verse 14 another prayer and promise, and verse 15 another; in verses 16–17 the verbs are indicatives again, as the psalmist again recognizes certain truths (as in vv. 4–6); and verses 18–19, perhaps added by a later hand, are a final request and what may be a final promise.

[496] John 7:37.   [497] Goulder, *Korah*, pp. 199ff.   [498] Cohen, p. 161.   [499] Ps. 40:8.

Either this is quite sophisticated verse-making, or it is simply, in Cohen's word, an outpouring, a stream of facts and feelings, pleas and promises, which come from the heart of a sinner through the mind of a poet and musician. Let us see what it tells us about him, and about ourselves, in our own frequent need of conviction and repentance. The statement verbs show his awareness of the facts, the imperatives express his pleas to God, the 'I will' passages are his promises for the future, and a 'you will' passage (not clear in the NIV) shows his confidence in the promises of God.

1. Realizing

In the heat of the moment, David began his psalm with pleading, but with hindsight and a cooler brain we shall look first at what he would in due course recognize as the facts of the case, in verses 3–6a.

He begins by saying *I know my transgressions*. He cannot simply mean 'I *acknowledge* them'; rather, he *knows* them – knows them only too well, for they are always there, a shameful waking nightmare, now that the word of God has convicted him of them. Then because that word has turned him round, he sees no longer before him the glamour of the woman he stole, nor even beside him the innocence of the man he killed, but behind him the judgment of the God he had turned his back on. This is how the rules work, *so that* when all secondary charges have been dealt with there remains *only* the One who is outraged by every sin. After the long account of David's wrongdoings in 2 Samuel 11, the chapter's bottom line (for once the cliché is a *mot juste*) is that 'the thing David had done displeased the LORD'.

In verses 5–6 David recognizes the fact of original sin, the fact that sin is a matter not just of what we do, but of what we are, and always have been. From birth – even from conception, before we 'were born or had done anything good or bad'[500] – the inherited warp in human nature was there. Indeed, the *inner parts / inmost place* of verse 6 may possibly mean the womb, and reflect a Jewish belief that divine truth is made known to (and refused by?) the unborn child.[501] But David in no way regards his innate sinfulness as an excuse. Far from saying 'It wasn't my fault. I couldn't help it,' he feels all the more responsible, all the more ashamed.

Corresponding to this passage near the beginning, verses 16–17 near the end are also the realization of facts which in spite of his distress David sees clearly. We know from Psalm 40:6–8[502] how to understand the statement that God does *not delight in sacrifice*. Both Old Testament and New use the 'not this, but that' turn of phrase for emphasis, when we should say 'not so much this, but rather

---

[500] Rom. 9:11.   [501] Tate, p. 20.   [502] See p. 1.143.

that'.[503] Here, the vital thing is not the sacrifice but the *broken spirit* which the sacrifice is meant to represent. Since it is a merciful God who brings sinners to this place of brokenness and contrition, they can for all their wretchedness be sure that he will not then turn them away.

2. Pleading

These truths are very real to David as he comes to prayer. Blinded though he is by his sin in 2 Samuel 11, God's word to him in the following chapter makes clear what needs to be clear, and he knows what he must ask.

In the first half of the psalm his pleas form its opening and closing lines (vv. 1–2, 7–9). He has much to repent of. The terms in which he describes his wrongdoing are familiar (we noted them in 32:1–2). Perhaps these words – transgression, iniquity, sin – are *too* familiar. Retranslate them, and our own conscience might be more sharply aroused by hearing this servant of God admitting to rebellion, perversion, and error.

Also worth pondering is what David asks God to do about them. *Have mercy*: he knows well that he deserves none, and that God would be well within his rights to abandon him to the punishment he does deserve. *Blot out my transgressions*: having in mind perhaps the engraving of Israel's names on the high priest's breastplate, and metaphorically on the Lord's own hands,[504] he hopes that his rebellion has been recorded in a less indelible form, so that somehow it can be wiped away. To *wash* ingrained dirt out of filthy clothes simply means for most of us the selecting of a different programme on the washing machine, but in other parts of the world and in other ages it is a long and painful process – especially for the clothes! To *cleanse* is to remove whatever hinders or disqualifies, so cleansing is just what is needed for the error that keeps us away from God.

David's pleadings in the second half begin with verses 10–12. He is looking to the future, in three verses linked by the word *spirit*. The passage in 1 Samuel which tells us that the Spirit of the Lord had come upon him when he was first chosen to be king, says in the very next verse that 'the Spirit of the LORD had departed from Saul'.[505] Perhaps David is fearing in verse 11 that because of his sin the same thing might happen to him. If so, we may ask how this squares with New Testament teaching, and why the verse is quoted in Christian

---

[503] Related scriptures are the Romans passage just quoted ('Jacob I loved, but Esau I hated,' Rom. 9:13 / Mal. 1:2–3), and Jesus' words about hating one's parents in order to follow him (Luke 14:26); and the *you only* phrase here in Ps. 51:4.

[504] See Exod. 28:21; Is. 49:16.   [505] 1 Sam. 16:13–14.

liturgy.[506] However, the meaning of the word may be the same in all three verses, something between a mere trait of character (vv. 10, 12) and the Third Person of the Trinity (v. 11). David may be asking for a spirit of steadfastness, of holiness, and of willingness, which is already part of God's character, to be given to him also.[507] This will have to be an act of creation, such as Genesis 1 speaks of; not that David does not already belong to God, but each day's cleansing will be a new bringing of good out of evil, of order out of chaos. It will be similarly an act of renewal, not a renovation of something he possesses naturally but an innovation in each day's frailty.[508]

Finally he asks once more to be saved from his guilt (v. 14), and prays that his lips may be opened (v. 15). Opened again, does he mean? Have his writing and composing dried up in recent months, for some reason – need we ask what? Be that as it may, this last prayer breathes something of a confidence for the future. To that sense of expectancy we turn next.

3. Expecting

David had long been aware of all that God had done for him. He had been chosen to be king of Israel, born a son of Abraham, loved as a man after God's own heart. Such a glory, such a privilege, and such a relationship belong to every Christian,[509] and enable us to put ourselves in David's shoes at this traumatic point in his life. For him and for us, these things can all be traced back to the *unfailing love* of verse 1.

What is the effect of the sinner's recalling that covenant love at the outset of this psalm of penitence? Three things, surely, in quick succession. First, he is mortified to find that one as richly blessed as he has been can fall so low. Secondly, he is realistic enough to accept that God's covenant promise has not yet made him proof against such temptations. Finally, he believes that that promise will hold good in spite of his sin. While he has no grounds for presumption, he has good grounds for hope. Though devastated by his shameful

---

[506] The Prayer Book, the versicles and responses at Morning and Evening Prayer. In the OT the Spirit was given to certain individuals for specific purposes, as in the case of these two kings. Ever since Pentecost he has been a permanent gift to every Christian (Acts 2:17; Rom. 8:9–11; Phil. 1:6; 2 Pet. 1:4). We cannot lose him. We can however grieve and quench him (Eph. 4:30; 1 Thess. 5:19) and so lose the awareness of his presence. He will always 'indwell' us but will not necessarily always 'fill' us, and without the latter we may be 'disqualified' from a particular service for God (1 Cor. 9:27). This of course was what Saul experienced and David feared, and in that sense v. 11b is as valid a prayer now as then.

[507] Tate, pp. 22–25.

[508] Jerome's two Latin translations of the Psalter differed over the word 'renew': *innova* in the earlier one, *renova* in the later. 'The old is better.'

[509] See, e.g., Eph. 1:20 – 2:6; Gal. 3:6–29; John 14:21–23.

exposure, he does humbly believe, and expect, that the covenant God of verse 1 will act again for his blessing.

When therefore some translators and commentators[510] insist that four successive verbs in verses 6–8 are not imperatives (e.g. 'cleanse me'), but imperfects, that is, futures ('you will cleanse me'), spiritual experience and not just grammar is on their side. An expectancy about what God will do is an integral part of this penitent's prayer.

The sequence of verbs begins in the middle of verse 6, suggesting that *inner parts / inmost place* does after all mean the psalmist's heart and not his mother's womb. It is there that God *desires truth*; but instead of giving up on this deceitful heart, he will teach it wisdom. He will cleanse it – a wonderful preview of Paul's teaching on justification; for as John Donne says in one of his sermons, verse 7a 'might be translated "Thou shalt un-sin me"; that is, look upon me as a man that had never sinned'.[511] God will wash the sinner 'whiter than snow', another forward glimpse, this time of the Lord's reasoning with his people in Isaiah 1:18 (one of many parallels between this psalm and the prophetic writings):[512] 'Though your sins are like scarlet, they shall be as white as snow.' And finally he will cause him to hear joy and gladness, so that the metaphorical *crushed bones* will dance (NEB).

4. Promising

Promises are an integral part of this very complete confession: not piecrust promises, made to be broken, but the genuine kind, emerging from all that the psalm tells us has happened. David admits what he has done against God and recognizes what God has done for him. He asks for cleansing and renewal, trusting what God will do for him, and now pledging what he will do for God.

After the pleas of verses 10–12 comes his promise *I will teach transgressors your ways*. Might this be what lies behind Psalm 32? After its testimony to sin confessed and forgiven, that psalm is concerned with instruction, teaching, and counsel (32:8). Who better to pass on the message of forgiveness than a real sinner who has himself been really forgiven, but whose humiliation in the process empties his words of all pomposity and gives them a real cutting edge? And what greater privilege does he now have than to tell others the good news?

After the single plea of verse 14a, *Save me from bloodguilt*, comes the promise *My tongue will sing of your righteousness*. Eager as David is for the blessing of sinners like himself, he is equally eager

---

[510] The LXX and the Vulgate; Coverdale's Psalter in the Prayer Book; Alexander, Kidner, Kirkpatrick. See Tate, p. 21. Tate himself takes the opposite view.
[511] John Donne, *Sermons* (1640).   [512] See Tate, pp. 9–10.

to uplift before them the God who 'has done everything well',[513] who is 'just' in condemning human guilt and yet at the same time 'justifies those who have faith'.[514] And after the still briefer plea of verse 15a, *O Lord, open my lips*, comes the promise *My mouth will declare your praise*. Sinners forgiven by a righteous God – what theme could be more worthy of praise?

It could be that the last two verses of the psalm are a later addition, perhaps even dating from after the exile. By that time the walls of Jerusalem had long since been broken down, as a consequence of the sins of many people over many years. A penitent Israel, looking for their rebuilding, would promise (as David had done) that forgiveness and restoration would mean renewed worship, not the mere formalities in which God does not delight (v. 16) but those which express true devotion and in which he does delight (v. 19). (There is of course no contradiction between these two verses, as some suggest.)

It could be, though, that David himself ended his psalm like this. He was king; he was not a private person; the kingdom could stand or fall with him. His restoration would mean the strengthening of his city and his people. A 'comeback' for me means a 'comeback' for them – that is the thought that lies behind verses 12a and 13b. Did Jesus have this in mind as he foresaw the equally calamitous fall of another of his chosen leaders? 'Simon, Simon, Satan has asked to sift you as wheat. But I have prayed for you, Simon, that your faith may not fail. And when you have turned back, strengthen your brothers.'[515]

Psalm 52

Although so many of the psalms from 51 to 72 have headings relating them to the life of David, they are not in chronological order: 51 is linked with 2 Samuel 11 – 12, and 52 with 1 Samuel 21 – 22. While the story of David and Bathsheba fits 51 like a glove, the same cannot be said for 52 and the story of Doeg. But there is some connection. Whether in this case the particular events were the germ of a psalm of more general application, or the psalm was composed independently and then connected back to the Samuel narrative, we can see in Doeg the Edomite something at any rate of this classic portrait of a 'man great in sin and substance'.[516]

If (like the AV, though unlike most modern translations) we keep to the Hebrew text of verse 1b,[517] we can readily see the symmetry of the poem.

---

[513] Mark 7:37.   [514] Rom. 3:26.   [515] Luke 22:31–32.
[516] The phrase is Spurgeon's.
[517] *The goodness of God endureth continually* (v. 1b AV). An altered text is followed

Your words, you man of might, express the pride of evil
  (though God's covenant love is always the same),
    and your words are destruction/deceit.
    But God plans your everlasting ruin;
    so our words are derision/confidence
  (for God's covenant love endures for ever),
and our words, we people of covenant, express the praise of good.

The first three steps of the chiasmus are verses 1a, 1b AV, and 2–4; its pivot is verse 5, and its remaining three steps are verses 6–8a, 8b, and 9.

1. You, the man of might (vv. 1–4)

Nob was the home town of a large priestly family. Doeg, Saul's 'head shepherd', happened to be there, under some kind of detention,[518] when David in flight from Saul arrived seeking help. In due course Doeg told Saul; and Saul, summoning the priests, in a paranoid rage accused them of fraternizing with the enemy and told his guards to slaughter them on the spot. What the horrified Israelite soldiers refused to do, Doeg the Edomite did.[519]

Are this man and the villain of Psalm 52 the same person? One is rich and powerful, the other a mere shepherd; one is a compulsive liar, the other speaks the truth all too effectively. But we can see how the historical incident could give rise to the broader picture here. Doeg was not a 'mere' anything; he was among Saul's leading 'officials',[520] no doubt ranking as a 'mighty man',[521] the same term in 1 Samuel as in Psalm 52:1. His words, though truthful, could not have been more harmful (v. 4). His confidence was not in God, but in the patronage of Saul, with whom he aimed to curry favour; he expected to grow *strong by destroying others* (v. 7).

There have been times and places in human history when people have been able to take the rule of law for granted. Nowadays, those of us who mercifully do not live under wicked and unjust regimes are keenly aware that many do. At the same time we have come to see that keeping the world informed is one thing, and keeping the world policed is quite another. We find ourselves, perhaps to our own astonishment, back in the days of the psalmists, when wealth and words, power and communication, are perverted to terrible ends, and no-one seems able to do anything to stop it. All such regimes, and those who lead them, are addressed in the person of Psalm 52's *mighty man*.

---

by NIV and others. See Motyer, p. 519; Tate, p. 33; Weiser, pp. 410ff.
[518] 1 Sam. 21:7.   [519] 1 Sam. 22:6–19.   [520] 1 Sam. 22:9.   [521] 1 Sam. 14:52.

2. He, the God of constancy (vv. 1b, 5, 8b)

The human race has seen the spread of evil halted, and tyrannies overthrown, a great deal more often than it deserves. It tends of course to ascribe these deliverances to anything rather than to God, though he gets the blame when they don't happen.

Yet oppression which goes on unabated, and the kind of *mighty man* who presides over it unchecked or retires from it unscathed, should turn our eyes towards the only person who can right such wrongs. Several times our psalm speaks of the constancy of God. His covenant love persists *all day long* (v. 1; see n. 517 above), indeed *for ever and ever* (v. 8). When it is from a position of *trust in God's unfailing love* that we face the intractable question of the wicked and their misuse of power, we are lifting that question on to a higher plane, into a different dimension. If God's love for his people is everlasting, so too is the ruin he will bring upon those who despise and ignore him (v. 5).

As so often, we are not told his method or his timing, the very things we should like to know. We ask 'How on earth can this evil be stopped? And how long must it be endured?' Those questions he does not answer.

But what he does say, in verse 5, is that the downfall of the wicked and powerful will in the end be *total*: like the demolishing of a house, the scattering of the embers from a fire (the regular meaning of 'snatch up'),[522] the evicting of people from their homes, and the uprooting of a tree. And it will be *final*. The idea of God's constancy brings together the *all day long* of verse 1 and the *for ever* of verses 8–9. He will sooner or later right all wrongs, whether in this world or the next, and in the meantime there is not a day, not a moment, in which the relentless process of his judgment is not step by step being carried to its conclusion. We need never feel in such circumstances that repeated prayer about a specific evil is vain repetition; we pray today for today's developments in the case for the prosecution.

3. We, the people of covenant (vv. 6–9)

Like the rest of Book II, Psalm 52 speaks of 'God' rather than 'the Lord'. It does not use his covenant name, but it does refer to it (*in your name I will hope, for your name is good*, v. 9) and to the covenant love which is expressed in it (vv. 1 AV, 8). One of the great privileges of us who are bound to him by his covenant is that we begin to see things as he does. The mighty men who spread evil across our world are blinkered. They see only what they want to see. From their field of vision God, and his people, and the whole

[522] Cf., e.g., Is. 30:14.

divine view of things, are excluded. By contrast, our God-given field of vision includes them as well as ourselves, evil as well as good; as the waking mind understands both waking and dreaming, whereas the dreaming mind understands only its own dream-world.

So we may laugh (v. 6) as God laughs (2:4; 37:13) at the ludicrous folly of the wicked – 'the wholly devastating penalty for the high and mighty'.[523] They seriously believed, and boasted of it, that their own resources were all they needed. They refused the longer, broader view, which takes God into account.

They perish, and verse 7 is their epitaph; we live, and verse 8 is our testimony. In contrast to the uprooted tree of verse 5, God's people are like *an olive tree flourishing in the house of God*. The tree image was planted, so to speak, in the Psalter's opening verses, and appears in many other parts of Scripture too.[524] The picture of the olive tree in particular has a special richness – evergreen, hardy, remarkably long lived, its fruit valuable, practical, versatile, life-sustaining, life-enhancing.

As on earlier occasions (22:31; 37:5) the emphasis in verse 9a is not on *what* God has done; the verb has no object, and the psalmist is praising God simply because he has 'done', that is, he has acted. It is because his people know how wonderfully he has been in action in the past that they can be confident in the darkest days of the present. More than that: we may take the verb to be a 'prophetic perfect' such as we met first in Psalms 9 and 10.[525] We may see the turmoils of history as he sees them, looking back from the end of time: as though we were already there with him, and from that vantage point, with an encouragement beyond words, he were saying to us, 'See, I was in action all the way through; and now in every sense I have done.'

Psalm 53

If, having worked your way through the first fifty-two psalms, it is with a sense of *déjà vu* that you look at Psalm 53, the reason is that the greater part of it duplicates Psalm 14. Why the repetition? And given that, why the variation?

For one thing, they are another reminder that our Psalter combines several collections of songs. Being accustomed in our own church life to a variety of hymnals and song books, we can see how a psalm might well appear in more than one collection, and how its

---

[523] Kidner, p. 195.
[524] Ps. 1:3. See Jer. 11:16; Hos. 14:8; John 15:1–8; etc.
[525] See pp. 1.42–43.

versions might differ slightly. Then when a number of books are combined, and the compilers leave two almost identical psalms where they are, instead of omitting one of them for the sake of tidiness, we may draw two conclusions. There is presumably some importance on the one hand in the differences between them, and on the other, in their positions in their respective books.

We can only guess what was in the minds of the anonymous compilers first of the smaller collections and then of the whole Psalter. Unlike modern editors, they did not write introductions to explain and justify themselves. But reading their work in order, and noting how it is put together, we find clues and insights that we might not notice in studying the psalms at random, simply as an anthology, when 'pick and mix' easily becomes 'hit and miss'.

1. Something familiar

This psalm, like its twin, is *for the director of music* and *of David*. It is about folly, in the biblical sense of the word: the fool being one who *in his heart*, that is, wilfully, organizes his life without reference to God. Sin and worldliness might be defined in the same way. With tiny changes in the wording (e.g. *God* for *LORD*, as almost everywhere in Book II), this version repeats the divine verdict on humanity: *no-one* is free from the infection of sin, *not even one*. It could as well be 53 as 14 which Paul quotes to this effect in Romans 3:10–12.

As before, God deplores the universal folly of mankind; and in the second half of each psalm his people too distance themselves from it. Again we ask, how can they, when they are themselves infected by it? And again the answer is, not with arrogance but with the deepest humility. They know that God has saved them from it, not because they deserved to be saved but purely because he showed them mercy. And they know that though they have been saved, they still have sinful hearts. But they do now stand on his side, over against the world of folly.

Both psalms therefore sing of the conflict between sinners *who do not call on* a divine Saviour, and sinners who do.

So much for the points that 14 and 53 have in common. It is of course where they differ that we hear their distinctive voices, and the new slant of Book II's version of the song.

2. Something new

Almost every verse of Psalm 53 differs in small and unimportant ways from the corresponding verse in Psalm 14. The heading here adds *Mahalath* (a tune? an instrument? no-one knows), and *maskil*, which we first came across in Psalm 32.

The major difference is in verse 5. This is the core of the second half of the psalm, which has to do with the conflict between *the evildoers* and *my people*, as the previous verse calls them. We should note in turn its broad historical setting, its narrower reference to David's time, and its message for all times.

We found reason to link 14:5–6 with the first such conflict, the prototype of all the rest, at the time of the exodus. The *evildoers* were the Egyptians, who did their best not only to *devour* God's people (v. 4 in both psalms) but to *frustrate the plans* God had laid for their escape (14:6). But when God acted Egypt was *overwhelmed with dread* (v. 5 in both psalms), as were many later antagonists in the course of Israel's history. The one whose discomfiture seems to tally most closely with Psalm 53 is the Assyrian king Sennacherib. Although an earlier foe was routed in a more obviously supernatural way,[526] this is the man who *says in his heart, 'There is no God,'* but in the event finds himself *despised* and *put ... to shame* by God and his people. The promise that *salvation for Israel* will *come out of Zion* is fulfilled, and Sennacherib retreats, leaving behind the *scattered ... bones* of many of his troops.[527]

All this took place in 701 BC. It was practically the last such deliverance recorded in the Old Testament, and may well be the one celebrated in this poem. In other words, Scripture itself is giving us an example of a psalm which looks back to the beginning of Israel's national history (14), yet which can quite properly be adapted for this latest experience of God's people, now in the days when Hezekiah reigns and Isaiah is prophesying (53).

Both psalms are linked with the name of David. This one, 53, belongs to a collection many of whose headings also mention specific events in David's career. To read the chapters suggested as background by the headings of 52 ('When Doeg ...') and 54 ('When the Ziphites ...'), namely 1 Samuel 21 – 26, is to discover a curious fact. In the course of that narrative a whole chapter is devoted to a man named Nabal, his wife Abigail, and their encounter with David; and in case we do not know the meaning of 'Nabal', it is explained for us: 'Nabal ... is just like his name – his name is Fool, and folly goes with him'.[528] A Hebrew reading of Psalm 53 therefore catches a reference which most of us would miss: 'The *Nabal* says in his heart ...'

[526] The Arameans abandoning the siege of Samaria, in 2 Kgs. 6 – 7. *Overwhelmed with dread, where there was nothing to dread* (v. 5), i.e. illusory fear, fits 2 Kgs. 7:5–7 exactly.

[527] 2 Kgs. 19:9–13, 21, 31–34, 35–36. In this connection Ps. 53:5 would better read, 'Overwhelmed with dread, where [previously] there *had been* nothing to dread', i.e. real but unexpected fear.

[528] 1 Sam. 25:25.

The effect is to remind us when we use these psalms that not only they, but also a sequence of narrative scriptures which are linked with them, may properly be applied to our own present situation.

Finally, both 14 and 53 convey a message for God's people in all ages. Both are meant to put heart into us, even though they deal with folly and corruption and the universality of sin. Where they diverge, 14 speaks to the wicked ('you evildoers'), defying them; 53 speaks to the righteous (about *those who attacked you*), encouraging them. Trust God, and you have nothing to fear. Ignore him, and you have everything to fear.

Psalm 54

We have already noticed how personal in tone the David psalms can be. In this second David Collection, a considerable number have been given not only headings but headings which mention people's names, and this fleshes them out still more with personal interest. As before, there is little reason why they should not have arisen directly out of the incidents in the books of Samuel to which the headings refer. But even if they did not, it must at the very least have been expected by the compilers that those who used them would make a connection between the poetry and the history.

The names noted in Psalm 54 are significant. They will help us to see what it is getting at.

1. The name of David's enemies

Our attention is caught at once, even before the psalm itself begins, by the name of the town of Ziph.[529] David in his outlaw days took refuge in the area. The story is told in 1 Samuel 23, and our psalm echoes its words: 'Saul had come out to take his life', and 'The Ziphites went up to Saul at Gibeah and said, "Is not David hiding among us …?"'[530]

The significant name is not however the one that is mentioned, but another that is implied. Every Israelite reader of this chapter would have known where Ziph was: it belonged to the tribe of Judah.[531] David was in home territory. In our reading of this group of psalms, we can see how he expected little but trouble from Doeg (52), who was not an Israelite at all,[532] and not much better from Nabal the Fool (53?), who though both an Israelite and a Judahite

---

[529] The Bible class leader of my youth who has provided me with more than one footnote was always hoping that one day he would get out of me a sermon with three points all beginning with Z: Zealot, Zamzummim, and Ziph. Alas, he hoped in vain.

[530] 1 Sam. 23:15 (cf. Ps. 54:3) and 23:19 (cf. Ps. 54, heading). [531] Cf. Josh. 15:55.
[532] Cf. 1 Sam. 22:22.

was 'surly and mean in his dealings'.[533] But he might have expected support from the Ziphites (54). The ironic words *Strangers are attacking me* (v. 3) pillory their 'unneighbourly behaviour',[534] which must have hurt him. In the next psalm the perfidy of a 'close friend' (55:13) will bring to a climax this escalating series of betrayals.

Four psalms in a row with the psalmist in the right and other people in the wrong – are we again to be embarrassed by David's self-righteousness? Hardly. The order of the second David Collection shows that there is no arrogance in his complaints about being let down by others, for it begins with the confession of his own catastrophic letting down of himself in Psalm 51. No self-righteousness there.

2. The name of David's rescuer

Whatever the relation between these psalms and their headings, they 'record how such situations should be faced'.[535] If you were ever to find yourself in real trouble through the ill will of someone you had assumed was a good neighbour, 54 would be the psalm for you.

At the heart of it (v. 4) stands the One to whom even in the darkest times David always looks. Before that, the first three verses are a prayer that sets out David's need. After it, the last three verses are a prayer that asks and then promises. Twice the psalm speaks not to God but about him, as if in asides that testify to others how good he is.

The core verse gives not exactly names, but titles and descriptions for David's great rescuer: God (Elohim) the helper, the Lord (Adonai) the sustainer. Unusually for this collection and for this book of the Psalter, but perhaps naturally in the circumstances, the use of the standard word for God (three times in vv. 1–3) thus moves, via verse 4, to David's calling on him by his own proper name in verses 5–7, the LORD (Yahweh).[536] The Ziphites have betrayed the name of their tribe in betraying its most distinguished member to his arch-enemy Saul. They might have argued that they had a higher loyalty to the Benjamite king than to the Judahite outlaw, but everyone, even Saul himself, knew that his days were numbered, and that David was God's choice for the future.[537] In contrast, the God of Israel would never betray *his* name. The name

---

[533] Cf. 1 Sam. 25:2–3; Num. 13:6; Josh. 15:55.

[534] Kirkpatrick, p. 305. *Insolent* (NRSV) translates a different Hebrew word. *Strangers* represents the standard text.

[535] Motyer, p. 520.

[536] The NIV, like many English translations, uses 'Lord' for Adonai and 'LORD' for Yahweh.

[537] It was at the very time of the Ziphites' betrayal that Jonathan came to tell David this: see 1 Sam. 23:15ff.

by which he makes himself known to his people – Yahweh, 'I am what I am' – means among other things that if he has told them he is their rescuer, then they will find he *is* their rescuer. He has made a covenant with them that it will be so. That is why Yahweh is his 'covenant name'.

The first part of the psalm therefore calls to God, *Save me ... by your name.* It is good to try to put our predicament into words: the Ziphite neighbours acting like hostile strangers, Saul as ruthless as ever (v. 3). It is even better to do so in the presence of a God who, because of what he is, can be relied on to do something about it.

And what, in the last part of the psalm, does David ask him to do? Although the prayer of verse 5 looks (yet again) like vindictiveness, we should note three things. It hands over to God the responsibility for punishing David's enemies; it asks him to do what is in line with his own *faithfulness* and truth, that is, the right thing; and it recognizes that unchecked evil has a way of recoiling on itself. Leaving the matter thus in God's hands means that the psalmist, and we too in like circumstances, can have confidence that God's people do win through in the end (v. 7, no doubt another prophetic perfect), can promise him our grateful obedience (v. 6a), and can already praise, as well as appeal to, his wonderful name (v. 6b; cf. v. 1). So the end of the psalm picks up its beginning, and for once even the editors of Book II, so sparing in their use of the sacred Four Letters, could not forbear to allow that name here: YHWH, the LORD, the covenant-keeping God who never lets you down.

Psalm 55

Since Book II of the Psalter has so many psalms which mirror David's life not only in their headings but in their content, and since 2 Samuel celebrates his poetic gifts and gives examples of his skill,[538] we take it that in this sequence *of David* means 'by David'.

Psalm 55 is his passionate reaction to some extraordinarily stressful events. The poem's structure, or lack of it, reflects this. It is quite possible, as we have often noticed already, for a psalm to be deeply felt and yet at the same time artistically constructed. However, there is so little agreement about the shape of this one, that perhaps David is not here thinking in terms of structure at all, but is simply pouring his heart out in distress and anger.

1. What is happening to David
Though the psalm is so largely an expression of feelings, the facts behind them can be seen clearly at several points in it. As on many

---

[538] Cf. 2 Sam. 1:17ff.; 22:1ff.; 23:1ff.

previous occasions, *the enemy* and *the wicked* are in evidence (v. 3), and their antagonism is shown in their bitter words and the *misery* they bring *crashing down* on David.[539] He is not imagining these things, for they are common knowledge (vv. 9b–11). He personifies them, as if he were drawing a political cartoon: the city patrolled by Violence and Strife, inhabited by Malice and Abuse, with Destruction at work in it and Threats and Lies dominating its public life.[540]

We note in passing that the second David Collection is, as it turns out, less concerned with following an historical sequence than with developing a spiritual theme. Recent psalms (52, 53, 54) may belong to Saul's reign and to the latter part of 1 Samuel, but 51 related to 2 Samuel, with David already king in Jerusalem, and now 55 has him again living in the city.

Betrayal is once more the cause of his troubles (vv. 12–14) now in this later time as it was before he became king. For this reason our present psalm (like some of those in Book I) seems to fit best into the period of the great rebellion, when David's throne was usurped by his son Absalom. People whom David had assumed were friends turned out to be foes. The treachery of the *companion* of verse 13 is something he cannot get over; he returns to it, spelling it out (vv. 20–21) as an attack on friends, the violation of a covenant, *speech ... smooth as butter, yet war ... in* [*the*] *heart, words ... more soothing than oil, yet ... drawn swords.*

It seems to many that David must be referring to Ahithophel, whose fame as an adviser, and whose perfidy, we have come across before.[541] There is no hint in 2 Samuel, however, of a close companionship between these two men such as verses 13–14 describe. The outstanding treachery was that of Absalom himself, who really was *a man like* David in rank and circumstance, certainly *close* to him and in a sense a *friend*, who without doubt had often been with his father *at the house of God* in earlier years. It was the smooth villainy of his words, as 2 Samuel 15:1–6 tells us, that sparked the civil war.

2. What is happening in David

The first five psalms of this collection, then, reorder the course of events so as to bring out the theme of ever more painful betrayal. First David's own guilt in this respect, as bad as anyone else's (51);

---

[539] V. 3 JB. See Kidner, p. 199.

[540] The 'streets' of a city like Jerusalem were the scene of transactions that affected the whole life of the community. Though the mind's eye is picturing something rather different, we similarly speak of Downing Street, Wall Street, or Fleet Street.

[541] Cf. p. 1.149, on Ps. 41:9.

then back to Doeg's (52), then perhaps Nabal's (53), then the Ziphites' (54); finally on to Absalom's, which hurt him most deeply of all (55). From the distress he felt on this last occasion we can learn much.

Our present psalm certainly seems disjointed, as we have noted. But there is no need either to suppose a complex and sophisticated poetic structure for it, or to assume obtuse editors whose work needs to be cut up and rearranged. David's frame of mind is quite enough to account for its violent changes of tone. What we have here is the 'collision of contradictory emotions which mark anybody passing through a situation of extreme stress'.[542] As Roy Clements' perceptive exposition says, it describes a classic case of anxiety.

While a number of scattered verses build up the picture of what is happening *to* David, a single passage, verses 2b–5, sums up what is happening *in* him. His mind is restless and distracted. It has gone into overdrive, racing round and round and so never reaching a conclusion or a point of rest. People are talking (about him?), looking (at him?); he is on edge, hypersensitive – even if they were not *the enemy* and *the wicked*, he would suspect they might be. Then when he really is at the receiving end of hard knocks and bitter words, these things are magnified, and perceived as *misery crashing down on him*. The emotional pain becomes practically physical: *trembling* and *anguish*, as you might say shivering and feeling sick.

What we see here is 'not a mild attack of nerves', but 'an acute anxiety attack'.[543] David's sore disappointment with the one who had been so close to him is still in the foreground of his mind, but from our point of view the cause of his anxiety takes second place to its effects. Some of us may have been betrayed as he was, but far more of us may find ourselves in a state of fear and panic like his, even if for quite different reasons. The question is, what can be done about it?

3. Opting out

Oh, that I had the wings of a dove! I would fly away and be at rest (v. 6). Opting out seems an obvious solution to pressures you cannot cope with. Why not just walk away from them? Can't you take a holiday? How about a sleeping pill, or if things are quite impossible, fifty sleeping pills? Almost as bad as the last suggestion is that you *fly away* from your anxiety by blocking it out of your mind, that is, repressing it. The likelihood then is that it will return in some even more dangerous form.

Someone who did try to opt out of such a situation, long after David's time, was the prophet Elijah. His great confrontation with

542 Clements, p. 55.   543 Clements, p. 56.

the Israelite paganism of his day, the combined forces of church and state in the persons of Queen Jezebel and the prophets of Baal, seemed to have achieved nothing. Seized with *fear and trembling*, he could well have cried to God in just these words: 'Lord, hear how they *revile me in their anger*!' Certainly he then fled *far away* to *stay in the desert*. Perhaps it was later still that the *selah* was placed against verses 7–8, by an editor suggesting 1 Kings 19 as a very apt Scripture reading at this point.[544]

But Elijah discovered, as David knew anyway, that flight was no answer. The prophet, trying to escape *far from the tempest and storm*, found waiting for him at Mount Horeb another wind and fire, and an earthquake too, and a God who lovingly but firmly made him face reality.

For David also the answer to fear and panic was not to run away from them, but to face them, as something the Lord had permitted and could use to his glory and David's blessing.

4. Opting in

Though still *overwhelmed* by his fear and distress, David grasps them as an opportunity. Instead of opting out, he opts in.

One aspect of this positive response is *prayer*. As we saw with regard to the facts of his situation, so also the style of his prayer comes into focus stage by stage in the course of the psalm. So far from being his last resort, it is his first (vv. 1–2a). The old hymn may seem simplistic – 'Have we trials and temptations? Is there trouble anywhere? We should never be discouraged; Take it to the Lord in prayer'[545] – but it should represent the natural response of the believer even to the most complex problems.

Sadly, of course, one can as time goes by move away from these simplicities. But they are still fresh and real to David, thanks partly to his deliberate practice of prayer, *evening, morning and noon*, and partly to his experience of having prayer answered – *the LORD saves me … hears my voice … ransoms me* (vv. 16–18).

It is almost at the end of this emotional roller-coaster of a psalm that David puts into one short sentence, and explains to other people, what he meant when he said in verse 1 *Listen to my prayer, O God*. The key words are *Cast your cares on the LORD* (v. 22). *Your cares* are *your lot*, the experiences that the providence of God allots to you. In this case they consist of a terrible betrayal and the resulting anguish. Talk about it, says David – don't try to hold it down or bottle it up, to block it out or keep it in! Talk about it to

[544] With 2 Sam. 15 perhaps at the other *selah* (v. 19).
[545] Joseph Scriven, 'What a friend we have in Jesus'. The line 'Do thy friends despise, forsake thee', later in the hymn, is especially apt in David's situation.

the one person with whom you really can say exactly what you feel. Throw it back on him.

And that includes expressing your *anger*, the other aspect of a positive response to such stress. Some will say, as before, that the angry words of verses 9, 15, 19, and 23 are simply examples of the vindictiveness of the psalmists. In fact they are not, as we have seen; but even if they were, they would still be showing us the right way to pray when in great distress. Spill it out! God can take it!

And if you know how he has dealt with such situations in the past, so much the better. Ask him to show himself the same kind of God now. Can he not *confuse the wicked* and *confound their speech*, as he did at the tower of Babel in Genesis 11:9? Can he not send them *down alive to the grave*, as he did with the rebel Israelites in Numbers 16:33? Cannot the God *who is enthroned for ever ... afflict* those who try even now to usurp his throne, as in 2 Samuel 15? Is he not able sooner or later finally to defeat evil? *Bring down the wicked*, cries David, confident that that is exactly what God will do in the end.

5. A pattern and a promise

'The spiritual eye', says Spurgeon, 'ever and anon sees the Son of David and Judas and the chief priests appearing and disappearing upon the glowing canvas of the Psalm.' As well as looking back to Genesis and Numbers, it looks forward to the Gospels. David's experience is as it were the same shape as that of Jesus in Gethsemane, in the shadow of a city full of malice and threats, where foes plot violence and 'friends' plan treachery. Jesus too fears the cup of suffering, yet entrusts his fate to God. Our own distresses will never be as terrible as his, but if like David we have to go through something of the sort, we can regard it as a privilege, 'the fellowship of sharing in his sufferings'.[546]

They bring with them the great promise of verse 22, for *he will never let the righteous fall*. Our part is to echo verse 23c, saying not that we trust God to do what we want him to do (in this case to relieve our distress), but that we trust *him*. For his part he assures us not that he will take the burden from us and carry it for us, but that he will sustain *us*. There is a personal relationship there which in the end triumphs over every adversity.

Psalm 56

It seems more than coincidence that almost the only Bible passages which link the words 'dove' and 'far away' should be in two successive

---

[546] Phil. 3:10.

psalms.[547] The heading here may mean that Psalm 55 and its tune were known by some such title, taken from 55:6–7, and that Psalm 56 was to be sung to the same tune.

A more important link is that this collection is still pursuing the general theme of trouble and distress, and the particular theme of David's life story. Four psalms (52 – 55) have shown how David copes with being badly let down, though without any sense of self-righteousness, since it has been shown at the outset that he is quite capable of letting both himself and others down equally badly (51). Now a new kind of distress emerges, as we return to the reign of Saul, and a time even earlier than the betrayals of 1 Samuel 22 – 26.

1. All day long (vv. 1, 2, 5): two enemies

If we follow the compilers' heading, and understand Psalm 56 to relate to the time *when the Philistines had seized* [*David*] *in Gath*, we can see perhaps why he labours the point about plots and attacks that seem to go on *all day long*. 1 Samuel 20 and 21 describe the final breakdown of relations between Saul and David, and tell us that on 'that day David fled from Saul and went to Achish king of Gath' (21:10). He stopped *en route* at the town of Nob, arriving there without companions, food, or weapons (21:1, 3, 8). Only later would a band of fellow-outlaws gather round him (22:2). For the moment he was alone, and he could not feel safe anywhere in Israelite territory.

Why did he go to the land of the Philistines? Did he think that as a rebel against their enemy Saul they would welcome him? Apparently not, for he seems at first to have hoped that he would not be recognized, though in the event he was (21:11). They saw him, as perhaps he had feared, not as a welcome defector but as a valuable hostage. 'While he was in their hands' he was in effect under house arrest, and eventually escaped only by a ruse (21:12–15).[548]

In any case he had perhaps been tempting providence by turning up in Goliath's home town armed with Goliath's sword, which he had found at Nob – the very weapon with which he had earlier killed the Philistines' famous champion. But the fact was that he had no choice. If he had to leave Israel, there was, from that part of the country, only Philistia to go to. At the beginning of 'that day' he had fled from hostility in the one, and by the end of it he had found, instead of safety, equal hostility in the other. *All day long*, as the psalm puts it, if it was not these it was those, misrepresenting him and assailing him.

[547] Is. 59:11 links the words in quite a different sense; Is. 60:8–9, more appositely, sees doves flying home and Israel's sons coming from afar.
[548] See Motyer, pp. 506, 521.

And what may give us the greatest reason to sympathize with David is that at this stage he had to cope with such unremitting stress *alone*.

2. In God I trust (vv. 4, 11): two refrains

Again a psalm of the second David Collection has a counterpart in the first. As David's great sin gave rise to both 32 and 51, so his flight to Gath gave rise to both 34 and 56. In each case the psalm in the earlier collection seems to be a later, more considered poem, while the one in the later group looks like an earlier, more spontaneous piece of work.

Although it is much less complex than the acrostic of 34, there is all the same a poetic shape to 56. It is divided by the refrain of verse 4, which recurs, slightly altered, as verses 10–11. Both times David speaks of God; but in verse 10 he also speaks of *the LORD*. Though the first time round the refrain is introduced by the words of simple faith *When I am afraid, I will trust in you* (v. 3), it seems a little half-hearted, since the next moment (vv. 5ff.) David is complaining as bitterly as ever. But it is specifically *the God of the word* whom he trusts, the God who spoke at Sinai to make a national covenant with Israel, and who has spoken through Samuel to make a personal one with David. By the time we reach verses 10–11 David has worked through the implications of all this, and adds to the refrain the extra line which gives God his covenant name Yahweh, rare in Book II.

Both times David also speaks of *man*. NIV's *mortal man* in verse 4 is literally *flesh* (NRSV). Hebrew regularly gives such words two meanings; in this case 'physical flesh, or meat', and 'human beings in their frailty, in contrast to God'.[549] So with *man* in verse 11. English has for centuries used the word 'man' to denote both 'an adult male human being' and 'humanity in general' (e.g. as distinct from God).[550] Hebrew is here doing the same. Compared with the Lord, in whom David trusts even as he tumbles out of the Israelite frying pan into the Philistine fire, both Saul and Achish are frail flesh (v. 4), mere man (v. 11). 1 Samuel 21:13 and Psalm 34's heading tell how David made his escape from Gath by acting as if he were mad. But it was God's grace, not David's cleverness, that saved him.

3. God is for me (v. 9), the light of life (v. 13): two gospel truths

At the climax of Psalm 56 David's hard-won confidence is expressed in words the New Testament will take up. Hebrews 13:6 might possibly be modelled on the refrain, but is more probably quoting

---

[549] See, e.g., Is. 31:3; Jer. 17:5. Similarly 'heart' can mean 'mind or will'; 'arm' can mean 'strength'; 'nose', 'anger'; 'bones', 'the real self' (see p. 32, n. 39), etc.

[550] See p. 1.20.

a psalm from Book V (118:6). The letter to the Romans and the fourth Gospel, however, speak of Christian experience almost exactly in the terms of our psalm.

The brave words of verse 4 do not seem to have cheered David up much. But he keeps praying; he tells God again about the pressures on him (vv. 5–6), asks for God's threats against godless nations to be fulfilled (v. 7), pleads for his heartfelt prayers to be noted, and expects them to be answered (vv. 8–9). In the process his confidence blossoms: *God is for me*, he can now cry. In Romans 8 Paul can say of the gamut of human experience, including stress like David's, that 'in all these things we are more than conquerors' if our trust is in Christ (v. 37). And what he has said in verse 31 about the people of God as a whole – 'If God is for us, who can be against us?' – the beleaguered David finds equally true for him individually.

The psalm ends with a commitment to *walk before God in the light of life* (v. 13). The first meaning of the phrase is that God will not let David be killed either by Achish or by Saul, and that he has many years yet in God's service before he descends to the darkness of the grave. But the New Testament gives it a second one. 'What to the psalmist was a present and temporal truth, receives for the Christian a spiritual and eternal meaning.'[551] To a commitment like David's Jesus promises that 'Whoever follows me will never walk in darkness, but will have the light of life.'[552] For him, and for us, 'never' really means never, and 'life' really means life, in the fullest possible sense.

Psalm 57

It is not hard to see the 'crossover', or 'pivot', pattern in Psalm 57:

> I pray (v. 1),
>> I pray confidently (vv. 2–3),
>>> though my foes are fierce (v. 4).
>>>> *Refrain (v. 5)*
>>> Yet my foes are doomed (v. 6);
>> I praise steadfastly (vv. 7–8),
> I praise (vv. 9–10).
>> *Refrain (v. 11)*

We may note alongside this chiasmus another poetic technicality, called epizeuxis: the 'fastening on' of an extra mention of a phrase, for emphasis – *Have mercy on me, O God, have mercy on me* (v. 1); *My heart is steadfast, O God, my heart is steadfast* (v. 7).

---

[551] Kirkpatrick, p. 320.   [552] John 8:12.

Technical terms like these are of course mere labels for an art which 'Israel's singer of songs' would have practised almost instinctively. But they have their uses. Analysing a psalm, even if in this case we do no more than notice that it has, like its predecessor, a repeated refrain (vv. 5 and 11), does help us to catch the drift of it.

Before we highlight four of its verses, we should just observe that it is linked with Psalm 56 also in some of its wording, and in being related by its title to a further stage in David's career.

1. The shadow of God's wings (v. 1): confidence

What the compilers understood to be the background of Psalm 57 was in fact the very next scene in the drama: 'David left Gath and escaped to the cave of Adullam' (1 Sam. 22:1). Soon others came, happy to make common cause with him, but at the outset he would have been alone. Isolation and solitude are not the same. He had felt the first in Gath; now he had to cope with the second as well. Would that make things even worse?

Strangely, he felt better. We sense a growing confidence. He may have been a fugitive hiding in a cave, but he was also a believer taking refuge in the shadow of God's wings. This beautiful phrase occurs several times in Scripture, most recently in Psalm 36:7. The wings of refuge figure also in the story of David's great-grandmother Ruth, a memorable page in his family history.[553]

The first three verses of our psalm give reasons for his, and our, confidence. If what has happened has been a total *disaster* (and for David it has), there is no point in pretending otherwise; but under God, he knows that one day he will be able to say that it *has passed*. Furthermore he knows that God is a God of action, who *fulfils*; as in Psalm 52:9, the verb is absolute, stressing not *what* he does, but the fact that he does *do* things. And David's escape from both Saul and Achish itself shows that God's covenant love and faithfulness are looking after him.

2. Lions and ravenous beasts (v. 4): trouble

When David speaks of teeth and tongues, and of spears and arrows and swords, obviously one set of nouns is real and the other is metaphorical. It is not equally obvious which is which. Are his enemies' mouths, accusing and betraying him, like hostile weapons? Or are their weapons like the mouths of wild beasts, eager to eat him up? Lewis points out how surprisingly often the Psalter 'protests ... against ... sins of the tongue';[554] we have just been reading 52:3 and 55:21, for example. On the other hand the beasts of verse 4a are a metaphor, so presumably in 4b their mouths are too.

[553] Ruth 2:12.   [554] Lewis, pp. 64–65.

206

Either way David is in a fearful situation. Whether he is himself fearful is another question. Although he is alone in the cave he is keenly aware of enemies on all sides. Does *I lie among ravenous beasts* express complaint ('I am forced to') or boldness ('I intend to')? The Hebrew tense could mean either. But previous verses have breathed such confidence, as indeed the rest of the poem does, that that surely is the spirit of this verse also. It reminds us of another evening prayer, earlier in the Psalter though later in the story, Psalm 4; and of course of Daniel 6 and a den of literal lions.

3. A net and a pit (v. 6): retribution
Already in the first David Collection we have seen the notion of 'the biter bit', the diggers of a pit falling into it themselves. David's prayer that this will happen (35:7–8) is really a recognition that it is what does happen (7:15) and that in the past it has happened (9:15). It is a principle of divine justice (9:16).

As in the previous psalm we may well have been able to empathize with David's isolation, so we may also know what he feels like now in a tight corner. For him it is literally so, in the recesses of a cave in the uplands of Judah. By the same token those of us who are in similar straits should be able to pray ourselves into the frame of mind which enables him to cope so well with his circumstances.

For at this point in the story his enemies have not yet fallen into their own trap. Far from it; humanly speaking all the advantage is at present with Saul. What David *can* do is to see the broad picture, both of the plan of God and of the progress of evil. The word of God, which he has praised in 56:4 and 10, is the whole long-term purpose of love and grace which is now in his mind when he speaks of a *God who fulfils* (v. 2). As the refrain twice declares, this God is *above the heavens* and *over all the earth*, in control of everything; and since he has already begun to show *his love and his faithfulness* (v. 3) by rescuing David from both Saul and Achish, the fall of his enemies is a matter only of time, not of uncertainty.

4. Harp and lyre (v. 8): praise
The harp and the lyre must be as metaphorical as the wings and the lions and the pit. If David had to leave home in such a hurry that he had no time even to pick up his sword, he is scarcely likely to have brought his harp to the party, so to speak. No; this verse gives us 'a bold and beautiful poetic figure'.[555] David has spent a chilly and uncomfortable night in unpromising surroundings, yet the sunrise does not awaken him – he awakens it! He is already alert, telling his

[555] Kirkpatrick, p. 324.

own soul, and the *harp and lyre* of his praising heart, and the dawn itself, that it is time to *sing and make music* to God.

The broad view we have just noted is even more in evidence in these closing verses. David has learned to think of his Lord as *God Most High* (v. 2), the God of *heaven* (v. 3), the God of *all the earth* (v. 5). It is sometimes said that the thought of praising God *among the nations* and *among the peoples* would never have occurred to an outlaw skulking in a cave near Adullam. But this God is also Yahweh, even though the covenant name is not mentioned here (*Lord* in v. 9 is Adonai). Before his covenant with David, indeed before his covenant with Moses, he had promised in his covenant with Abraham that all nations would be blessed through him and his descendants. The fulfilment of this promise may have seemed remote to David the fugitive, but David the king was to become just such a 'city on a hill ... a lamp ... on its stand'[556] to the nations of his day.

Two points from the psalm's heading are worth recalling. Like its four neighbours, it is a *miktam*, and in connection with the only other *miktam* in the Psalter (Ps. 16) we have noted this word's possible meaning of 'hidden' or 'covered', and therefore of its aptness for David's time in hiding in the cave of Adullam.[557]

It would be similarly apt to set such a psalm to a tune called *Do Not Destroy*. The phrase is found in other Old Testament scriptures, two in particular. In Isaiah 65:8 the Lord quotes a song sung in the vineyards: 'As when juice is still found in a cluster of grapes and men say, "Don't destroy it, there is yet some good in it," so will I do on behalf of my servants; I will not destroy them all.' In Deuteronomy 9:26 Moses prays to God at a time when his people are rebelling against him, 'Do not destroy your people.' In Psalm 57, David seems to be in a minority of one, but to the eye of faith it is the all-powerful Saul who is riding for a fall, and God will, as ever, assuredly preserve his faithful remnant.

Psalm 58

Psalm 58 presents us with difficulties both obvious and hidden. The latter have to do with the meanings of words, and we spot them only when we compare different translations and see how widely they vary. Here we shall notice such variations only briefly; details are in the commentaries, and the general sense of our psalm is not affected by them.

The former kind of difficulty is most obvious in verses 6–9. If we home in on them straight away, we shall see why this is the psalm

---

[556] Matt. 5:14–15.   [557] See pp. 1.56–57.

which the 1980 Service Book excused Anglicans from ever having to use in worship.

1. An imprecatory psalm (vv. 6–9)

Where the NIV has arrows, a slug, and pots, other translations propose grass, an abortion, and an uprooting, while verse 9 is 'a thoroughly tangled text, on which no two versions reach the same answer'.[558]

In spite of these uncertainties, the gist of the prayer of verses 6–9 is plain. On our way to it, the word *venom* in verse 4 may have caught our eye, and now returns to our mind. Whoever the psalmist's venomous foes may be, he sounds just as bad himself. It is precisely this sort of language that to many people makes Psalm 58 unfit for Christian use.

Concerning all such imprecatory psalms, a great deal of what was said in connection with Psalm 35 applies here also. We must not let the violence of *Break the teeth in their mouths* deter us from trying to look coolly at the problem as a whole. And indeed we are in a fair way to misunderstanding this by having gone straight to the allegedly most offensive verses without considering them in context. So we begin again where we should have begun in the first place.

2. An indignant psalm (vv. 1–2)

You rulers conceals a puzzle: the Hebrew consonants *'lm*, for which at least half a dozen translations have been suggested.[559] But clearly the psalm is addressed to those who govern or administer justice. That at least is what they are supposed to do, but instead it is violence which the scales of justice in their hands *weigh out* (RV).

This then is a psalm with a social conscience. It is concerned with the kind of wickedness in high places which has not only bungled or neglected those things which it ought to have done, but has also done those things which it ought not to have done – indeed, planned and perpetrated them with ruthless care. Could we arraign the villains of history, we should not simply express our horror at their deeds; what really appals us, we should tell them, is that coldly, deliberately, *in your heart you devise* such things.

If it is right to be indignant about this state of affairs in government and administration, how much more in the realm of law? When it is a judicial system or a police force which is thus perverted, then most of all there is a place for 'hot anger' (the literal translation of *dry* in v. 9). In Kidner's words, where there is a well-founded 'sense of outrage', which is more appropriate – 'an

---

[558] Kidner, p. 210.   [559] See Kidner, p. 208; Tate, pp. 82–83.

impassioned curse', or 'a shrug of the shoulders or a diplomatic silence'?[560]

3. A theological psalm (vv. 3–5)

What makes people act so? And what is to be done about it? The psalm's reaction to this political scandal is couched not in political but in theological terms. It is not society which is ultimately to blame: *even from birth the wicked go astray.* Nor is it an infamous minority who happen to be born bad, for even David, just seven psalms back, has admitted that he 'was sinful at birth' (51:5). So are we all, 'separated from the life of God',[561] until the grace of God in Christ takes away our sin and baptizes us with the Holy Spirit.[562] Without that, any of us may be capable of unthinkable wickedness.

Why then has that grace not halted these wicked people in their tracks? Because they are like *a cobra that has stopped its ears.* It is by God's doing that the saved will be saved; it is by their own doing that the lost will be lost. Psalm 58 has in view the evildoer who refuses to change, the terminally wilful, the mindset which has resolutely turned against God, as we saw in Psalm 35.[563]

4. A zealous psalm (vv. 10–11)

One further offensive statement is worth grappling with: *the righteous will be glad ... when they bathe their feet in the blood of the wicked.* Do we catch a glimpse of one of the arenas of the ancient world, with (in this case) the righteous filling the stands with shrieking glee and the wicked down below, noble in defeat, 'butcher'd to make a Roman holiday'?[564] No, we do not. The imprecatory psalms do indeed renounce personal vengeance, and explicitly leave their cause to God; nevertheless the singers of these songs are not mere onlookers. This is not an arena, but a battlefield, and the righteous are not spectators of, but participants in, the 'struggle ... against the powers of this dark world'.[565] 'With justice' the Rider on the white horse 'judges and makes war'.[566] It is entirely right for his soldiers to rejoice in his victory, that is, in the destruction of evil, here graphically described as *the blood of the wicked.*[567]

Our psalmist does however seem to imagine onlookers, the *men* of verse 11, perhaps people of goodwill who are as yet uncommitted. *God* in verse 11 has a plural verb; it could suggest that people such

---

[560] Kidner, p. 209.

[561] Eph. 4:18, where Paul uses the same Greek word that the LXX has here for *astray* (v. 3).

[562] Cf. John 1:29, 33.　　[563] See p. 1.121.　　[564] Lord Byron, *Childe Harold*, cxli.

[565] Eph. 6:12.　　[566] Rev. 19:11.　　[567] Cf. Rev. 18:1ff. with Rev. 19:1ff.

as these have despaired of finding *rulers* (*'ēlîm*) who will judge uprightly (v. 1), and are glad to think, as they grope towards the truth, that there may after all be gods (*'elōhîm*) who do judge as they ought to (v. 11). These related Hebrew words would provide a satisfying inclusio to begin and end the poem.

5. A Davidic psalm?
Without actually giving Psalm 58 the label of some event in David's life, the compilers have dropped some interesting hints. Its lions gnash their teeth alongside those of Psalm 57, and singers are directed to sing about them to the same tune. It is another of the six *miktams*, most of which do have Davidic connections.

Looking at this psalm in isolation, we have seen in it an attack on powerful people who misuse their power by ruling or judging unjustly. When we have found this fierce kind of language in psalms which seem to relate very naturally to David's life and times, it is directed against his enemies: before he came to the throne, Saul; afterwards, Absalom. Bringing the two thoughts together, we realize that the *rulers* of Psalm 58 could have been Saul and his powerful supporters, or Absalom and his.

But whether or not that is the historical background to the poem, its spirit is needed in all ages. Watts entitled his version of it 'A Warning to Magistrates', meaning the would-be saboteurs of the 1689 Toleration Act, which protected the liberties of thousands of non-Anglicans like himself: 'Yet you invade the rights of God, And send your bold decrees abroad To bind the conscience in your chains.' We have here a lesson in justified indignation – 'worth the attention of Hitler', was Manning's comment in the 1930s.[568] A dispensable psalm? By no means; rather, we should say, an indispensable one.

Psalm 59

Bad people *snarling like dogs* and a good God who is *my fortress*: a verse about each of them appears twice here, and these repetitions reveal the shape of the psalm. The NIV, which sets out verse 10 slightly differently from most other translations, makes this very clear: two stanzas, each followed by a refrain, much as in Psalm 57.

1. The heading
When the Psalter was compiled Psalm 59 was understood to be related to the occasion *When Saul had sent men to watch David's house in order to kill him*. The story is told in 1 Samuel 19, and is

[568] Manning, p. 90.

the earliest of all the incidents referred to by such psalm headings (except possibly that which lies behind Psalm 7). 'Now the Spirit of the LORD had departed from Saul, and an evil spirit from the LORD tormented him,' says 1 Samuel 16:14. Two chapters further on the troubled king is developing a paranoid jealousy of David, and by the time of this ambush he has already made no fewer than five attempts on his life.

David's wife Michal, Saul's daughter, learns of the new plot and helps him to escape from their home (in Gibeah, Saul's capital?). From that point on until the death of Saul David is an outlaw on the run.

Although much of the psalm seems to reflect these events, much else does not. Hence the doubts often expressed in the commentaries as to whether not only this but any of the historical references in these psalm headings has a basis in fact. Psalm 59 provides a good opportunity to grasp this nettle.

2. Stanza 1 (vv. 1–5)
The cry for help in verses 1–2 could certainly have been David's, as it has been that of many servants of God since. The plural *enemies*, too, fits 1 Samuel 19. True, Saul was the individual to beware of, and in his madness could be personally dangerous (19:9–10). But when less mad, though no less malicious, he understandably *sent men* (19:11; Ps. 59 heading) to do secretly what he himself could not do publicly to the successful and popular David. The two scriptures are likewise connected by David's innocence (19:4–5; Ps. 59:3–4). This is, as we have noted earlier, nothing to do with sinlessness – simply that, as Jonathan protests to his father, 'He has not wronged you.'

So nearly everything in this first stanza fits the proposed setting. The odd feature is the prayer that God will punish *wicked traitors* and *all the nations*. Would not such words seem more appropriate at a later stage in David's career, if not at a later period in Israel's history?

The answer is 'Yes, but.' They would indeed suit David the king, and some of his successors too. But from the time of his anointing by Samuel,[569] the young David's sense of destiny would lead him to identify the Lord's enemies as his enemies, and those who tried to destroy him as traitors to the cause of God. And already when he is challenging Goliath he shows a great breadth of vision: 'the LORD will hand you over to me … and the whole world will know that there is a God in Israel'.[570]

---

[569] 1 Sam. 16:1–13.   [570] 1 Sam. 17:46.

3. Refrain 1 (vv. 6–10a)

This section, beginning with the dogs and ending with the fortress, is the psalm's refrain, which recurs with inner variations after the second stanza (vv. 14–17). In two or three ways the language here seems rather excessive for the intended assault on David's house at Gibeah. The *return* of a pack of vicious strays (v. 6) pictures something repeated, and noisier than we should expect. *Swords from their lips* (v. 7) is the kind of metaphor that has elsewhere meant slander and treachery, not the grunts and oaths of a bunch of hoodlums in the small hours. And are such men, evil though they may be, really on a par with *those nations* at which the Lord will *scoff* (v. 8)? A poem could certainly have shaped itself in David's mind from the distress of this sixth attempt to kill him; it was after all the incident which finally made him a fugitive and an outlaw. But is this that poem?

Perhaps the answer is again 'Yes, but.' Yes, David may well have written a psalm at the time; why not? But, with the dogs returning and the swords continuing to flash on later occasions and in other ways, it could equally well have been amplified for repeated use later on. Verses 9–10a are a response of believing prayer which will bear repetition. Escaping from Gibeah, evading Saul in the wilderness, surviving Absalom's rebellion years afterwards, bequeathing his songs to his people and to his successors, David learned to *watch* – to be constantly on the alert – not just for possible enemies but for his Strength, his Fortress, his God of covenant love.

4. Stanza 2 (vv. 10b–13)

Assuming a simpler original poem whose author and occasion were as the heading says, and the more developed one we have today, we can see in the second stanza how it was expanded.

The God who is *before me*, either coming to meet me or leading me forward,[571] *will let me look in triumph on my enemies* (NRSV). David could have spoken thus even from his earliest times of trouble. When however he asks God to deal with them so that *my people will [not] forget*, the words are no doubt possible on the lips of the younger David, but they do sound more appropriate to David the king. It is the 'national' section of some older English hymn books that includes lines based on the AV of verse 11: 'O Lord our God, arise, Scatter our enemies, And make them fall.'[572]

---

[571] See Kidner, p. 213. Most translations, as we have noted, include the whole of v. 10 in the refrain.

[572] The rest of the almost-forgotten second verse of the British National Anthem is even more splendidly unfashionable: 'Confound their politics, Frustrate their knavish tricks; On thee our hopes we fix, God save us all.'

In fact, of course, the prayer is about the enemies of *God's* nation. It asks that their destruction will be complete but gradual, so as to be an object lesson to Israel. The word *wander* recalls the punishment of Cain, driven away as a 'restless wanderer on the earth', bearing a divine mark forbidding any to kill him, so that he, the first murderer, might provide just such a lesson.[573]

The sins of their mouths and *the words of their lips* figure increasingly in David's story, and we know what a prominent theme this is throughout the Psalter. So it is in our own world. As modern communications drown us in words, we need all our wits about us to distinguish truth from falsehood ('When words are many, sin is not absent'),[574] and to pray fervently for the destruction of the latter.

Finally, stanza 2 speaks of the longing that it should *be known to the ends of the earth that God rules over Jacob*. As far back as his fight with Goliath, and on to the end of his long reign, this was always David's desire, and is ours too whenever we pray 'Your kingdom come, your will be done.' As with the Davidic psalms, so with all the truths of Scripture. They seem to begin relatively small and local, yet they prove to have an elasticity that allows them to embrace a world of possibilities and an age of experience.

5. Refrain 2 (vv. 14–17)

The repetition of the refrain, with its changes, is like the rest of the psalm a prayer which belongs in embryo to those early days yet applies equally to all later ages.

Again David looks realistically at the enemy first. But then he deliberately looks away. In the first stanza, the powers of evil are all around, *but you, O LORD, laugh at them* (v. 8); in the second they are still prowling, *but I will sing of your strength* (v. 16). And as he looks to God, he declares first *I watch for you* (v. 9), alert with expectancy, then *I sing praise to you* (v. 17), rejoicing in promises fulfilled.

This psalm too is tied together with an inclusio. The words for *protect* in verse 1 and *fortress* in verse 17 are related: they both have to do with a high place, strong and secure above the turmoil. It is easy to be cowed by these numberless enemies, from the lurkers in the shadows outside David's house to 'the spiritual forces of evil in the heavenly realms'.[575] It is easy to fear that we may be overwhelmed by them. But, says David, when these *rise up against me*, lift me higher still into a place of safety; and that high place (three times by the end of the psalm) is *you, O God*.

---

[573] See Gen. 4:12, 14, 16 ('Nod' = wandering).   [574] Prov. 10:19.   [575] Eph. 6:12.

Psalm 60

One of this psalm's difficulties is that many of its Hebrew words give us a choice of meanings. In opting for this rather than that as a translation, one useful guide is an eye for a consistent overall meaning for the psalm. Another is an idea of its structure; a third is its possible background.

The general sense of it will become clear as we go on. Its shape is, I think, a simple division of its twelve verses into three equal stanzas; partly because that accords well with this general sense, partly because of the *selah* after verse 4, and partly because the lengthy quotation from it in Psalm 108 comprises the eight verses beginning at the same break. As for its background, we have first to consider the rather detailed heading.

1. The heading

Much modern opinion, as we know, dismisses introductory words like these as pious guesswork, and connects verse 9 not with David's wars but with later Edomite campaigns, whether in the reign of Amaziah,[576] or in the days of the exile,[577] or even in post-exilic times. It is worth reminding ourselves that myriads of worshippers, far closer than we are, both in time and in culture, to all these events, saw nothing odd in editorial notes which linked familiar Davidic psalms with equally familiar Davidic history, and would have expected each to shed light on the other.

Practically all the nations mentioned in Psalm 60 figure in the account of David's wars in 2 Samuel 8. The king of Zobah was re-establishing Aramean control in the Land of the Two Rivers (Naharaim, in our terms northern Iraq), when David took the opportunity of invading his territory from the south (Zobah, or central Syria). The psalm's cry for help would be explained by an equally opportunist invasion of David's territory while *he* was campaigning elsewhere, by Israel's unfriendly neighbours and kinsmen the Edomites.

'David became famous', says 2 Samuel, for his simultaneous victories on both fronts. He sent his commander-in-chief Joab hotfoot to cope with the deadly threat to Israel's heartland, and it seems that Joab's brother Abishai played a leading part in the battle of the Valley of Salt, where Edom was soundly defeated.[578]

But while the LORD 'gave David victory wherever he went',[579] he did not always give him his approval. Psalm 60 implies an Edomite

---

[576] Cf. 2 Kgs. 14:7.   [577] Cf. Ps. 137:7; Obad. 10–14.

[578] The three names appearing in 2 Sam. 8:13; 1 Chr. 18:12; and Ps. 60 (heading) are thus readily accounted for. The difference in the casualty figures is probably a copyist's error.

[579] 2 Sam. 8:6, 14.

invasion which was a real threat, and a punishment, perhaps for a war God had not sanctioned.[580]

2. Stanza 1 (vv. 1–4)

It may be Edom which has attacked us, says David, but it is God who has *rejected us, broken our defences* (NRSV), *shaken the land,* and so on. In fact seven verbs in quick succession all point back to him as the first cause of these woes. They describe an experience which is traumatic and destructive. Can a loving God be responsible for such things? Yes, he can, in the sense that 'no discipline seems pleasant at the time, but painful'. Discipline is what this is, designed of course to produce 'a harvest of righteousness and peace for those who have been trained by it': a sharp lesson with a positive purpose.[581]

This is a bigger God than many people are disposed to believe in, but by the same token a God worth praying to. If he set up the whole Edomite operation, he can close it down when it has achieved its aim.

Verse 4b is one of the psalm's great word puzzles. *Be unfurled* could be 'rally' or 'flee', *against* could be 'because of' or 'from', *bow* could be 'truth'. Of the many permutations the best seems to be 'to flee from the bow', that is, from the battle. Even that may be taken in three ways: reproachful ('You raise a banner to rally them *in the battle,* and they run away from it!'), or punitive ('You raise a banner … to bring them to defeat'), or gracious ('You raise a banner *over a place of refuge,* to which they may run from the battle'). This last suits well as a direct lead in to stanza 2, and its four verses of prayer and promise. It is in these that God intends his people to find their rallying point.

3. Stanza 2 (vv. 5–8)

Those God has temporarily rejected (v. 1) are still those he loves (v. 5). To their words of prayer he responds with words of promise. Some commentators picture the Jerusalem cultus, with God's people in *his sanctuary* singing the prayer to him and a prophet bringing the message of verses 6–8 from him. Such a message would have become from its first utterance an integral part of the psalm; there is no reason why David, prophet as well as psalmist, should not have put it there from the start. It was in any case a summary of much that God had already said in earlier scriptures.

It is not so much that he is speaking *from his sanctuary,* as that he has spoken *in his holiness* (AV). His holy word declares that not only Israel but all the nations are under his control. *Moab is my*

---

[580] See Motyer, p. 523.   [581] Heb. 12:11.

wash-pot, a sentence which I remember from childhood exposure to the Prayer Book psalms as second only to 'Why hop ye so, ye high hills?'[582] for peculiarity, is in fact part of a majestic declaration of the power and plan of God. Succoth, east of the Jordan, and Shechem, west of it, were the first two places where Jacob – Israel the individual – pitched camp when he came back from exile.[583] When Israel the nation came out of slavery in Egypt, lands east of the river (Gilead, Manasseh) and west (Ephraim, Judah) were allocated to and occupied by her tribes. Moab, descended from Israel's cousin Lot, and Edom, descended from his brother Esau, were not part of God's chosen family, but they had their place in his scheme: as it were the menial servants who took the master's shoes and washed his feet when he came in from work. So did even rank outsiders like Philistia. As he would declare through his prophet Amos, he brought not only 'Israel up from Egypt' but also 'the Philistines from Caphtor and the Arameans from Kir'.[584]

'God dominates the scene': it is not a case of 'rivals fighting for possession'.[585] All things shall be as he decrees they shall be. The promises of God (stanza 2) are far greater than the miseries of his people (stanza 1).

4. Stanza 3 (vv. 9–12)
We can recapture the image that Israel at the time would have had of Edom, for the latter's *fortified city* was a well-nigh inaccessible place in the mountains where later the amazing Nabatean capital of Petra would be cut out of the rock. David has been humbled, and knows that even he, the extraordinarily able man of war, cannot penetrate that fastness without the help of God. But the God who will not *go out with our armies* while our hearts are not right with him, *will trample down our enemies* when we turn back in repentance and trust.

The effect of the prophetic declaration in stanza 2 is thus the paradox known to all God's servants: that David recognizes both his total inability in himself, many and great though his gifts may be, and the unlimited power that is his in God.

Psalm 61

Symmetry and content, together with the placing of the *selah*, suggest that this psalm divides into two equal stanzas. If the psalmist is praying for himself in verses 1–4 and for the king in verses 5–8, the train of thought is disjointed, and the division is then so marked that the two halves seem unrelated. If the psalmist is himself the

[582] Ps. 68:16 Prayer Book.   [583] Gen. 33:17–18.   [584] Amos 9:7.   [585] Kidner, p. 217.

king, and in verses 6–7 is praying for himself in the third person,[586] everything falls into place. And as with the second David Collection in general, we may take him to be David, and the occasion to be once again his temporary exile at the time of Absalom's rebellion.

1. Personal need (vv. 1–4)

He first puts into words, and of course they are the words of a prayer, how his need is felt. His escape across the Jordan and away to the uplands beyond means that he is at 'the ends of the *land*', as verse 2a could be translated, instead of at the centre of it, at Jerusalem, his capital. To say that he is at *the ends of the earth* is a wild exaggeration, but that is what it feels like. He may even mean that to him it seems he is at 'the edge of the world', about to fall off into the abyss; at death's door, in other words. In any case he feels a long way from where he would like to be.

Along with this sense of being far – far from home, and in a way far from God, though quite near enough to pray to him[587] – is the sense of being faint, in verse 2b. He is fainthearted, not as a coward is, but as a man *overwhelmed* by his circumstances is (that is the AV's word for it). He cannot cope any longer.

And how is his need met? By thinking of God as he knows him to be. None of the four graphic pictures of verses 2c–4 is new to the Psalter. The safety of the inaccessible *rock* we heard about as recently as Psalm 60, except that there it was the refuge of the Edomite enemy. David looks to God to give him the same kind of security, as he does in many psalms from 18 onwards.[588] A famous Korah psalm has drawn attention to the *towers* of Zion (48:12), which David already knows. The *tent* too he knows, the 'sanctuary' of 15:1; and he has appealed for the shelter of God's *wings* on several occasions, including the last time he was a fugitive, according to the heading that prefaces 57:1. No doubt he did long for Zion's literal towers and tent, but if in this context rock and wings are metaphors, probably all four are. They provide our imaginations with the kind of pictures that can make our own praying real and vivid.

2. National vision (vv. 5–8)

Recalling what God is reminds David also of what God has done. The *heritage* of Israel is primarily the land, with the promises that

---

[586] Cf. Jer. 38:5: 'The king', says Zedekiah (meaning himself), 'can do nothing to oppose you.' So similarly Shakespeare's Julius Caesar declares (II.ii.28), 'Caesar shall go forth.'

[587] See p. 1.154.

[588] Ps. 18:2a (*sela'*), 2b (*ṣûr*). Both words for 'rock' are frequently used as a metaphor or name for God.

attach to it, and that (says he) you have given to me; though at present I may be far from it, it is inalienably mine. Behind his vows to God lie God's vows to him. So on the strength of God's word to the king – 2 Samuel 7 is the classic passage – David claims in verses 5–8 enduring blessings which are in complete contrast to the insecurity expressed in verses 1–4: increased days, *many generations, for ever*, the permanence of God's covenant love and faithfulness.

In praying for himself as king, he is praying equally for his kingdom, whose welfare is bound up with his own. Stanza 1 was a deeply personal prayer, yet with stanza 2 the psalm is seen to have a national vision. We can imagine David's successors also using the prayer, and they too will be bringing the needs of their kingdom to God. At the same time the form of it is such that the people in their turn can use it to pray for their king, and thus indirectly for themselves.

Nor do the fall of the monarchy and the exile put an end to its usefulness. The phrase *the ends of the earth* in stanza 1 turns out to have a new and unforeseen dimension when the nation of Israel is scattered worldwide. A still greater breadth of meaning is given to stanza 2's words *enthroned in God's presence for ever*. The collapse of the Davidic kingdom in 587 BC refocused the thoughts of God's people on to a new kind of king, the coming Messiah. The significance of the psalm is not being perverted, but fulfilled, when we see Christ in it. Rightly do Christians use such a prayer for their King's glory and his people's blessing.

Psalm 62

Jeduthun, or Ethan, was one of the leading musicians of the Jerusalem cultus, along with Asaph and Heman. All these names appear in the headings of psalms,[589] and here, where David also figures, the reason is more uncertain than usual. Was Psalm 62 for the choir which Jeduthun led, or which in later years bore his name? Did he provide the setting – 'write the tune' – for it? An English version as non-committal as the original might simply say that this is in some sense or other both a 'David psalm' and a 'Jeduthun psalm'.

We have met much of its language elsewhere, especially the string of titles for God in verses 6–7 (as in 18:2). We have seen very recently poems structured like this one, with two or three equal stanzas (as in 60 and 61). Four features here call for particular notice.

---

[589] Jeduthun has already appeared above Ps. 39.

1. Liturgy and life

Scholars give much thought to how the psalms generally would have been used in the temple cultus in Jerusalem, and who would have sung this or that section.[590] This poem's *I* and *you* and *people* – who did the worshippers suppose them to be? To whom was verse 10 addressed? Did the temple liturgy expect a prophecy at verse 11?

As we have seen, however, the real-life situations that lie behind so many of the psalms are of still greater interest. Even if we cannot be certain what they were, we do know that David himself, for example, both talked and listened to God, just as the Davidic psalms do. How such things did happen historically is likely to be of more practical value to modern readers than how they may have happened liturgically.

Once again the meaning of the phrase *A psalm of David* could include authorship, and once again it could have been the great rebellion that prompted the writing of it. *How long will you assault a man?* cries our psalmist, echoing a psalm in the first David Collection which seems to belong to the same period (4:2). The downfall (v. 3) of one so eminent (v. 4a), brought about by a man of deceit (v. 4b; see 2 Sam. 15:1–6), fits these circumstances. So does the sense of desperation: in spite of many loyal friends, the outlook is so serious that if God does not rescue the psalmist he is doomed. If this is not the King David of 2 Samuel 15 – 16, it must (as the schoolboy said of Second Isaiah) be another person of the same name.

2. Truly and only

At this period of his life maybe more than at any other it is borne in on David that his hope really is in God alone. Six times he expresses that quivering awareness by the little word *'ak*. It can mean 'truly' (v. 4, *fully*), or 'only' (vv. 1, 2, 5, 6, *alone*), or perhaps both (v. 9, *but a*).[591] Instead of trying to find a word for it, an English translation might simply put in italics the words that follow it. 'It is *in God* that my soul finds rest,' says David, '*he* is my rock ... They *really mean* to bring me down ... Yet a *breath*, a *lie*, is all they are.'

The Hebrew adds to the emphasis by putting each *'ak* at the beginning of its line. Then after the first five of them the same facts are stressed in a different way, for verse 7 is a very effective little chiasmus, which might be translated, 'On God rests my safety and honour; my rock and my refuge is God.'[592] As Tate says, *'ak*

---

[590] See pp. 1.74ff., 2.189ff.

[591] One *'ak* at the beginning of the verse covers both 'lowborn' and 'highborn'.

[592] Curiously, the NIV turns this chiasmus inside out, while conveying a similar effect.

statements 'do not come naturally and easily'.[593] We may mouth them glibly at any time, but Psalm 62 is for the times when bitter experience makes us mean them.

3. Silence and speech

Finding rest (vv. 1 and 5) is perhaps misleading. God can certainly give rest to the weary, a chance for repose and recuperation, but something rather different is David's conviction here. What he states in verse 1, and reminds himself to ensure in verse 5, is that his soul is silent, or still, in God's presence.

Silence too may not seem quite the right word, since he obviously has plenty more he wants to say. He will, indeed, be encouraging others to pour out their hearts to God (v. 8), as he has poured out his own at other times. But then we notice that scarcely more than a single verse out of the twelve is addressed to God. Perhaps David's prayers were done before he began the psalm. Prayers of confusion – 'Lord, I don't know what to say'? Prayers of exhaustion – 'Lord, I don't know what else to say'?

The point of these verses, however, is not that the mouth should cease to speak, but that the mind should compose itself to stillness. It aims to get beyond the earthquake, wind, and fire of Horeb, to the 'sound of sheer silence';[594] to have the divine rebuke to the storm on Galilee bring about a 'great calm'.[595] There one begins to see things God's way, and the facts come into focus.

4. Vanity and dependability

We should note how the thought of the psalm develops from stanza to stanza. The soul in stillness may see clearly that God alone is all it needs, but it is not in some mystical trance that enables it to ignore the nastinesses of life: stanza 1 (vv. 1–4) is brutally realistic, and sees also the envy and malice of the enemy.

Though stanza 2 (vv. 5–8) has almost the same first half as stanza 1, it shows that the soul in stillness is not inactive, any more than it is unrealistic. It knows that the inner calm needs to be maintained; the statement of verse 1a becomes the encouragement of verse 5a. In the same way, it turns from the enemies of verses 3–4 to the friends of verse 8, to encourage them also.

The contrast between those who with David put their confidence in God and those who are out *to topple him* is then drawn in a new way in stanza 3 (vv. 9–12). The latter are only a *breath*, yes, truly, just a breath. It is the word used for 'vanity', that which is 'meaningless', in Ecclesiastes.[596] Absalom may have advanced in

[593] Tate, pp. 120–121.   [594] 1 Kgs. 19:12 NRSV.   [595] Mark 4:39 AV.
[596] Eccles. 1:2 AV, NIV.

wealth and power as he steals the kingdom, but in the scales of God
he is a mere nothing. The former have found their rock and refuge
and fortress (all the great solid, weighty, dependable metaphors)
where alone (*'ak!*) they can be found. This is the *one thing God has
spoken* (v. 11), though in his mercy he causes us to hear it twice,[597]
indeed 'at many times and in various ways'.[598]

Between the two, God's friends and God's enemies, there is a
great gulf fixed. That fateful division is the fundamental truth set at
the Psalter's beginning, in Psalm 1. The New Testament sets it
likewise at the end – the end of all things, that is, as Paul says when
quoting verse 12b: 'the day of God's wrath, when his righteous
judgment will be revealed'.[599]

Psalm 63

Unlike its predecessor, this psalm has no very clear shape. There may
be a reason for that, as we shall see. What does help us to grasp
something of its riches is a pairing of themes such as we used in
Psalm 62.

1. Desert and sanctuary

The question of what is metaphorical and what is literal reappears
here. Commentators who focus on how the psalms may have been
used in worship tend to assume that Psalm 63 was for the king to
recite[600] when he was actually *in the sanctuary* (v. 2) but felt as if he
were *in a dry and weary land* (v. 1). Conversely, one could of course
argue for a real desert and a metaphorical temple!

But if we focus instead on how the psalms were composed, the
possibility that the heading of 63 might be something more than
mere fancy suggests that practically everything here could be literal.
The Desert of Judah was the scene of the start of David's journey
into exile at the time of the great rebellion – truly a *weary land*.[601]
He was leaving behind him the Jerusalem sanctuary, where he had
often had a real awareness of God among his people. He did still,
even now, feel safe under the shadow of God's wings (now that *is* a
metaphor), and expected the day to come when treason would be
punished literally by the sword.

Three psalms in the first David Collection, 3, 4, and 5, are
morning or evening prayers, and the first of them was understood
to relate to the time of the great rebellion. This one has a similar
theme, as we shall see in a moment. Might it be the equivalent, here
in the second collection, of those three in the first, as 51 and 56 seem

[597] So NRSV.   [598] Heb. 1:1.   [599] See Rom. 2:5–6.
[600] Speaking of himself in the third person in v. 11, as in 61:6.
[601] The words for *desert* and *weary* figure several times in 2 Sam. 15 – 17.

to be the counterparts of 32 and 34? In each case Book I would contain the more carefully constructed poems and Book II would preserve the earlier, more artless outpourings.

In speaking of the soul that longs for God and values the place where he may be met, this psalm is paralleled also in both Korah Collections, by 42/43 in the first and by 84 in the second.

2. Morning and evening
Clear divisions we may not find, but we do notice that the soul which is thirsty at the beginning of the psalm is by its midpoint confident of being satisfied. Verse 1 and verses 5–6 answer to each other in this way, and in another way also. For *earnestly* the older versions had *early*; there seems to be a connection with a word meaning 'dawn' which should not be lost sight of. This was no doubt in David's mind when halfway through the poem he spoke of the satisfied soul's thinking about God in *the watches of the night*.

We could certainly see this as a double marker (in the morning the thirsty soul, at night the satisfied soul), and use the psalm ourselves in the light of it. Verses 1–4 are very visual. The day stretches before us, and we *can see* what it looks like: a wearisome way with nothing refreshing about it. On the other hand, we remember things we *have seen* in the past, in places where God made himself known to us (and David would have in mind the gathering of God's people rather than a private experience). Verse 2 is not describing a mystical glimpse of the divine. *Seen ... and beheld* means 'gazed ... and realized'; what God is like has been set forth before me in all its richness, primarily of course by his word, and as I have meditated on it it has become real.

When I go to bed, then (vv. 5ff.), and for better or worse can see nothing, whether past glory or present misery, my thoughts of him have a further effect. God not only becomes real, he becomes real in his relation to me. He is my help. My darkness is the shadow of his wings.[602] I do not need to see; I hold on to him (as Ruth 'clung to' Naomi),[603] and he holds on to me.

3. Love and justice
'What God is like', his character, is summed up in his covenant name Yahweh, and his covenant love, or *ḥesed*. Everything that Psalm 63 tells us of these twenty-four hours in the life of David, with prayer and the answers to it at both dawn and dusk ('a day hemmed by prayer rarely unravels'), is an experience of God's covenant love. That, says David, *is better than life* (v. 3).

[602] Cf. Francis Thompson, 'The Hound of Heaven': 'Is my gloom, after all, Shade of His hand outstretched caressingly?' See pp. 2.258–259.
[603] Ruth 1:14, as here in v. 8 ('stay close to').

We may see verses 9–11 as a third and final section of the psalm, or as part of its second half. What we should not imagine is that it brings about an awkward change of gear and does not really belong with the rest. It fits historically, if our psalmist is David at the time of Absalom's revolt. He personally would be heartbroken by his son's death, but he knew all the same that those who set themselves against the Lord's anointed can expect only defeat, and there must in the end be joy – though not a cheap joy – when destroyers are themselves destroyed.

This is justice; so this final part fits into our psalm theologically also, for justice is the other side of the coin of covenant love. God has made his covenant with his people. All of us are either bound by it, or rebels against it. Once again we are confronted with the personal choice, the taking of sides, of Psalm 1. Once again we are made to see, as in Psalm 2, its cosmic and eternal importance. Perhaps it was the last line of Psalm 63 that Paul had in mind when he spoke of the judgment by which 'every mouth' will 'be silenced and the whole world held accountable to God' (Rom. 3:19).

Psalm 64

With regard to its contents, this sits well alongside Psalm 63. True, its structure does seem rather more sophisticated than that of its companion piece, or of others in this second David Collection. However, even the most impromptu verses of a psalmist like David might fall naturally into poetic forms like this chiasmus:

> In God, protection (v. 1);
>   secret conspiracy (v. 2);
>   tongues, arrows, sudden shooting (vv. 3–4);
>   hidden cunning (vv. 5–6);
>   sudden shooting, arrows, tongues (vv. 7–8);
>   public proclamation (v. 9);
> in the Lord, refuge (v. 10).

1. The complaint of the psalmist (v. 1)

Again we shall take it that the heading represents a true tradition of authorship, that the conspiracy of verse 2 is Absalom's, and that the psalmist is David. His circumstances could be similar, perhaps identical, to those of Psalm 63. The difference is that there he was (as it were) seeing them as white on black, while here they are black on white. That is, in 63 he and his security in God were in the foreground, and his enemies and their schemes loomed in the background; here in 64 it is the other way round.

The leaders of the revolt, then, dominate the scene, and give rise to David's *complaint*. The word means not that he is moaning, but that he is simply telling God what is on his mind. For the first verse, like the last, has more to do with his state of mind than with *the threat of the enemy*. Here too we might find a better word, as David asks to be protected not from an outward *threat* but from an inward *dread* of the threat (RSV). By the end of the psalm there is joy instead, as in 63:11. Again we have to remind ourselves that here, as there, it would be a joy derived only from a broad, deep knowledge of God, for it would have to coexist with the anguish of a fearful bereavement, and to survive it. 2 Samuel 18 tells of the 'very foolish, fond old man'[604] (not so old, neither), personally devastated by the loss of his worthless son. The joy in the psalm has to be a deeper and more enduring emotion than the grief in the story.

2. The conspiracy of the wicked

What David and his fleeing loyalists expected to see following hard on their heels was a host of Absalom's armed men. These, like Saul's thugs in Psalm 59, were the *evildoers* who 'carry out the ringleaders' designs'.[605] Behind them were the ringleaders themselves, the *conspiracy of the wicked*. For the nouns *conspiracy* and [*noisy*] *crowd* we find in Psalm 2:1–2 the corresponding verbs, 'gather together' and 'rage'.[606] This psalm is describing a classic instance of the rebellion against God of which that one warned us in the Psalter's preamble.

Behind *them*, the conspirators, is the all-pervading wickedness of the human heart (v. 6), which is 'deceitful above all things and beyond cure'.[607] David's, and ours, are just the same as Absalom's; we do well to confess our own sins when we deplore other people's – the reason perhaps why 51, a 'confession' psalm, was placed at the head of a sequence of 'betrayal' psalms.

Yet again the emphasis on the sins of the tongue is remarkable. The conflict of 2 Samuel 15 – 18 involves real swords and arrows aplenty, but it is the *words* of the wicked, metaphorical swords and arrows (v. 3), which are their deadly weapons throughout this passage. And it is Absalom and Ahithophel plotting behind David's back, not Ziba flattering and Shimei cursing him to his face,[608] who are reflected in Psalm 64. We recognize this world: a world where words are used to rob and deceive, to discredit and hurt, and where the culprits go undetected, for '*Who will see them?*'

No wonder David cries out to the only one who can 'see', and 'consider', and 'take it in hand' (10:14).

[604] William Shakespeare, *King Lear*, IV.vii.60.   [605] Kidner, p. 228.
[606] So AV/RV/NIV (1979).   [607] Jer. 17:9.
[608] 2 Sam. 15:1–6; 16:15 – 17:13; 16:1–4; 16:5–14.

3. The works of God (v. 9)

When it does come, God's response to the convoluted schemings of the wicked is forthright. He pays them back in their own coin (vv. 4 and 7). 'They shoot, and shall be shot,' says Spurgeon; 'a greater archer than they shall take sure aim at their heart'. More than that, he repays them *with* their own coin, using not merely weapons like theirs but their very own weapons, words they themselves have spoken returning to destroy them (v. 8). Furthermore, his justice is sudden, catching them as unprepared as their victims were. And their downfall is sure; the future tenses of verses 7–9 are in fact all perfects, the 'perfect of certainty' or 'prophetic perfect', meaning that if we could look back from some viewpoint in the future we should see that it really had happened: 'God *has* shot them! They *have* been struck down!' we should say.

Most encouraging of all, he will act in such a way that *all mankind will fear* and *proclaim the works of God*. Not until the end of our age, maybe; but the day when wickedness in high places is finally called to account will be the day of his universal glory.

Psalm 65

The next four psalms are also called songs. Though we can only guess at the precise meaning of this double title, it does at least serve to mark off 65 – 68 as a group. Certainly we are here breathing a different air from that of 51 – 64, a sequence of psalms so readily identifiable with many of the conflicts that harassed David.

This, the first of the group, divides into three sections so clearly that some suppose it to be a combining of poems which were originally separate. The fact is that the psalm as a whole sings not only of one and the same God as we see him in the temple, in the world, and in the harvest, but also of the way in which each of these aspects of him is related to the others. It has a profound unity.

1. God in the temple (vv. 1–4)

Perhaps with some relief, after following for so long the wanderings of David, we find ourselves back in God's house in Jerusalem. The psalmist assures us at the outset that *temple* in verse 4 means Zion; it is the literal temple (or tabernacle if the psalm comes from David's time),[609] not the metaphorical one of 29:9. Conversely, *Zion* in verse 1 means the temple, rather than simply the hill, or the city on it.

It is not temple liturgy that concerns us here, though that is an interest we could pursue with this or with any psalm. The beating heart of the Jerusalem cultus was not its liturgy but its system of

---

[609] See p. 2.257.

animal sacrifice. For the temple to be a meeting place between God and his people, they had to be reminded incessantly that they met him there on the grounds not of their merit but of his grace. Every one of them, even the high priest, was a sinner needing forgiveness, and 'without the shedding of blood there is no forgiveness'.[610]

It is in exactly this sense that the Lord's supper, by whatever name we call it, is at the heart of New Testament worship. It looks back to Christ crucified as the Old Testament sacrifices looked forward to him. There is of course far more to worship than this. By the shed blood, God brings his people to himself in order to speak to them; the preached word in all its variety equips them for the godly life; and that in turn comes back to him in praise and prayer. Yet they must be brought home repeatedly to the sacrifice that deals with sin.

So each of these four verses goes to the heart of the temple worship. The psalm as a whole is one of the most exuberant in the book, but verse 1, appropriate to this solemn opening theme, begins literally 'Praise is stillness' (as in 62:1). The hush centres our thoughts on the most important thing of all, in New Testament terms the cross. It is the gospel of the shed blood, when it is 'lifted up', that 'will draw all men' (v. 2; John 12:32–33). It is for those who are keenly conscious of the power of sin (v. 3).[611] It is the only way in to the enjoyment of the *good things* we find in his presence (v. 4).

2. God in the world (vv. 5–8)

The God *of* Israel is not confined *to* Israel, as the first section has already said. The RSV may be right in combining verses 2 and 3: *To thee shall all flesh come on account of sins*. The Saviour who answers us, here among his people, is also *the hope of all the ends of the earth*. The earth's physical structure is his: the mountains may seem 'massively secure' and the seas 'menacingly wild', but we neither trust the one nor fear the other; rather, we trust and fear him who is Maker and Master of both.[612] Its nations too are his, their turmoil as much under his control as that of the ocean. It is surely not just the beauties of sunrise and sunset that are called to glorify him, but people, even *those living far away … where morning dawns and evening fades*.

In this section's heading, *world* has not its bad sense (those who oppose God, contrasting with the church), but its good sense (the rest of God's creation, complementing the church). The first two sections of the psalm illustrate one of the grand themes of Scripture.

---

[610] Heb. 9:22.

[611] *Overwhelmed* means not so much drowned in its quantity as gripped in its power.

[612] Kidner, p. 231.

The Lord of Exodus, who calls Israel to be his people, is also the God of Genesis, who made them and their world in the first place. At the other end of the Bible, Revelation celebrates both the Creator of all (4:11) and the Redeemer of his own (5:9–12).

Yet all this may raise a question. Grand theme though it may be, this pairing of church and world, of God as Creator and Redeemer, what is it doing here? Does verse 3 refer to a particular deliverance from sin, and verses 7–8 to a particular stilling of the turmoil of the nations which brings praise to God? Or is this simply a psalm which sings of God's grace and power in quite general terms?

3. God in the harvest (vv. 9–13)

Before we address that question, we should briefly answer an earlier one: whether this third section really belongs with the first two. These verses clearly have to do with a harvest, and a good one, either on its way or reaching its climax. If verses 1–4 are about the hidden work of the Redeemer who takes away our sin and makes us his own, and verses 5–8 about the visible work of the Creator who controls our environment, it is not hard to see their logical (and theological) link with verses 9–13. What God has done for us spiritually, as Redeemer, he assures us of concretely, as Creator, by bringing his creative power to bear on the provision of our needs. He is the Provider, not of riches or luxuries, but of necessary and appropriate blessings. For a farming community like Israel, that meant a good harvest.

Just so, in Mark 2:1–12 Jesus is concerned first with the sins of the paralysed man, then with his practical and physical needs; and as he deals with both, God is glorified by the visible fact of the man's cure.

Was Psalm 65 for a particular occasion? It could have been. Half a dozen of its general observations would come into sharp focus if it were taken to be a reflection of events during and after the Assyrian assault on Jerusalem in 701 BC. A string of evidences in Isaiah 37 latch on to verses in the psalm. A particular prayer of King Hezekiah's (v. 2 here) is recorded at length there. He saw the attack as a rebuke for the nation's sins (v. 3). God routed the invaders by awesome deeds (v. 5), stilling the turmoil of the nations (v. 7). As a confirming sign to his people that it was indeed the Lord their Redeemer who was also controlling the world scene, he promised them unexpected harvests in both the years of invasion, even though they would not be able to resume normal farming until the third year (vv. 9–13; Is. 37:30).

In such real-life circumstances the truth of God becomes equally real. It is he – the repeated *You* of verses 9–11 – who brings about the harvest, both in principle and in detail, and to him that the rich farmlands are pictured as returning praise. We of the supermarket culture may smile at the rustic image of God the farmer driving a great waggon along the country lanes, so laden with produce that the surplus tumbles off it. But in a world where so many are hungry, those of us who do have enough to eat should be moved to say perhaps more often than we do, 'God has done this.'

Psalm 66

The occasion for a psalm like 65 to be sung in Old Testament times would have been, not what we call a harvest festival (a fairly recent invention of our own), but one of the three historic festivals in Israel's calendar. The harvesting of a variety of crops began in April and ended in October, and Passover, Weeks, and Tabernacles fitted into that sequence.[613] The second in this group of four song-psalms, 66, would similarly have suited one of these.

It divides into two major sections: verses 1–12 are for *us*, the congregation, to sing, and at verse 13 *I*, an individual lead singer, or cantor, takes over. Two *selahs* divide the first section into three, and another divides the second section into two. As we work through these five stanzas, the possible identity of both festival and lead singer will emerge.

1. Great expectations (vv. 1–4)

Except for Book II's regular *God* instead of *LORD*, Psalm 66 begins with the same words as Psalm 100. Some years ago an updated version of the latter turned them into 'Jubilate everybody'! While singers in a modern congregation would naturally take themselves to be encouraging one another with these words, the psalmist had a bigger vision. He expected his singers to be looking out to the wider world – to be telling those who did not yet recognize the Lord of Israel that they, and not just God's own people, should take note of what he had done, and bow before him.

What was more, if they meant what they were singing they would be expecting this to happen. Does that raise an awkward question? Both they and we should be able to answer it, in at least four ways. The earth itself, as distinct from the sinners who live on it, does recognize its Maker in this way; the world of nature obeys his laws. Then there is a response of men and women from many other nations besides God's nation, who already do see what he has done and come to worship him. Thirdly, there is the eagerness of his people to tell others of him so that they too will do so. And there is the confidence that the day is coming when 'every knee' will in fact 'bow' before this great Lord.[614]

[613] See Lev. 23.   [614] Phil. 2:10.

The world is being urged to *sing the glory of his name* and *give to him glorious praise* (v. 2 NRSV). As the theme of its worship is to be his glory, what he has done and what he is, so the quality of its worship is to be equally glorious, as far as it can make it so. If we require such standards of others, how much more should our own worship be appropriate to such a God – 'never trivial, never pretentious'?[615]

2. Vivid recollections (vv. 5–7)

What the church bids the world look at is God's *tremendous ... dealings with mankind* (v. 5 NEB). That means first and foremost the events of the exodus. When the worshippers say, *He turned the sea into dry land; they passed through the river on foot. There we rejoiced in him* (v. 6 NRSV),[616] the sea and the river could be the Red Sea at one end of Israel's journey to freedom and the River Jordan at the other end, each crossed by a miracle, or else both terms could be describing the first of these. But in either case, why *we rejoiced*?

A liturgical re-enactment of those events, which some suppose to be the setting for our psalm, would no doubt be very dramatic. But far profounder is the biblical view that the once-for-all drama of the exodus set an eternal pattern, which reappears in the New Testament as the crucifixion, and which is a present reality to all God's people. 'Were you there when they crucified my Lord?' Yes, I was; that was where Egypt was destroyed for me, where the power of sin was broken and new life began. By faith, in solidarity with the church of all ages, we know that *we were there*, and it is that climactic event of history that we invite the nations to *come and see*. Passover is clearly the most fitting festival for the psalm; and if *selah* means the point at which Scripture is to be read, suitable readings are not far to seek.[617]

3. Hard times (vv. 8–12)

The other side of the exodus experience, contrasting with the heady days of deliverance, was the long years of misery from which Israel was at last being rescued. That too would be real to this later congregation. They would know their own equivalents of the enslavement, the burdens, and the cruelty of verses 11–12. They could put themselves in the shoes of those who had suffered for four centuries in the furnace of Egypt[618] and had marvelled at the events

---

[615] Kidner, p. 234.

[616] So the Hebrew, followed by the earlier English versions (AV/RV/RSV).

[617] Viz., in OT days key passages from Exod. 12 – 15, and for us, NT references to Passover and the exodus such as 1 Cor. 5:7.

[618] See Gen. 15:13; Exod. 12:40–41; Deut. 4:20; 1 Kgs. 8:51.

of that single night that brought them dry-shod across the Red Sea, *through fire and through water ... to a spacious place.*[619]

But with the reading of Psalm 65 fresh in our minds, we may think it more likely that the Jerusalem congregation was not simply identifying with the experience of its ancestors, but was looking back on a recent experience of its own. Perhaps this psalm, like that one, belongs to the days of the Assyrian invasion of 701 BC. Again there are parallels with Isaiah 37, which tells us how the Assyrian king rose up against the God of Israel (v. 7 here) and how Hezekiah prayed that God would see his pride (v. 7) and the nations would see his downfall (v. 5). It is Isaiah, too, who speaks elsewhere of the testing and refining of Israel (v. 10) and her preservation through fire and water (v. 12).[620] It is in that light that Israel is to see the traumas of the invasion of her land and the siege of her capital.

Such testing, whether long ago, or recent, or both, is very clearly seen to be God's doing. The repeated *you* in verses 10–12 parallels that in 65:9–11. Both psalms go back behind second causes to see God as the first cause of everything. There it was the blessings of harvest, here it is the hardships of discipline, for which he is responsible. He is a God who knows exactly what he is doing, both in the happy times and in the hard times.

4. Wholehearted offerings (vv. 13–15)

Now the solo voice takes up the theme of praise. If we ask whose words these will be, the first and obvious answer is the psalmist, who composed them. Then we take it that the singer of them, if not the psalmist himself, would be a cantor or choir leader. We can go further. We know that temple worship was not, as its equivalent so often is today, the interest of a religious minority, but something in which the leaders of the nation regularly played an active part. We know of occasions in the period of the monarchy when the king himself would take a prominent role in the cultus.

In a psalm like 66, then, we may imagine the *we* sections being sung by the choir or the congregation, and the *I* sections perhaps by the king. As in governing he represented God to the nation, so in worship he would represent the nation to God.

However, if these verses really are spoken or sung by the king, there is something personal about them which strikes a deeper note than a merely formal act of worship on behalf of his subjects. And if the background to verses 1–12 really is Sennacherib's invasion, the king is Hezekiah, and he has every reason to speak personally. He,

---

[619] Ps. 66:12 NRSV. *A place of abundance* (NIV) would suit better the crossing of Jordan into the Promised Land.

[620] Is. 1:25; 43:1–2.

with his people, has been in real trouble. He has brought agonized prayers and made heartfelt vows to God. And now he comes to say thank you, with burnt offerings, the kind which literally go up in smoke: nothing is left, for this is a symbol of the giving of everything to God, the total devotion of the grateful heart. It is not too far-fetched to suppose him himself to be both author and first singer of the psalm. Certainly the rest of it lends weight to the supposition.

5. Personal testimonies (vv. 16–20)

Is it fanciful to imagine Hezekiah as a worthy successor to his illustrious ancestor David, not only as a great and godly king, but as the composer of memorable psalms? Isaiah 37 – 38, chapters which describe some of the crucial events of his reign, also give us one of his compositions in full. They could be the background to this one too. The trouble already mentioned in verse 14 would have been double trouble: as well as the terrifying onslaught of Sennacherib's armies, he had had to cope with an illness that threatened to be fatal. In both cases he *cried out* for help (v. 17), keenly conscious of the need to repent of his sin (v. 18), and could in due course testify to answered prayer (v. 19).

This closing section of the psalm has the genuine ring of personal testimony. It is one of the happy paradoxes of such scriptures that the more definitely they seem to belong to a particular individual, the more readily usable they are by any of us. And how God can use a church where this happens – where an individual says to his or her fellow-believers, *Come and listen … let me tell you what he has done for me* (v. 16), and where the fellowship as a whole then says to all around, *Come and see what God has done* (v. 5)!

Psalm 67

In a more concise form, Psalm 67 shows the same spirit and has the same themes as its neighbours, and may belong to the same occasion.

1. Two roots

Rather like 65, with its twin roots in the Genesis story of creation and the Exodus story of redemption, 67 grows both from a blessing in Moses' time and from an earlier one in Abraham's.

Very familiar are the words God gave to Moses, for his brother Aaron and every succeeding high priest to use in blessing Israel. Its opening lines are clearly the model for those of our psalm: 'The LORD bless you and keep you; the LORD make his face shine upon you and be gracious to you' (Num. 6:24–25).

Our psalmist builds his poem on this text, developing it in the light of the original blessing given centuries before to Abraham: 'I will make you into a great nation and I will bless you; I will make your name great, *and you will be a blessing* ... All peoples on earth will be blessed through you' (Gen. 12:2–3). In Abraham's time God chose this family; in Moses' time he would make it his people, his nation; yet it is the smaller company that is given the greater prospect. Standing further back, we can see further ahead, and that is the vision of Psalm 67.

2. *Two themes*
All four psalms in this group touch on the theme of harvest. It does not have the prominence that the NIV of verse 6 seems to give it ('If verses 1–5 happen, then what we are really hoping for, i.e. the harvest, will follow'). What the psalmist is looking forward to is something infinitely greater than that. Abundant crops are his starting point, not his goal. *The earth has yielded its increase* (NRSV), and that is a metaphor for his other, grander, theme.

In New Testament terms, this is the spread of the gospel. The simple chiastic shape of the poem helps us to see it:

> Bless us, and all the nations (vv. 1–2);
>> may all the peoples praise you (v. 3)
>>> for the joy of your universal rule (v. 4)!
>> May all the peoples praise you (v. 5)!
> Bless us, and all the ends of the earth (vv. 6–7).

Verse 3, repeated word for word as verse 5, is a kind of refrain. What is the great object? That God should be glorified by all the nations: the refrain states it twice over. How would such a thing work out? The core or pivot of the poem, verse 4, sees it happening only when God governs and guides them. And how could that come about? By their seeing the gospel, say verses 1–2 and 6–7, *in a blessed and radiant Israel*. The gathering in of the nations – now that *is* a harvest. Jesus said the same (Matt. 9:36–38; John 4:30–35).

3. *Two applications*
'Lord, the light of your love is shining,' sings a twentieth-century psalmist, Graham Kendrick; 'Shine, Jesus, shine, fill *this land* with the Father's glory.' Isaac Watts versified our psalm in a similar way back in 1707: 'Shine, mighty God, *on Britain* shine'! These are worthy prayers; but they are not what Psalm 67 is about.

The 1834 version by Henry Lyte got the point: 'God of mercy, God of grace, Show the brightness of thy face: Shine upon us, Saviour, shine, Fill *thy church* with light divine.' It is when the people of God are alight with joy and praise, and are themselves ruled and guided by him, that his ways and his salvation will be known among the peoples around.

The 1552 Prayer Book had set its own version, the Deus Misereatur, alongside the 1549 book's Nunc Dimittis, the Song of Simeon (Luke 2:29–32). A song of praise from the New Testament, about Christ who is the light, was backed by one from the Old, about the church which reflects the light. That is the best kind of evangelism. Indeed it is the regular way (to revert to our other metaphor) in which the field of the world is to be harvested.

Psalm 68

This is the fourth and last of the great poems in Book II that share the heading 'song-psalm', and deal, even if only briefly, with the theme of harvest. Psalm 68 has been used traditionally in Jewish synagogue worship at the feast of Weeks, or Pentecost. For Christians too it is a Pentecost psalm, for reasons we shall see later.

1. Impressions

The old Prayer Book version of this psalm would present many oddities to new readers today. God's name of Jah, the high hills that hop, someone who has 'lien among the pots' – all very strange; though they might find some of it striking, perhaps even familiar, like the man who was surprised to discover, when he first read *Hamlet*, that it was full of quotations.

However, you may get to know it and may try to understand it and yet still find that its problems do not evaporate. If it seems a difficult psalm at the outset, that impression will be confirmed, not dispelled, as you go on. An exposition based on the NIV, like this one, may not always make sense to readers with a different version of the Bible open beside them. Is it the men in the camps or the women at home who divide the spoil (v. 12)? Is it *campfires* or *sheepfolds* in verse 13, *assembly* or *fountain* in verse 26, *envoys* or *bronze* in verse 31? Does the Lord bear us or our burdens (v. 19)?

Even where the translation is certain, the meaning may be far from clear. Is the gold-and-silver dove of verse 13 a trophy captured in battle, or the victors' womenfolk dressed up in plundered finery, or Israel enjoying the fruits of conquest? In verse 14, is the snow on the Black Mountain of Zalmon the scattered enemy armies, or their weapons, or their bones; or does it mean that they were blown away as if by a blizzard? And whatever are the *hairy crowns* of verse 21?[621] No wonder this has been called 'the most difficult of all the psalms'.[622]

---

[621] Perhaps a style that warriors affected, indicating strength, recalling Samson's long hair.

[622] Tate, p. 170, quoting W. F. Albright.

2. *Connections*

In a tapestry so full of glittering but perplexing detail, there are at any rate some indicators to tell us where we are. Like its predecessor, this psalm looks back to Moses, and to the brief but pregnant liturgies he gave to Israel. As 67 grew out of his blessing in Numbers 6:24–26, so 68 elaborates (though at much greater length) his prayer in Numbers 10:35.

This in turn connects with the days of David, and suggests that we may have here another 'David' psalm which the poet king himself composed. If the words 'Rise up, O LORD! May your enemies be scattered; may your foes flee before you' were used, as Numbers tells us, 'whenever the ark set out', they would most certainly have figured among the ceremonies of the last splendid stage of its journey. It had taken hundreds of years to get from Mount Sinai, where it was made, to its final home on Mount Zion (v. 17).[623] To David fell the privilege of organizing the procession for that day (vv. 24–27). The event is described in 2 Samuel 6:12–19. What could be more likely than the composition of a choral work specially for the occasion, what could be more apt than an extravagant fantasia based on the three-line prayer of Moses used every time the ark moved, and who but 'Israel's singer of songs' would have written it?

David, if he is indeed the author, has in mind a further famous event, one between Moses' time and his own, the classic instance of an Israelite triumph over Canaanite forces in the days of the judges. Verses 7–8, 12, 13, and 18 all echo the Song of Deborah in Judges 5.[624] The first of these four passages is of particular interest. For Deborah, the God who had led her colleague Barak and his army to victory was the God of Sinai, Moses' God. Whether literally or metaphorically, the earth quaked and a storm raged when God fought for Israel in their time, just as when God met with Israel in Moses' time.[625] For David, both what God did when Israel left Egypt and what he did when she settled in Canaan are prime examples of the kind of thing he does regularly. The installation of the ark in Jerusalem is for him the latest and greatest instance of the same thing: *Our God is a God who saves* (v. 20).

3. *Suggestions*

Such pointers do not alter the fact that Psalm 68 bristles with problems. How can it be user-friendly when we repeatedly trip over its mystifying details?

[623] If that is what the verse means. See below.
[624] In order, Judg. 5:4–5; 30; 12; 16.
[625] Cf. Judg. 5:4–5, 20–21; Heb. 12:18.

One approach is to think of it as a television commentary, or the soundtrack of a film, which for some reason is not coming over clearly. (In v. 4, for instance: 'I didn't quite catch – did he say "the rider of the *deserts*" or "the rider of the *heavens*"?') Although every word of Scripture is important, some matter more than others; the truths we need to hear plainly God has spoken plainly, and what is less plain is less important. God rides both upon the clouds and through the deserts, and there are other scriptures to back each of these two statements, whichever David originally wrote. What we must do in such cases is to try to grasp the gist of the passage – not to fret over what we can't hear, but to appreciate what we can hear. What we see, the 'visuals' or picture language, is generally clear enough.

To put it another way, we are especially likely to be unable to see the wood for the trees if we spend too much time scratching our heads over this or that specimen which we cannot identify. If in a psalm like this one we stand back from the individual trees, we shall be in a better position to get an overall picture of the wood, and shall find ourselves exclaiming at its magnificence.

The main image that David has in his own mind's eye is a moving picture, not a static one. He sees in the arrival of the ark in Jerusalem a miniature of the history of Israel, from the exodus to his own time: the events of that entire period have been *the procession of my God and King into the sanctuary* (v. 24). It is a procession notable more for excitement than for stateliness – David 'danced before the LORD with all his might'.[626] Indeed in yet another metaphor the poem as a whole has been likened to a cataract ('the wild cataract leaps in glory', we might say),[627] such is its phenomenal vigour.

4. Explanations

As always, it is helpful to try to see the way a psalm is put together. In this case we seem to have nine stanzas averaging four verses each, mostly following the paragraphs of the NIV.

If the general picture is as has just been suggested, we might put verses 1–3 into the mouth of Moses as God is about to rescue Israel, *the righteous*, and destroy Egypt, *the wicked*. Let him arise, and act! His destruction of his enemies is balanced in verses 4–6 by his care for his own, whether he is riding with them through the desert or coming down to meet them in the thundercloud of Sinai. *His holy dwelling* is of course wherever he happens to be, and this memorable description of the gracious acts of God will be recognized by all who cry to him, whoever they happen to be.

[626] 2 Sam. 6:14.   [627] Kidner, p. 238; Lord Tennyson, *The Princess*, iv. Introd.

Next, forty years are condensed into four verses (7–10). God marches at the head of his people out of Egypt, *through the wasteland*, and into Canaan. Earthquake and storm mean Sinai, just after the start of their journeyings, and perhaps also the victory of Deborah and Barak, after the end of them. A gentler rain refreshes God's *inheritance*, the people or the land or both, once they have *settled in it*; here, briefly, is the harvest theme. But the main picture of the stanza is the march. Long after Isaac Watts wrote the hymn 'Come ye that love the Lord', it had a refrain added to it by some well-meaning Victorian editor, 'We're marching to Zion'. Whether he would have approved, we do not know; but the hymn does use the 'marching' metaphor, and two verses of it suggest that he had Psalm 68 in mind:

> The God that rules on high,
> That all the earth surveys,
> That rides upon the stormy sky,
> And calms the roaring seas;

> This awful God is ours,
> Our Father and our love;
> He will send down his heavenly powers,
> To carry us above.

In spite of the puzzles with which verses 11–14 tantalize us, they are clearly about Israel's conquest of *the kings in the land*. There are as we have seen two or three references to Judges 4–5; such conflicts persisted well into the reign of David (2 Sam. 8). All God's victories are to be seen as rescue, or salvation. All the way from Moses' time to David's time,[628] it was the privilege of women to be 'proclaimers' of these victories. The word in verse 11b is feminine; and it means one who tells good news. Isaiah too uses it in his thrilling later chapters – 40:9; 52:7; and especially 61:1–2, since that passage is taken up by Jesus as the key to his own ministry in Luke 4:18.

But now at last (vv. 15–19) the ark has arrived at Mount Zion. There, rather than on any more imposing height, God *chooses to reign*. What the Hebrew strikingly says in verse 17 is that *the Lord is among them, Sinai is in the sanctuary* (RV mg.). All the glories that you have heard were there then, you can experience here now.

In the next four verses, the rescuings and bringings out achieved by God's victory (so v. 20 calls them literally) are bound to involve destruction as well as salvation. Verse 23 recognizes the fact, without

---

[628] Exod. 15:20–21; 1 Sam. 18:6–7, and v. 25 here.

revelling in it. But from this point on, all is joy and praise. The cultus in action, so often reconstructed by the scholars, is described in verses 24–27 by someone who knows it, as it is in 2 Samuel 6. Two southern and two northern tribes stand for the whole *assembly of Israel*. Benjamin, being Saul's, and Judah, being David's, are also royal tribes, and Jerusalem stands on the border between them.

Verses 28–31 call on God finally to subdue the nations that oppose his will (the *beast among the reeds* is Egypt), and verses 32–35 call on the nations to recognize him. His people in particular know his majestic rule, and his world in general is under his powerful control.

5. Implications

When Paul refers to half a verse from this psalm, we should not imagine that he is lifting a dozen words out of their context to suit his own purposes. On the contrary, that one sentence distils the entire psalm, which is what the apostle has in mind in quoting it. Its quotation brings together not only Ephesians 4:8 and Psalm 68:18, but Judges 5:12 as well. The fine phrase about leading *captivity captive* appears in the AV and RV of all three, and in the Prayer Book version of the psalm. Our chief interest, however, is the lines on either side of it, not drawn from Judges, about ascension and gifts.

Here, as elsewhere, something clear stands alongside something obscure. God the King, represented by the ark, and David his viceroy, are going up to the holy mountain in their victory procession (v. 24). Paul takes the event to be a foreshadowing of the great going up, the ascension of Christ after his victory on the cross. Nothing can be clearer. What is not clear is the curious change in the wording: *received gifts from men* in David's psalm, 'gave gifts to men' in Paul's letter.

If Ephesians 4 understands the whole sweep of the psalm, from Egypt to Zion, as a picture of the saving work of Christ, then both phrases are equally true. All, friend and foe alike, pay tribute to the great Old Testament victor: naturally his people also will be enriched by his conquests, but the psalm focuses on what they give to him. All God's people will be blessed by the triumph of the greater King: of course all will give him their tribute too, but the New Testament passage focuses on what he gives to them.

Paul saw, as David could not, how the *kingdoms of the earth* would be brought to *sing praise to the Lord* (v. 32). What the ascended Christ would give to his people was infinitely more wonderful than anything they could give to him: the gift of his own Spirit, the manifold gifts the Spirit would bring with him, the gift of Spirit-filled leaders, all in order to transform them themselves into the means of making God known throughout the world. Yes, this is a psalm for Ascension and Pentecost, and it celebrates harvest too. *When he ascended on high ... and gave gifts to men*, the first result was a gathering in of 3,000 souls. 'Exalted to the right hand of God, he has received from the Father the promised Holy Spirit and has poured out what you now see and hear,' says Peter in Acts 2:33.

Psalm 69

The suggestion that Psalm 68 might have seemed to be 'full of quotations' meant that readers might have found it to be the original home of a heap of familiar biblical phrases whose whereabouts they had forgotten. To say the same about Psalm 69 means rather more than that. Many phrases here are familiar from other parts of the Bible as well. It has similarities to other psalms; it may tie in with other Old Testament books; and along with 22 and 110 it is one of the three psalms most often quoted in the New Testament.

1. Echoes from Book I
Here in Book II, the cry of the fainting heart has been frequent in the shorter poems of the second David Collection. Even among the Korah psalms, normally so buoyant, 44:13–16 has bewailed the kind of 'reproach', 'scorn', 'disgrace', and 'shame' which so burdens this one.

If we return to Book I, and work back through the longer psalms in the first David Collection, we are reminded of at least three which spoke in terms now echoed in 69. Assuming for the sake of argument the same author in every case, in 40 he had already been rescued from the mire and the pit in which here he is still sinking (vv. 2, 14, 15). There he was already singing the new song which here comes into view only towards the end (v. 30). In both psalms it is clear that a right attitude to God is more important than animal sacrifice, that is, formal religion (v. 31).

In 38, we found earlier signs (in admittedly different circumstances) of his distress (here in v. 2) and of his failing strength and sight (v. 3), of the fact that his enemies hated him without reason (v. 4) although he did recognize his guilt and folly (v. 5), and of his desertion by those close to him (v. 8).

Already 31:9–11 had spoken of 'distress' and 'eyes ... weak with sorrow'; not only of 'enemies' but of 'the utter contempt of my neighbours' and of 'friends ... who ... flee from me'. 69 is also foreshadowed in the sudden change from wretchedness to praise with which 31 ends.

Closest of all the Book I parallels to 69 is 22. We should look at this comparison in more detail.

2. Parallels with Psalm 22

It is not that the wording of one psalm often appears in the other also. Here in 69, verse 3 recalls 'my tongue sticks to the roof of my mouth' (22:15), verse 19 recalls 'scorned by men and despised by the people' (22:6), and verse 32 recalls 'the poor will eat and be satisfied; they who seek the LORD will praise him – may your hearts live for ever!' (22:26); but that is practically all. No; it is much more a matter of a common theme. These are two poems each of which is a heartfelt cry to God from someone in great distress, the object of general scorn, yet confident in the end of an outcome which will bring praise to God. The three pairs of verses just noted represent these three thematic strands in each psalm.

There is a further correspondence, of a different kind. In 22 we noticed a feature which suggested a sensible way of dividing the psalm. It started with 'me' and 'my groaning'; 22:3 began 'Yet you …'; 22:6, 'But I …'; and 22:9, 'Yet you …' To-ing and fro-ing of this kind was observable at least down to 22:21, and possibly further. We find that in 69 the psalmist's attention shifts in the same way, and the alternation gives this psalm also a satisfying shape. On this basis, it has five sections, beginning successively with the words *Save me* (v. 1), *You know* (v. 5), *But I pray* (v. 13), *You know* (v. 19), *I will praise* (v. 30). We shall work through them in order in a moment, considering first who the psalmist, the *I*, might be.

3. Cries of Old Testament pain

Is the *David* in this psalm's heading the author of it? If so, there is, as with 22, no obvious event in his life which 69 might reflect. The nearest we can get to it is to suppose that his enthusiasm for the temple his son was to build (*zeal for your house*, v. 9), including a big financial contribution as well as detailed plans,[629] landed him in some deeply embarrassing affair. He was *forced to restore what [he] did not steal* (v. 4). Whatever lies behind that phrase, enemies contrived to make him seem guilty, when he had been at worst merely foolish, and most people believed them.[630]

However, it is odd that a calamity like the one described here is nowhere alluded to in the histories, not even in Samuel/Kings, which is brutally honest about the failings of its great men. Nor does such an event readily fit in to the life and times of David's descendant Hezekiah, another suggested author for 22, except that when the Assyrians invaded his kingdom he would certainly have prayed that God would *save Zion and rebuild the cities of Judah* (v. 35).

A hundred years later the prophet Jeremiah lived through similar upheavals. He too has been canvassed as a possible author of both

[629] Cf. 1 Chr. 28:11 – 29:5.   [630] So Motyer, pp. 528–529.

the psalms in question, and 69 in particular is full of echoes of his prophecy.[631] In his case the *miry depths* were quite literal; King Zedekiah had a sneaking regard for him, but was putty in the hands of the powerful men who were Jeremiah's enemies, and the prophet was imprisoned in a pit of mud (vv. 2, 14–15; Jer. 38:6). In his time Israel would actually become a *captive people* (v. 33), and there really would be a need for God to *rebuild the cities of Judah* (v. 35).

Whichever of the Old Testament poets wrote 69, whether famous or obscure, it is like 22 in one further respect: the New Testament relates it directly to Christ. From start to finish 22 could have been uttered by him, with truth and passion, at Calvary. It is not quite the same with 69 – he could not, for example, have spoken of his folly and guilt, as verse 5 does – but a similar wealth of quotations and allusions shows how the early church regarded our present psalm.

4. 'The sufferings of Christ' (vv. 1–29)

The first section, verses 1–4, is centred on *me*, the suffering servant of God. There could scarcely be a more unnerving image of what it was like for Christ to be forsaken by his Father. Psalm 22:1 gave him his words; these verses give a picture – a flood, or (worse) a quicksand, with nothing firm to grasp in any direction, as the psalmist vainly calls for help and looks for God. If that kind of disorientation is your nightmare, Christ has been through it before you, and for you. It is verse 4, however, that he actually quotes, and that not on Good Friday but on Maundy Thursday, in the calm before the storm. To the disciples in the upper room he explains that he will go to the cross because of those who *hate [him] without reason.*

> Why, what hath my Lord done?
> What makes this rage and spite?
> He made the lame to run,
> He gave the blind their sight.
> Sweet injuries!
> Yet they at these
> Themselves displease,
> And 'gainst him rise.[632]

According to the passage in John (15:18–25), such hatred is born precisely where the evidences of the gospel are seen but rejected.

We do not know in what sense the psalmist was *forced to restore what [he] did not steal* (v. 4), or why it was reckoned as folly or guilt

[631] See the many references in Kirkpatrick, pp. 396–407.
[632] Samuel Crossman, 'My song is love unknown'.

(v. 5). It led, at all events, to two further foreshadowings of Christ in verses 5–12, the second section. Christ too could have told his Father *You know* – not of course how he had sinned (in that respect he would obviously have distanced himself from the psalmist), but how he had identified himself with his Father's house (v. 9a) and with his Father's cause (v. 9b). In his cleansing of the temple his disciples saw a zeal for God's house like the psalmist's zeal (John 2:17). It would in due course open out into a passionate concern for the temple in its widest sense, that is, the church, not as a building or an organization but as his own holy people. And he was so committed to his Father's will that Paul could see the second part of the verse also come true in its fullest sense in him (Rom. 15:3). As Jesus said, Father and Son stand together: insult the one, and you insult the other.[633]

The third section, verses 13–18, begins with the words *But I ...* Again we hear of the mire and the flood, and now too of the pit. In this section however the psalmist seems to be in touch with God again. His pleas for rescue from his distress are no less agonized, but the repeated *I* and *me* and *my* of the first section are now in the context of repeated prayer to *you* for *your great mercy*. Here God is no longer inaccessible. Perhaps this part of the pattern corresponds to Christ's prayer in Gethsemane ('Not my will, but yours be done')[634] or his last words from the cross ('Into your hands I commit my spirit');[635] the New Testament is silent on the matter.

On the fourth section (vv. 19–29) it has much to say. Verse 20, beginning *Scorn has broken my heart*, is linked with the crucifixion (very aptly, it must be said) in Handel's *Messiah*,[636] not in the New Testament. Verse 26, though it reflects the thought of Isaiah 53:4 and the events of Calvary, is not quoted there either. But verses 21–25 are. Most of this passage we shall consider under our final heading; here we simply note verse 21, the *gall* mixed into wine as an anaesthetic drug and offered to Christ before he was crucified, and the *vinegar* given him just before he died, according to Matthew's account.[637] John, without actually quoting, says that Scripture was fulfilled in the latter incident.[638]

5. 'The glories that would follow' (vv. 30–36)
We have already seen something of what this final section might have meant in Old Testament times. As a prefiguring of Christ, it is, like

[633] Cf. John 5:23.
[634] Luke 22:42.   [635] Luke 23:46.
[636] Though Handel sets the words 'Thy rebuke ...' as if it were God's reproach, not that of his enemies.
[637] Matt. 27:34, 48.   [638] John 19:28–30.

the last part of Psalm 22, the 'happy ending' of the story: the resurrection and ascension, 'the glories that would follow'.[639] Curiously, for a psalm tied at so many points to the suffering of Christ, nothing in these last seven verses is quoted or even alluded to in New Testament accounts of its glorious aftermath. The previous section more than made up for the lack, and in connection with this one we should now look back briefly to the core of that one, verses 22–25. We skimmed over it earlier. In fact the passage is one of those that some would like to ignore altogether: *May their eyes be darkened ... May their place be deserted*, and in verse 28, *May they be blotted out of the book of life*. If such things are embarrassing on the lips of the psalmist, how much more so on the lips of Christ!

Yet as Lewis says, 'where we find a difficulty we may always expect that a discovery awaits us. Where there is cover we hope for game.'[640] Paul and Peter matter-of-factly apply the greater part of this passage to those in Israel who rejected Christ (Rom. 11:9–10 = vv. 22–23) and betrayed him (Acts 1:20 = v. 25). We need to remind ourselves of two things. First, it occurs in a *You* section of the psalm, not an *I* section; it is a prayer. The speaker is explicitly handing over to God the responsibility for judgment on his opponents. God's justice is perfect and unerring, and it is he, not the one who is praying to him, who will exact from the wicked a penalty corresponding to the evil they intended for their victims.[641] Secondly, to the suggestion that such prayers are even less fitting on Christ's lips than on the psalmist's, the reply is that, on the contrary, no-one has ever had a greater right to utter them. None knew better than he the enormity of the crime and the irredeemable wickedness of those who committed it. He had in mind of course not the soldiers who nailed him to the cross – 'Forgive them,' he prays, 'they do not know what they are doing'[642] – but those who, as Paul says, 'were hardened',[643] who saw the evidences and rejected them, and who in that sense knew perfectly well what they were doing.

It is to the great comfort of all right-thinking people that determined, destructive evil should in the end meet its match and be itself destroyed. That is why so many of the psalms rejoice in God's coming judgment. It is as it were from the *pain and distress* of Good Friday (v. 29) that the terrible condemnation arises. But it is only on that basis, the assured overthrow of the gospel's enemies, that the ecstatic praises and glowing promises of the psalm's closing lines make sense. Whatever its origin, it becomes a coherent statement of New Testament truth.

[639] 1 Pet. 1:11. See on Ps. 22, p. 1.84.
[640] Lewis, p. 29.   [641] Cf. Deut. 19:16–19.   [642] Luke 23:34.   [643] Rom. 11:7.

Psalm 70

What now follows two heavyweight psalms is not a lightweight (that would be a misleading epithet for any psalm), but one which is at any rate considerably briefer than either.

1. Its theme

It is a cry for help, and an urgent cry at that. In form, it is an ABBA chiasmus; it encloses between the psalmist's two prayers for himself a prayer about those who seek him (he is a wanted man!) and one about those who seek the Lord.

Since there is a tone of urgency in the outer verses, we are not surprised that the inner ones are somewhat revealing; under pressure we tend to blurt out what we really think. The psalmist is asking for more than a personal rescue from his own predicament. He is, he tells God, one of *those who love your salvation*. He and his fellow-believers will rejoice when *all who desire* [*his*] *ruin* are *turned back*, when they retreat or *shrink back* (NEB) in shame at the failure, or even the exposure, of their evil plans.

Is he being naïve? This general sorting out of everyone into two teams, 'us' and 'them', so that it becomes obvious who are the goodies and who are the baddies – is it not a primitive and oversimplified idea of what God can properly be asked to do?

No, for it takes us back from this point, almost at the end of Book II, to the black-and-white simplicities of Psalms 1 and 2, at the beginning of Book I. In the last analysis there will be no greys. We have here in another form the psalmists' frequent longing for God's judgment, which will show up everyone for what he or she really is. The distinction will be made anyway at the end of time. There is no reason why we should not ask God, in his grace, to *come quickly* and start making it rather sooner.

2. Its connections

Among these psalms which close Book II, 70 not only shares its particular 'language of faith' with 69 and 71, but puts in a nutshell what 69 has said at length. Here as there, a threatening situation has given rise to prayer both on the psalmist's own account and also against his enemies and for his friends. Far closer in its wording, though further away in the Psalter, 40 (the last psalm but one in Book I) has a sequence of five verses, 13–17, that are almost identical with 70 (the last but two in Book II). It is the kind of duplication we have seen once before, with 14 and 53. Such differences as there are make 70 just a little sharper than its twin. It is hard to know which version came first, and, if 70 is an excerpt taken out of 40, rather than 40 an expansion of 70, whether the shorter of the two was an adaptation for public or for private use.

This psalm is also very like 35, especially the latter part of that fearsome, much longer, prayer (vv. 17–28). It was there, we recall, that we first had to face squarely the problem of the imprecatory psalms. It brings to mind as well the ultimate suffering of 22. There too the psalmist cries 'Come quickly to help me' (v. 19), but anticipates the day when 'they who seek the LORD will praise him' (v. 26). The distress here may not be so extreme, but it is severe all the same. It is good to have ready to hand, perhaps even memorized, words that can express it as an arrow prayer, and to be confident that we shall in due course be able to say 'Let God be exalted!' – a worthier cry than what Spurgeon calls 'the dog's bark of "Aha, aha"'.

Psalm 71

This is the only psalm in Book II (assuming that 43 belongs with 42) that has no heading. Possibly 71 was similarly attached to 70, in this case as a longer, freer, composition on the same theme. It has a voice of its own, however.

1. Many voices

Before we become aware of its distinctive note we hear in it the echoes of several other psalms. They all bear the name of David, and come from the first David Collection (Book I). If 71 is related to 70, it is by the same token related to 40, of whose closing verses 70 is practically a duplicate. Furthermore, verses 9–12 here are similar to the end of 38, and the latter part of our psalm often recalls 35. The beginning of 31 is almost the same as our verses 1–3.

Then as well as the familiar cry for help (v. 12), 71's backward look to God's care for the psalmist since his birth (vv. 5–6) and its forward look to the encouraging of future generations by the telling of that tale (v. 18) both recall very similar passages in 22. And it was in 18 that we first noted a cluster of metaphors for God, fortress and refuge and both words for rock, that reappears here in verse 3.

To put it another way, this psalm is largely a mosaic of allusions to or even quotations from others. Where then do we find its individuality?

2. The individual voice of old age?

Three passages seem to show that this, alone among the psalms, is obviously the composition of an elderly person: verses 5–6 (*My hope ... since my youth ... From my birth*), verse 9 (*Do not cast me away when I am old*), and verses 17–18 (*since my youth ... Now also when I am old*). This last phrase is the AV's translation, which is followed by several modern versions. Of course if the NIV is correct, *When I am old* does not necessarily mean 'Now that I am old'. The psalmist could be looking ahead, as well as back, from his middle years. He still feels quite able to *shout for joy* (v. 23), a faculty he may well lose in old age.

But there may be a different kind of indication that he is already *old and grey*. It is hard to find a clear shape to Psalm 71, and that together with its many reminiscences of other psalms could point in this direction. The psalmist is as articulate and as fluent as ever. But greater use of familiar words, and less concern with a disciplined structure, are for writers and speakers one of the privileges of age – *experto credite*!

Elderly or not, he can certainly look back over many years of experience of the great deeds of an incomparable God (v. 19).

3. The individual voice of long experience

In verse 3 NIV, as in 31:3, God is the psalmist's *rock of refuge*. In fact the Hebrew text here uses another word, which differs by only one letter, and calls him a *rock of habitation*. I may often have found him my refuge in my earlier years (perhaps the psalmist is saying), but long experience has led me to see him as something more: my *home, to which I can* always *go.*

In verses 5–6, the psalmist looks back to his youth, indeed to his birth, and even beyond that to his *mother's womb*, and recognizes the reliability of God's care throughout. This God has been unfailingly true to his word, and that is one aspect of his righteousness, a favourite concept in this psalm.

In verse 15 the term itself appears: *My mouth will tell of your righteousness ... though I know not its measure. Tell* and *measure* are related words, as if the psalmist were to say, 'I may not be able to *count* the righteous acts of God, but I intend to *recount* them.' Paul has a similar paradox in Ephesians 3:19, praying that his readers may know the love of Christ, even though it surpasses knowledge.

In verse 16, the familiar AV phrase *I will go in the strength of the Lord GOD* well expresses a great Bible truth, though not the one the psalmist has in mind! Still with the intention of telling what God has done, he is saying not that he will *go in* God's strength, but that he will *come with* God's mighty acts (cf. RSV).

Lifelong experience of this kind, and the grateful testimony that flows from it, were Joseph Addison's theme in another of his memorable hymns.

> When all thy mercies, O my God,
> My rising soul surveys,

Transported with the view, I'm lost
In wonder, love and praise.

He was not here versifying our present psalm, as he versified 19 and 23, but his lines breathe the same air as our psalmist's.

Unnumbered comforts to my soul
Thy tender care bestowed,
Before my infant heart conceived
From whom those comforts flowed.

When in the slippery paths of youth
With heedless steps I ran,
Thine arm unseen conveyed me safe
And brought me up to man.

In one respect Addison falls short of the psalmist: for him God's grace is a theme for praise, as in verse 14 –

Ten thousand thousand precious gifts
My daily thanks employ,
And not the least a cheerful heart
Which tastes those gifts with joy –

but not so readily a theme for preaching, as in verses 15–18. He is after all a cultured gentleman of the early eighteenth century, not the kind of 'enthusiast' who will rejoice in the rise of Methodism in the generation following! But in another respect he can go beyond the psalmist: with him in verse 18 –

Through every period of my life
Thy goodness I'll pursue –

and then, with the New Testament's greater knowledge, past him:

And after death in distant worlds
The glorious theme renew.

Through all eternity to thee
A joyful song I'll raise,
For O, eternity's too short
To utter all thy praise.

4. *The individual voice of misunderstood affliction*

The psalmist is surrounded by troubles. Verse 20 tells us that they are *many and bitter*, such as might be described as taking him down to *the depths of the earth* – as we might say to 'death's door', perhaps?

The result is that people regard him as a *portent* (v. 7). God is making an example of him, they say: this is what happens to those who commit dreadful sins, he must be a dreadful sinner. So Job was regarded by his friends.

As if that were not enough, some who see him in this light are already his enemies, and aim to take advantage of his misfortune (vv. 10–11). His troubles are those of the author of Psalm 69; if that is David, suffering the consequences of some otherwise unknown folly of his later years, this psalm could conceivably be the same person's response to the same situation, though in a very different spirit.

More to the point is the example to us of how our psalmist copes not just with his afflictions, but with the way that others misunderstand them. There are few scriptures which touch on this particular misery, with the exception of Job, as we have noted. But our author has available to him a grasp of God which Job, in very similar circumstances, did not have. He appeals beyond his own personal experiences of divine grace to the *praise* and *splendour* revealed in God's *mighty acts* and *marvellous deeds*, the *great things* he has done throughout the history of his people: in a word, his *righteousness* – his *righteous acts* (vv. 8, 16, 17, 19, 24). Such a God cannot in the end let the psalmist down. Verse 1 (or its twin, 31:1) rounds off the Te Deum, that grand old Christian hymn of corporate praise in which the repeated 'we/us' suddenly becomes 'I/me' only in that very last verse: 'O Lord, in thee have I trusted: let me never be confounded.'

5. *The individual voice of living tradition*

It goes without saying that our psalmist does not *declare* [God's] *marvellous deeds* (v. 17) because he likes the sound of his own voice. He speaks so that others may hear; he sings so that they may join in. Specifically, he says, *I declare your power to the next generation* (v. 18). There is no shadow of doubt in his mind that God's great acts in the past are meant to benefit the people of the future. The notion that the mere passage of time renders Bible truth obsolete is one of the more idiotic of modern ideas. There is nothing more old-fashioned than yesterday's new thinking, and today's, if we had the nous to realize it, is about to go the same way. There is nothing more relevant *to all who are to come* (v. 18) than the vital proclamation of what God did in Bible times, and of the truth that that embodies.

He is, after all, the incomparable God. *Who, O God, is like you?*

says verse 19. 'Who is like you?' sang Moses, long before.[644] 'Who is a God like you?' Micah will cry long after – it is the very meaning of his name.[645]

Psalm 72

One of Isaac Watts's best-known hymns is based on Psalm 72. As the title of his book of paraphrases tells us, they are *The Psalms of David, Imitated in the Language of the New Testament*, and the very first word of this one shows how he updated the Old Testament original: '*Jesus* shall reign where'er the sun Does his successive journeys run.' A hundred years later, James Montgomery versified it comprehensively in his equally well-known 'Hail to the Lord's Anointed'. He too saw the psalm as a prophecy. Watts and Montgomery of course used the AV, and its unvarying future tenses (the word *shall* thirty-one times in vv. 2–17) point in that direction. Modern translations however read many of these futures differently, and take much of the psalm to be a prayer.

1. Hail to the Lord's Anointed (v. 1)
At once the general question of prophecy or prayer is raised. Who is this king? Is the psalmist's chief aim to pray for a contemporary Old Testament monarch, or to prophesy the coming Messiah?

In one sense he is concerned primarily with his own time. He gives God's people a liturgy for an enthronement ceremony in Jerusalem. This is one of only two psalms in the Psalter bearing Solomon's name, the other being 127; and while this need not imply anything more than a collection under that name, it could mean a psalm by him (for Rehoboam, his successor?) or for him (by his father David?). There is no strong reason why it should not be the latter. A good deal of it reminds us of Solomon as king[646] or indeed of David as psalmist.[647]

In another sense the kingship of Christ is primary – the primary concern of all Scripture. Although the New Testament nowhere connects this psalm with Christ, the connections it does make show that everything right and good about the Israelite monarchy foreshadowed Messiah's kingdom. The English hymn writers were not wrong in Christianizing Psalm 72.

---

[644] Exod. 15:11.
[645] Mic. 7:18. 'Micah' (like 'Micaiah', of which it is an abbreviation) means 'Who is like Yah[weh]?'
[646] Cf. 1 Kgs. 1:39; 3:5–14 (*give* [four times] is the same word as *endow with* in Ps. 72:1); 4:21, 34; 10:1–29; 1 Chr. 22:9–10.
[647] Cf. 2 Sam. 23:2–5.

2. *He shall come down like showers (vv. 2–7)*

Verse 2 raises the question of prophecy and prayer in a different way. In the NIV this verse prophesies: *He will judge.* In the NRSV it prays: *May he judge.* Which did the psalmist mean?

The AV takes every verb in the psalm to be a Hebrew imperfect, and translates them uniformly as English futures. But for the most part there is no difference in form between imperfects and what are called *jussives* – that is, *May his name endure* (v. 17) or *Let its fruit flourish* (v. 16) – and nearly all these verbs could be either. The imperfects/futures are the language of prophecy; the jussives, that of prayer. Normally (though not invariably) we depend on the context to show which verbs have which function.

In a few cases the form of the verb leaves no room for doubt. Verse 2 begins with a definite future (*pace* the NRSV), *He will judge,* which sets the direction as far as verse 7. Verse 8 is certainly a jussive, *May he rule* (cf. NRSV), so we should expect the next few verbs to follow suit. In the second half (vv. 1, 11, and 17b mark the beginning, middle, and end of the psalm, vv. 18–20 being a postscript) we seem again to have a sequence of futures (vv. 12–14), which again changes tack with a definite jussive at *Long may he live* in verse 15. All this is simpler than it sounds. It gives a clear shape to the seventeen verses of the psalm proper:

> *Introduction* (v. 1);
>   prophecy (vv. 2–7);
>   prayer (vv. 8–10);
> *refrain* (v. 11);
>   prophecy (vv. 12–14);
>   prayer (vv. 15–17a);
> *refrain* (v. 17b).

This shape is, incidentally, very like that of Montgomery's hymn; hence our section headings, which are taken from it.

How rich is the blessing of God's people under this king's rule, as the beautiful language of verses 2–7 spells it out! *Shalom* (technically *šālôm*, but it has become familiar in the simpler form) is a grand word. Something better than *peace* (AV) or even *prosperity* (NIV), it means total wellbeing: potentially theirs under Solomon – it is what his name signifies – and certainly ours under Christ. For how secure is the promise of it, if the king's rule is based on righteousness! Real peace is 'the fruit of righteousness' (Is. 32:17), and grows nowhere else. What was given to Solomon, the first *royal son*, in answer to the prayer of verse 1, he eventually lost. Christ, 'great David's greater Son', is himself both our righteousness and our peace (1 Cor. 1:30; Eph. 2:14), and that for good and all.

3. Arabia's desert ranger (vv. 8–10)

The first glimpse of a vision of empire stretching *from sea to sea and from the River [Euphrates] to the ends of the earth* had been given to Israel at the time of the exodus.[648] It began to take shape in the days of Solomon.[649] We can imagine the great congregation uniting in prayer for the success of his reign, and in due course seeing an answer to their prayer. Within the 'fertile crescent' which curved beyond Israel north and east to Mesopotamia and south-west to Egypt, peoples both independent and hostile (v. 9) came to recognize him. So did more distant nations, at the end of long journeys by sea westwards or by land south-eastwards (v. 10).

> Arabia's desert ranger
>   To him shall bow the knee;
> The Ethiopian stranger
>   His glory come to see;
> With offerings of devotion
>   Ships from the isles shall meet,
> To pour the wealth of ocean
>   In tribute at his feet.

After Solomon there followed, albeit with a few blips on the graph, a long decline, with such glories receding ever further into the past and therefore the more readily looked for in a future Messiah. Rightly, the New Testament duly crystallized these prayers in one of its own: 'Your kingdom come.'

What do we make of the prayer formulas our psalm suggests? They are slightly odd in English, these jussives (for that is what they are, as in the NRSV: *May he have dominion,* and so on). 'May he' sounds like asking permission, 'Let him' sounds like giving it! Such prayers are far stronger than that. It will help us to understand them if we use 'Let' rather than 'May', and recall God's own words in Genesis 1:3: '"Let there be light," and there was light.' Oh, but (you say) surely no prayer of mine is a divine fiat of that kind. No? But the more closely your prayers are aligned with what God has said he is going to do anyway, the more like they will be to the great jussives of creation. 'Let him rule!' you will cry; and rule he will.

So it turns out that in this case prayer and prophecy amount to much the same thing when one is totally in tune with the mind of

[648] Cf. Exod. 23:31.   [649] Cf. 1 Kgs. 4:24.

God. Lord, what do you say you will do? Then, Lord, let that be done!

4. Kings shall bow down before him (v. 11)

What it means to be a royal son endowed with God's righteousness (v. 1) has been spelt out in the intervening verses, and is now summarized here at the midpoint of the psalm: *All kings will bow down to him and all nations will serve him.*

Of the royal line of David, it was his immediate successor who saw the prophecies and prayers of verses 2–10 most nearly fulfilled. 'Solomon ruled over all the kingdoms from the River to the land of the Philistines ... These countries brought tribute and were Solomon's subjects all his life ... Men of all nations came to listen to Solomon's wisdom, sent by all the kings of the world, who had heard of his wisdom.'[650]

With even better reason, the New Testament uses just such language of Christ, the language of universal authority and recognition, 'that in everything he might have the supremacy'; although of course 'at present we do not see everything subject to him', as we were shown in the New Testament's treatment of Psalm 8.[651]

Again we see that this psalm is in a broader sense both prayer and prophecy. As originally composed, it is a prayer for use presumably at the enthronement of an Israelite king – Solomon, surely, in the tenth century BC. As adopted by the Christian church, it is a prophecy: it prophesies 'something greater than Solomon',[652] the reign of Messiah, which was to begin a thousand years later and has been growing ever since.

> For he shall have dominion
> O'er river, sea and shore,
> Far as the eagle's pinion
> Or dove's light wing can soar.

The historical reality never quite measured up to the vision of the poem; the final reality will far surpass it.

5. He comes with succour speedy (vv. 12–14)

The psalmist now develops what he touched on in verse 4, the confidence that the king will *defend the afflicted ... save the children of the needy ... crush the oppressor.* He who will rule *to the ends of the earth* will be equally concerned with the felt needs of its

---

[650] 1 Kgs. 4:21, 34.   [651] Col. 1:18; Heb. 2:8; cf. Matt. 28:18. See pp. 1.39–40.
[652] Matt. 12:42 NRSV.
[653] Kidner, p. 254.   [654] Gal. 3:16, 19.

individual men and women. He cares, as Montgomery puts it, for 'those who suffer wrong', for 'the poor and needy' and 'the weak', for 'souls condemned and dying'.

The message is clear, and immensely comforting. Yet within the psalm, the background to this compassion is still the righteousness of God. It is not a case of the demands of justice being shelved while the demands of pity are met. It is not in that sense that 'mercy triumphs over judgment', to quote the often misused words of James 2:13. The king does not forget the sins of the oppressed, any more than he ignores the needs of the oppressor.

The point is well illustrated by the broader background of Scripture against which we should read this passage. The word *rescue* in verse 14, *redeem* in the NRSV, points us to the early chapters of Exodus, and we realize how well these three verses sum up the events of those days. That prototype of redemption set the pattern of God's saving grace and love for all time. Yet not for a moment did it lose sight of righteousness and justice. Egypt was punished, which was judgment, and Israel was rescued, which was mercy; yet Egypt was also offered mercy, and Israel was also faced with judgment. So will it be under the rule of God's King.

6. Prayer unceasing and daily vows (vv. 15–17a)
Montgomery's paraphrase of these verses is half-forgotten today.

> To him shall prayer unceasing
> And daily vows ascend;
> His kingdom still increasing,
> A kingdom without end.
> The mountain dews shall nourish
> A seed in weakness sown,
> Whose fruit shall spread and flourish
> And shake like Lebanon.

This ignores one oddity in the AV he would have had before him, and reproduces another. He left out *they of the city* in verse 16 AV, as the NIV also does, though it should probably be there (*May people blossom in the cities* NRSV). He put in, in the form of 'a seed in weakness', the *handful of corn* which the AV has in the same verse, and which modern versions correct to *abundance of grain* (NRSV).

Even if the phrase was a mistranslation, the image of a mere *handful of corn* which produces fields of grain so vast as to cover mountains, waving in the wind like the forests of 29:6, is a powerful one. It reflects the real theme of the passage. That is *growth*, and unlimited time for unlimited growth – 'his kingdom still increasing, a kingdom without end'. We cannot miss this dominant thought: *Long may he live, ever, all day long, for ever, as long as the sun [continues]*, ample time for this unheard-of increase in the grain crop. Grain represented of course the staple wealth of an agrarian economy like Israel's.

Unbroken economic growth is something no government can deliver. Even in Solomon's days this vision of it could be no more than an ideal, the wording of the psalm was what Kidner calls 'courtly extravagance',[653] and the prosperity Solomon brought to Israel ended when his reign ended.

Yet, remarkably, such visions become ever more positive as the possibility of their fulfilment in Old Testament Israel grows fainter. Some real, solid, permanent quality of life, of which these rich and endless fields (Thomas Traherne's 'orient and immortal wheat'?) are a picture, awaits us yet in the coming kingdom of Christ.

7. All-blessing and all-blest (vv. 17b–20)

The postscript to the psalm has two parts. Verses 18–19 are a doxology like that which rounds off each of the first four books of the Psalter. Verse 20 is a note indicating that Book II contains all the David psalms the editors had available for, or wished to include in, this particular compilation (we shall find others in later books). Neither part of the postscript belongs to Psalm 72 as such, though Watts no doubt had verse 19 in mind when he wrote, 'Earth repeat the loud Amen'. Montgomery, on the other hand, goes back to verse 17a for his closing lines ('The tide of time shall never His covenant remove; His name shall stand for ever').

It is verse 17b which corresponds to verses 1 and 11, and completes the psalmist's poem: *All nations will be blessed through him, and they will call him blessed.* This goes back beyond the Exodus references of verses 12–14 to three key scriptures in Genesis – beyond God's acts in the time of Moses to his promises in the time of Abraham. 'All peoples on earth will be blessed through you,' Abraham is told when God first calls him; 'Through your offspring all nations on earth will be blessed' is the promise when his faith is proved by the offering of his son Isaac as a sacrifice; and the same words are in due course repeated to Isaac in his turn (Gen. 12:3; 22:18; 26:4).

Abraham might have assumed that the offspring meant Isaac, and Isaac that it meant Jacob. David might have assumed it would be Solomon. But always God has something better in store, until Paul can confirm for us that 'the Seed to whom the promise referred' is Christ.[654]

O'er every foe victorious
   He on his throne shall rest,
From age to age more glorious,
   All-blessing and all-blest;

for he who blesses all with righteousness and peace is himself blessed by all in songs of praise and thanksgiving.